A. N. SHANBHAG is a bestselling author and a very widely syndicated columnist on personal finance and taxation. Mathematics is his passionate pursuit.

SANDEEP SHANBHAG is a chartered accountant and has practised as a tax and investment adviser for over 20 years. He writes regular columns on investment and tax planning for financial websites and newspapers. He has addressed a number of seminars and lectures arranged by corporates and other organizations.

No government has the right, in the process of extracting tax, to cause misery and harassment to the taxpayer and the gnawing feeling that he is made a victim of palpable injustice.

— Nani Palkhivala

Other Books by the Same Authors Published by Vision Books

1. In the Wonderland of Investment	38th Edition
2. In the Wonderland of Mathematics	2nd Edition
3. Taxpayer to Taxsaver	24th Edition

IN THE WONDERLAND OF INVESTMENT FOR NRIs

FINANCIAL YEAR 2019-2020

A N SHANBHAG

SANDEEP SHANBHAG

VISION BOOKS

www.visionbooksindia.com

www.vision**books**india.com

This publication is sold with the understanding that neither the publisher nor the authors will be responsible for the result of any action taken on the basis of this work, whether directly or indirectly, for any error or omission, to any person, whether a buyer of this publication or not.

The greatest reward any author can get is feedback, good or bad, from his readers. All suggestions for improvements are most welcome.

Wonderland Investment Consultants
A/11, Kastur Mahal, Opp. Canara Bank,
Sion, Mumbai 400 022
OR call: 2409 1317, 2409 4522
E-mail: anshanbhag@yahoo.com

Readers are welcome to send their personal queries through
www.anshanbhag.com
This is a pay channel

Twentieth Edition, 2019

ISBN 10: 93-86268-34-5
ISBN 13: 978-93-86268-34-1

Published by
Vision Books Pvt. Ltd.
(Incorporating Orient Paperbacks & CARING imprints)
24 Feroze Gandhi Road, Lajpat Nagar 3
New Delhi 110024, India.
Phone: (+91-11) 2984 0821 / 22
e-mail: visionbooks@gmail.com

Printed at
Anand Sons
C-88, Ganesh Nagar, Pandav Nagar Complex
Delhi 110092, India.

Contents

~

Preface

~

Amongst the non-residents across the globe, Indians shine bright because of their inherent multi-professional and multi-technological expertise. This is coupled with the Indian cultural and traditional attitude towards result-oriented application to the job on hand. Therefore, the NRIs are the most respected and sought after resource for foreign entrepreneurs. As a corollary, they have become an affluent group which can influence the world economy. The combined wealth of NRIs is estimated to be close to the current GDP of India of more than $350 billion! Tens of thousands of such Indians are now offering these professional and entrepreneurial skills to boost the economy of the country they serve. If such Indians sow some seeds of foreign remittances **In the Wonderland of Investment** that India is, they are bound to reap a rich harvest which can be enjoyed by them and their family members at their chosen "El Dorado".

Incidentally, this is the title of our first book which, fortunately happens to be a best-seller and is currently in its 37th edition. It deals with the various investment avenues available for an individual and the related Indian tax implications. We have also written **Taxpayer to Taxsaver** that deals with many strategies an individual can adopt taking advantage of the current tax provisions to obtain the maximum mileage from his investible funds and also addresses *Kinks in Tax*.

Both these books contained a large portion dealing with NRIs. This portion was becoming larger and larger, edition by edition, purely because of the demand. We have therefore, taken out the relevant portion from both the books and added the long overdue meat and flavour, which we could not do because this would be unkind to the residents who were not interested in the material dealing with NRIs.

Thus was born **In the Wonderland of Investment for NRIs**.

As is the wont with all dedicated professionals, their preoccupation with work leaves very little time on hand for a heavy-duty exercise on their investible funds. A little objectivity will make them realise that they would be doing themselves, their families as well as their motherland a great favour if they use their reservoir of funds optimally to make it richer over the passage of time. It is a known fact that India, especially after its new liberated economy, provides the greenest pastures for them to graze on.

Unfortunately, some prophets of doom and gloom have emerged advising the NRIs to adopt the policy of sitting on the fence, waiting and watching the Indian scenario with indifference. Instead of brooding over imaginary negative features which have little relevance for the Indian economy, it would be prudent to inspect hard-core facts.

Important amongst these opportunities are availability of cheap skilled and unskilled labour, abundance of untapped resources and most important, the sops offered by government in terms of subsidies and tax concessions, with repatriation facilities. NRIs planning to return to their motherland in the foreseeable future for good, will do well to look at non-repatriable avenues, where the returns are significantly higher.

1st August 2019

A. N. SHANBHAG
SANDEEP SHANBHAG

Glossary of Abbreviations

~

AAR Authority for Advance Rulings
AD Authorised Dealer / Bank
ADR American Depository Receipt
AY Ass essment Year
BSE Bombay Stock Exchange
BTQ Business Travel Quota
CCP Customs Clearance Permit
CD Convertible Debenture
CGAS Capital Gains Accounts Scheme, 1988
CII Cost Inflation Index
CIT Commissioner of Income Tax
CTT Commodity Transaction Tax
Co-FDs Fixed Deposits of Public Limited Company
DDT Dividend Distribution Tax
DP Depository Participant
ECB External Commercial Borrowing
ECS Electronic Clearing System
EEFC Exchange Earner's Foreign Currency Account
ELSS Equity-Linked Saving Scheme
EMI Equated Monthly Installments
ESOP Employees Stock Option Plan
F&O Futures & Options
FA18 Finance Act, 2018
FCCB Foreign Currency Convertible Bond
FCNR Foreign Currency Non-Resident Account
FCRA Foreign Contribution (Regulation) Act, 1976
FDI Foreign Direct Investment
FE Foreign Exchange
FEA Foreign Exchange Asset

FEMA	Foreign Exchange Management Act, 1999
FEMR	Foreign Exchange Management Rules, 1999
FERA	Foreign Exchange Regulation Act, 1973
FI	Financial Institution
FII	Foreign Institutional Investor
FMV	Fair Market Value
FPI	Foreign Portfolio Investment
FY	Financial Year (1st April to 31st March)
GDR	Global Depository Receipt
HNI	High Networth Individual
HUF	Hindu Undivided Family
ICC	International Credit Card
IDC	International Debit Cards
IDR	Indian Depository Receipt
IPO	Initial Public Offer of Shares
IRDA	Insurance Regulatory & Development Authority
ITA	Income Tax Act, 1961
ITO	Income Tax Officer (= AO, Assessing Officer)
JV	Joint Venture
KYC	Know Your Customer
LIC	Life Insurance Corporation
LLP	Limited Liability Partnership
LRS	Liberalised Remittance Scheme
LT	Long-Term
LTA	Leave Travel Assistance
LTCG	Long-Term Capital Gains
MAT	Minimum Alternate Tax
MFs	Mutual Funds
MoF	Ministry of Finance
NAV	Net Asset Value
NBFC	Non-Banking Financial Company
NCD	Non-Convertible Debenture
NHB	National Housing Bank
NOC	No Objection Certificate
NPA	Non-Performing Asset
NRE	Non-Resident External Rupee Account
NRI	Non-Resident Indian

NRO	Non-Resident Ordinary Account
NSE	National Stock Exchange
OCB	Overseas Corporate Body
OCI	Overseas Citizen of India
PE	Permanent Establishment
PIO	Person of Indian Origin, not a citizen of India.
PMS	Portfolio Management Scheme
PoA	Power of Attorney
PODs	Pure-growth Open-ended Debt-based Schemes
POEM	Place of Effective Management
PPF	Public Provident Fund, 1969
PSU	Public Sector Unit
QFI	Qualified Foreign Investor
RBI	Reserve Bank of India
RD	Recurring Deposit
RFC	Resident Foreign Currency Account
RNOR	Resident but Not Ordinarily Resident
ROI	Resident Outside India
ROR	Resident and Ordinarily Resident
SCRA	Securities Contracts (Regulation) Act, 1956
SBI	State Bank of India
SCSS	Senior Citizens Savings Scheme
SEBI	Securities and Exchange Board of India
Sec.	Section
SPV	Special Purpose Vehicle
ST	Short-Term
STCG	Short-Term Capital Gain
STT	Security Transaction Tax
SWP	Systematic Withdrawal Plan
TCS	Tax Collection at Source
TDS	Tax Deduction at Source = Withholding Tax
TR	Transfer of Residence
u/s	under section
ULIP	Unit Linked Insurance Plan
w.e.f.	with effect from
w.r.e.f.	with retrospective effect from

Taxes are the lifeblood of any government, but it cannot be overlooked that the blood is taken from the arteries of the taxpayer and therefore the transfusion is not accomplished on dictate of political expediency but in accordance with the principles of justice and good conscience.

— Nani Palkhiwala

FA 2019 for NRIs

~

Interim FA19 by Interim FM

Sec. 16(1a): Standard Deduction

This has been increased from ₹40,000 to ₹50,000 for salaried class, including pensioners. This is useful for those NRIs who get Indian sourced pension

Sec. 23, 24 and 54

At present income tax on notional rent is payable if one has more than one self-occupied house. Levy of income tax on notional rent on a second self-occupied house has been exempted. Moreover, the tax concession on LTCG if the gains are invested in purchasing or constructing one residential house within certain stipulated time frame has been extended to two residential houses for a tax payer having capital gains up to ₹2 crore. This benefit can be availed once in a life time.

Surcharge on Super-Rich Individuals

There are no changes in the base income tax rates. However rich individuals were subjected to pay surcharge @10% having total income exceeding ₹50 lakh but not exceeding ₹1 crore and @15% on total income exceeding ₹1 crore. FA19(2) has further imposed surcharge for super-rich @25% on total income exceeding ₹2 crore but not exceeding ₹5 crore; and @37% on a total income exceeding ₹5 crore. The marginal relief is applicable in all these slabs. Consequently, the highest rate has become 42.7440%!!

There are about 9,400 foreign portfolio investors registered in India who have invested nearly $50 billion in Indian equity, debt and hybrid instrument markets.

Around 40% of them, registered as trusts, could be affected by the new rules. FPIs prefer the route of private trusts mainly to navigate cumbersome disclosure rules and other compliance requirements. If structured as a corporate, they may have to pay a minimum alternate tax of 18.5%. In a trust structure, it is easy for investors to move capital in and out of trusts without paying high taxes.

FPIs registered as trusts are taxed as AoPs. at the new rates. Though they will continue to be charged at the basic tax rate of 15% and 10% on short-term and long-term capital gains the increase in the overall income tax rates will raise their tax bills substantially. w.e.f. 1.9.19

Payment to Resident Contractors, Professionals, Brokers and Commission Agents

At present there is no liability on an individual or HUF to apply TDS on any payment made to such entities when it is for personal use even if the payer is carrying on business or profession which is not subjected to u/s 194C. A new Sec. 194M is inserted to provide for levy of TDS @5% on the aggregate of sums, paid or credited if it exceeds ₹50 lakh in a year. The TDS may be deposited by using PAN if the deductor does not possess a TAN.

w.e.f. 1.9.19

TDS on Purchase of Immovable Property

Explanation to Sec. 194-IA dealing with application of TDS @1% on transfer of immovable property other than agricultural land on the amount of consideration paid for transfer of such property has been amended to clarify that such payments are inclusive of fees for club membership, car parking, electricity and water, maintenance, advance fee or any other charges incidental to the transfer. w.e.f. 1.9.19

Deemed Gift Made to a POI

Gifts by Residents to NRIs can be claimed to be non-taxable in India as the income does not accrue or arise in India. To plug this loophole Sec. 2(24xviia) has been amended so as to consider such gifts shall be deemed to accrue or arise in India. However, the existing provision for exempting gifts as provided in proviso to Sec. 56(2x) will continue to apply. In a treaty situation, the relevant article of applicable DTAA shall continue to apply for such gifts as well. w.e.f. 5.7.19

Mandatory Furnishing of Return by Certain Persons

Sec. 139 has been amended so as to provide that a person shall be mandatorily required to file his return, if during the previous year, he has —

(a) deposited aggregate of the amounts exceeding ₹1 crore in one or more current accounts maintained with a banking company or a co-operative bank; or
(b) incurred expenditure of aggregate amounts exceeding ₹2 lakh for himself or any other person for travel to a foreign country; or
(c) incurred expenditure of aggregate amount exceeding ₹1 lakh towards consumption of electricity;

Further, at present a person claiming exemption from capital gains tax on investment in specified assets like house, bonds etc., is not required to furnish a return of income, if after claim of the exemption, his total income is not more than the maximum amount not chargeable to tax. Sixth proviso to Sec. 139 has been amended to provide that a person who is claiming such benefits on investment in a house or a bond or other assets, u/ss 54, 54B, 54D, 54EC, 54F, 54G, 54GA and 54GB shall necessarily be required to furnish a return, if before claim of the benefits, his total income is more than the maximum amount not chargeable to tax. w.e.f. 1.4.20

Inter-Changeability of PAN & Aadhaar

Sec. 139A has been amended so as to provide that —

Every person who is required to furnish or intimate or quote his PAN under the Act, and who, has not been allotted a PAN but possesses Aadhaar, may quote his Aadhaar in lieu of PAN. Such a person shall be allotted a PAN in due course.

Every person who has been allotted a PAN and who has linked his Aadhaar u/s 139AA, may quote his Aadhaar in lieu of a PAN.

Sec. 139AA(2), provides that the PAN allotted to a person shall be deemed to be invalid, in case the person fails to intimate the Aadhaar. In order to protect validity of transactions previously carried out through such PAN, the proviso has been amended so as to provide that if a person fails to intimate the Aadhaar, the PAN allotted to such person shall be made inoperative. w.e.f. 1.9.19

TDS on Cash Withdrawal to Discourage Cash Transactions

A new Sec. 194N has been inserted to provide for levy of TDS @2% on cash payments in excess of ₹1 crore made during the year, by a bank or post office, unless such a recipient is exempt. w.e.f. 1.4.20

Tax Incentive for Affordable Housing

A new Sec. 80EEA has been inserted to provide a deduction in respect of interest up to ₹1,50,000 on loan taken for residential house property from any financial institution subject to—

(a) loan has been sanctioned by a financial institution during FY 19-20.

(b) the stamp duty value of house property does not exceed ₹45 lakh.

(c) assessee does not own any residential house property on the date of sanction of loan. w.e.f. 1.4.20

Tax Incentive for Electric Vehicles

A new Sec. 80EEB has been inserted to provide for a deduction in respect of interest on loan taken for purchase of an electric vehicle from any financial institution up to ₹1,50,000 provided the loan has been sanctioned by a financial institution including an NBFC during 1.4.19 to 31.3.23 and the assessee does not own any other electric vehicle on the date of sanction of loan.

w.e.f. 1.4.20

Buy-back

Sec. 115QA provides for the levy of additional Income-tax @20% of the distributed income on account of buy-back of unlisted shares (STT not applicable) by the company since this distributed income is essentially deemed to be dividend. Listed companies pay STT and therefore buy-back was not taxable either in the hands of the company as well as the shareholder. To curb the malpractice of listed companies resorting to buy backs to replace dividend, this Section has been extended to listed companies. As additional income-tax has been levied at the level of company, the consequential income arising in the hands of shareholders has been exempted from tax u/s 10(34A).

w.e.f. 5.7.19

Amount of TDS when NRI Sells House

U/s 195(2) person who is responsible for paying any sum to an NRI can make an application to the AO to obtain a certificate/order indicating the amount of TDS to be applied. This process is manual. The portion related with prescribing the form and manner of application to the AO and also for the manner of determination of appropriate TDS by use of technology.

w.e.f 1.11.19

1

~

General Provisions

FEMA has Replaced FERA

The Foreign Exchange Regulation Act (FERA) was enacted way back in 1973. A myriad amendments and clarifications were issued in the name of liberalisation reaching a situation where it became difficult to differentiate between the wood and trees. Therefore, FEMA replaced FERA with effect from 1.6.2000.

FEMA is a civil law, whereas the FERA was a criminal law. Contravention under FEMA is dealt with civil procedures resulting in no prosecution, arrest or imprisonment. It has also curtailed the powers of Directorate of Enforcement. Most importantly, it has provided for compounding of penalty. The burden of proof will be on the enforcement agency and not on the implicated person. FEMA describes an elaborate redressing machinery for total justice and fairness while deciding on the question of contravention. It has also narrowed down RBI's role only to supervise and control by giving all executive powers to Authorised Dealers (ADs) within the framework of FEMA.

An AD Category-I is a bank specifically authorised by the RBI to deal in forex and foreign securities. For providing greater reach, the RBI grants licenses to certain entities by authorising them as AD Category-II or Category-III or Full Fledged Money Changers to undertake a range of non-trade current account transactions. All transactions undertaken by a Resident that do not alter his assets or liabilities, including contingent liabilities, outside India are current account transactions.

List of activities handled by different categories is available on www.fedai.org.in.

Basic Conditions

With a view to avoid repetition, the following is a list of general conditions applicable to all the areas. You are requested to keep these in mind while reading the rest of the book.

ROI, PIO and NRI

The Act uses these nomenclatures rather loosely. For the sake of clarity, throughout this book we shall stick to the following nomenclature —

1. "ROI" is a person Resident Outside India. Obviously, such a person may be a rank foreigner, PIO or NRI.
2. "NRI" is an Indian citizen (Indian Passport) who is not Resident.
3. "PIO" is a foreign citizen (Foreign passport) of Indian origin.

Since most of the rules, regulations, provisions, etc., are common for both NRIs and PIOs, for the purpose of this book, NRI would include PIO, unless otherwise separately mentioned.

Currency

The definition includes debit cards, ATM cards or any other instrument by whatever name called that can be used to create a financial liability.

Know Your Customer (KYC) Compliance

Investments of all investors related with banks, Depository Participants for shares, units for MFs, life and general cover for insurers, etc., should be compliant with "KYC" and also Anti Money Laundering guidelines. It is also mandatory to possess a PAN in most cases. Each of these entities required separate KYC, causing a lot of inconvenience to the investors. Fortunately a Centralised KYC (CKYC) has been established w.e.f. 1.2.17 to allocate a number to new applicants and the current KYC-compliant investors. The new application form is available on the sites of all these entities. Unfortunately CKYC has not yet seen daylight. Unfortunately, the CKYC appears to be non-functional.

Clubbing of NRE & FCNR

NRE and FCNR accounts are forex in nature and all rules are common for both. Therefore, reference to FCNR is dropped in all such cases. However, take note of the fact that since FCNR is a term deposit, where withdrawals, though legal, are virtually impossible.

Close Relatives

ITA has defined "close relative" in Sec. 56 (Refer Chapter *Wealth & Gift Tax*). FEMA refers to Sec. 6 of Companies Act. This results in confusion.

For FEMA, a person shall be deemed to be a "relative" of another if, and only if —

(a) They are members of Hindu undivided family.
(b) They are husband and wife.
(c) Relative as defined by Schedule-IA which is as follows:

Father	Father's father	Father's mother
Mother	Mother's father	Mother's mother
Son	Son's wife	Son's son
Son's son's wife	Son's daughter	Son's daughter's husband
Daughter	Daughter's husband	Daughter's son
Daughter's son's wife	Daughter's daughter	Daughter's daughter's husband
Brother	Brother's wife	Sister
Sister's husband		

Note: Mother, son, daughter, brother and sister include step entities also.

Prohibited Transactions

An ROI shall not make investment in India, in any form directly or through any entity, whether incorporated or not, which is engaged or proposed to be engaged in —

(a) Chit fund or Nidhi Company.

(b) Agriculture or plantation activities. These exclude —

(c) Floriculture, Horticulture, Development of seeds, Animal husbandry, Pisciculture, Cultivation of vegetables, mushrooms, etc., under controlled conditions and services related to agro and allied sectors and Plantations (other than tea plantations).

(d) Housing and real estate business or construction of farm houses. "Real estate business" means dealing in land and immovable property with a view to earning profit therefrom and does not include development of townships, construction of residential commercial premises, roads or bridges, educational institutions, recreational facilities, city and regional level infrastructure. Further, earning of rent income on lease of the property and also investment in units of Real Estate Investment Trusts (REITs) shall not be treated as real estate business.

(e) Trading in Transferable Development Rights (TDRs). This is a certificate issued in respect of land acquired for public purpose by government for surrender of land by the owner without monetary compensation. These are transferable in part or whole.

(f) Lottery, gambling and betting in casinos or otherwise, including government, private or on-line lotteries.

(g) Partnership firms and proprietorship concerns having investments as per FEMA are not allowed to be engaged in print media sector.

(h) Retail Trading except single brand product retailing.

(i) Atomic Energy.

(j) Manufacturing of cigars, cheroots, cigarillos and cigarettes, of tobacco or of tobacco substitutes.

The same restrictions are applicable to a Resident in respect of the amount borrowed, if any.

Prohibited Remittances

Prohibited remittances out of India by any person or entity are —

1. Income from lottery winnings, racing, riding, or any other hobby.

2. For purchase of lottery tickets, banned or proscribed magazines, football pools, sweepstakes, etc.
3. Payment of commission on exports of equity investment in Joint ventures or wholly owned subsidiaries abroad of Indian companies or on exports under Rupee State Credit Route except commission up to 10% of invoice value of tea and tobacco.
4. Dividend by any company to which the requirement of dividend balancing is applicable.
5. Payment related to “Call Back Services” of telephones.
6. Drawal of exchange for travel to Nepal or Bhutan and also transactions with a person resident therein, unless specifically exempted by the RBI by general or special order.

However, remittance of prize money or sponsorship of sports activity abroad by a person other than international, national or state level sports bodies, if the amount involved exceeds US$ 1 lakh requires permission from Ministry of Human Resources Development, Department of Youth Affairs and Sports.

Transactions with Terrorist Countries

Capital account remittances directly or indirectly to countries identified by the Financial Action Task Force (FATF) as “non-cooperative countries and territories” and remittances directly or indirectly to those individuals and entities identified as posing significant risk of committing acts of terrorism, are banned. Further, AP (Dir) Circular 28 dt 25.1.17 prohibits an Indian Party from making direct investment in an overseas entity (set up or acquired abroad directly as JV / WOS or indirectly as step down subsidiary) located in such countries. The list of these is available on www.fatf-gafi.org.

Repatriation v Remittance

Repatriation is sending money abroad which was originally remitted from abroad. Such an amount received from abroad can be credited to NRE account and is repatriable. This amount along with income generated therefrom can be sent outside India without any restrictions. It is mandatory for all the receipts and dispatches to be made through normal banking channels.

Funds on non-repatriable basis cannot be remitted abroad. The income from such funds or their maturity proceeds should be credited only to the NRO accounts. Depositor transferring funds from NRE to NRO loses repatriability.

Export & Import of Currency to or from Nepal and Bhutan

Release of forex is not admissible for travel to and transaction with Residents of Nepal and Bhutan. Investments in Nepal are permitted only in Indian Rupees. Investments in Bhutan are permitted in Indian Rupees as well as in freely convertible forex. All dues receivable on investments made in freely convertible currencies, as well as their sale or winding up proceeds are required to be repatriated to India in freely convertible currencies only. Use of International Credit Cards for payment in forex in Nepal and Bhutan is not permitted.

FEMA allows (a) citizen of India, Nepal or Bhutan, resident in Nepal or Bhutan, (b) a branch in Nepal or Bhutan of a company or corporation in India or Nepal or Bhutan and (c) a branch in Nepal or Bhutan of a partnership firm or otherwise of citizens of India, Nepal or Bhutan are permitted to deal in INR freely. Such persons can invest in shares and convertible debentures of Indian companies under FDI Scheme on repatriable basis, subject to the condition that the amount of consideration for such investments shall be paid only by way of inward remittance in forex.

An individual travelling from India to Nepal / Bhutan or vice versa, may carry notes of only ₹100. The new notes freshly introduced of ₹200 and ₹2,000 or replaced the old ones of ₹500 have not yet become legal tender. The cap of ₹25,000 appears to have been untouched.

Prohibition on Export of Antique Indian Coins

No person shall take or send out of India the Indian coins which are covered by the Antique and Art Treasure Act, 1972.

Repatriation Subject to Tax Compliance — Forms 15CA/CB
Sec. 195 mandates application of TDS (= withholding tax) from payments made or credit given to NRIs at the rates in force. RBI also requires that except in cases of specifically exempted personal remittances, no remittance shall be allowed to an NRI unless he has obtained a no objection certificate from the Department. Such a certificate is not required if the NRI submits a letter of undertaking (Form 15CA) along with an accountant's certificate (Form 15CB) stating that tax, if applicable has been paid on the amount contemplated to be repatriated or transferred to his NRE account.

There was a huge confusion related with Forms 15CA/15CB. While CBDT notification 67/2013 required these Forms only for taxable transfers, the confusion was created by the Income Tax (14th Amendment) Rules, 2013, which specified a list of 28 (expanded to 33) nature of payments under Rule 37BB which were exempt from furnishing these Forms. This list did not cover even the non-taxable transfers. To bypass this contradiction, the banks asked for the Forms for all transfers.

To remedy this situation, FA15 has substituted Sec. 195(6) as follows — "The person responsible for paying to a non-resident, (not being a company) or to a foreign company, any sum, whether or not chargeable under the provisions of this Act, shall furnish the information relating to payment of such sum, in such form and manner, as may be prescribed." (Forms 15CA and 15CB.) Thankfully, this amendment has brought clarity to the procedure.

Henceforth, Form 15CA as well as 15CB has to be furnished.

To monitor and track transactions properly, Circular 04/2009 dt 29.6.09 has laid down the following revised procedure:

- Remitter obtains certificate of Accountant (Form-15CB).
- Remitter accesses www.tin-nsdl.com.
- Takes printout of the undertaking (Form-15CA), fills the remittance details, signs it electronically and uploads it.

- Takes printout of filled Form-15CA with system generated acknowledgement number.
- Submits both the forms to the AD in duplicate.
- If the remitter has obtained a certificate from AO for applying tax at lower or nil rate, this certificate is required to be submitted in place of Form-15CB.
- AD remits the amount.

In the case of NRIs who do not maintain NRO account and have no taxable income in India, ADs can allow remittances after obtaining a simple declaration from them.

GSR 978(E) dt 16.12.15 states that Form 15CB is required only if such payment made to an NRI is chargeable to tax and it exceeds ₹5 lakh.

Note that the FA17 inserted a new Sec. 271J to levy penalty on an accountant, merchant banker or registered valuer who furnish the incorrect information in a report or certificate. The amount of penalty shall be ₹10,000 for each such inaccurate report or certificate.

Prohibited Foreign Contributions

Sec. 4 of Foreign Contribution (Regulation) Act, 1976 (FCRA) prohibits acceptance of foreign contribution by any candidate for election, correspondent, columnist, cartoonist, editor, owner, printer or publisher of a registered newspaper, judges, government servants or employees of any corporation, members of any legislature, political party or its office bearers. Associations having a definite cultural, economic, educational, religious and social programme should get themselves registered with the Ministry of Home Affairs, before receiving any foreign contributions. These should be received only through a designated bank branch as specified in the application for registration. Those who are not registered with the ministry may obtain prior permission of the Central Government. Indian citizens abroad do not fall in the purview of "foreign source" and therefore do not attract the provisions of FCRA.

Capital Account Transactions

These are transactions altering assets or liabilities, including contingent liabilities, outside India of Residents or ROIs such as —

For Residents

(a) Investment in Foreign Securities.
(b) Forex loans raised in India and abroad.
(c) Transfer of immovable property outside India.
(d) Guarantee in favour of an ROI.
(e) Export, import and holding of currency or currency notes.
(f) Loans and overdrafts from and to an ROI.
(g) Maintenance of forex accounts in or outside India.
(h) Taking an insurance policy from an insurer outside India.
(i) Remittance outside India of capital assets.
(j) Sale and purchase of forex derivatives in India and abroad and commodity derivatives abroad.

For ROIs

(a) Investment in securities issued by a body corporate or an entity in India and contribution to the capital of a firm or a proprietorship concern or an AOP in India.
(b) Acquisition or transfer of immovable property in India.
(c) Guarantee in favour of an ROI.
(d) Import, export and holding of currency or currency notes.
(e) Forex accounts in India.
(f) Remittance outside India of capital assets in India.

Current Account Transactions

These differ from capital account transaction and include —

(a) Payments due in connection with foreign trade, other current business, services, and short-term banking and credit facilities in the ordinary course of business.
(b) Payments due as interest on loans and as net income from investments.
(c) Remittances for living expenses of parents, spouse and children residing abroad, and

(d) Expenses in connection with foreign travel, education and medical care of parents, spouse and children.

GST on Forex Conversion Service

Service of supply of foreign currency, including money changing will be taxed under the newly introduced GST as follows:

1. Up to ₹1 lakh : 1% of gross amount subject to minimum of ₹250.
2. ₹1 lakh to 10 lakh : ₹1,000 + 0.5% of amount exceeding 1 lakh.
3. Over ₹10 lakh : ₹5,000 + 0.1% of amount exceeding ₹10 lakh.

The value of supply of services in relation to purchase of sale of FE including money changing shall be equal to the difference in the buying rate or the selling rate and the RBI reference rate for that currency at that time multiplied by the total units of the currency.

Master Circulars

We have strived hard to incorporate the provisions as mandated by the latest master RBI circulars.

2

~

Residential Status

When I read FEMA, I was reminded of a couplet —

I am the parliamentarian draftsman, I make the laws
For most of the litigations, I am the cause.

FEMA is a classic case of an armchair drafting of the legislation with little application of mind and no contact with reality.

Let us first study the definition of an NRI as per ITA.

Residential Status under ITA

Tax liability in India is directly determined by residential status of an assessee under ITA and it depends on change in such status.

There are 3 statuses —

1. Resident and Ordinarily Resident (ROR),
2. Resident but Not Ordinarily Resident (RNOR), and
3. Non-Resident Indian (NRI).

An individual is treated as a Resident (ROR) for the FY (April to March) if he satisfies, during the year, any one of the following 2 conditions — He is in India for at least a period or periods amounting in all to —

(a) 182 days in the FY, OR
(b) 365 days out of the preceding 4 FYs AND 60 days in the FY.

Most of those going for the first time may not be eligible to be an NRI because of the "b" clause above which allows stay in India only for 60 days. This problem is bypassed by the following additional provisions —

(i) Where an *Indian citizen* leaves India in any year for the purpose of employment, or as a member of a crew of an Indian merchant ship, the period of "60 days" is to be replaced by "182 days". Consequently, an Indian citizen going abroad for employment can stay in India up to 181 days for obtaining NRI status for that very year, even if he is in India for 365 days or more during the 4 preceding years.

(ii) When an *Indian citizen or a person of Indian Origin* (PIO) who is abroad comes to visit India, the period of "60 days" is to be replaced by 182 days.

Finally, an NRI is a person who is not a Resident.

Note that the condition-i above is applicable only to Indian Citizens and not PIOs whereas condition-ii is applicable to both of them. None of them is applicable to rank foreigners.

We strongly feel that the word "employment" has various shades of meaning. Dictionary defines it as "work", "occupation", "keeping busy". Therefore the period of 60 days can be replaced with 182 days, not only for rendering service to an employer but also for undertaking of business or profession. Moreover, the person going abroad may be either employed in India or abroad.

Note also that for those who return to India permanently (not on a visit), the period of "60 days" is not replaced by 182 days. Consequently, anyone who has been in India for 365 days or more in the preceding 4 years and returns before February finds that his NRI status is lost right from the year of his return.

HUFs

As per Sec. 6(2), an HUF (or a partnership firm or Association of Persons) gets it Residential status for a financial year, depending upon where, during that year, the control and management of its affairs is situated wholly.

In other words, it can be an ROR, RNOR or NRI. Note carefully that the HUF status does not depend upon the status of its Karta, unless, it is the Karta who handles its affairs and is an NRI. Consequently, an NRI Karta may give a Power of Attorney to any trustworthy Resident person, preferably a member of his HUF, even a female one, for handling its affairs.

Alternatively, he may ask the bank to redesignate the HUF account as an NRO account.

We prefer the first option. If you are not in a position to come to India for donating the PoA, you may do so from your host country abroad, but you will require the attestation thereon of an Indian consulate located in your host country.

Crew Members on Ships with Indian & Foreign Flag

Crew members are required to submit the correct declaration before Custom authorities with respect to the currency, gold ornaments and electronic goods, etc. in their possession on arrival as well as departure.

Most of the persons working on Indian ships oscillate between NRI and RNOR because of the contractual nature of their job. For some years they may even become full-fledged Residents.

In the case of *CIT* v *Avtar Singh Wadhwan* (247ITR260), Bombay High Court has held that income from salary, in the case of crew of even an Indian vessel operating in international waters, is to be treated as having accrued outside India.

As per Sec. 5(2a) only such income of a non-resident shall be subjected to tax in India that is either received or is deemed to be received in India. Circular # 13/2017 dt 11.04.17 has clarified that salary accrued to an NRI seafarer for services rendered outside India on a foreign going ship (with Indian or foreign flag) shall not be included in the total income merely because the said salary has been credited in the NRE account maintained with an Indian bank by the seafarer. Other NRIs should carefully ensure that their income is first received in their host country before it is dispatched to India.

Members of a crew of a merchant ship with a foreign flag are treated as having left India for employment; not so for crew of an Indian ship. In an attempt to bring both of them on par with each other, FA90 extended the benefit of 182 days to Indian citizens who are members of the crew of an Indian ship. But again this is a shoddy correction. It merely states that if a crewman on an Indian ship passes the test of being an NRI, he will not be charged to tax on his forex earnings earned while working outside Indian waters. It is silent about the taxability in the hands of an individual when he travels from the status of an NRI to RNOR.

Moreover, as per Sec. 10(*6viii*), salary of a Non-resident foreign national as a member of a ship's crew is exempt provided his stay in India does not exceed an aggregate period of 90 days in the FY. Therefore, the members of a crew of a merchant ship with an Indian flag are still not on par with those with a foreign flag.

In the case of foreign bound ships where the destination of the voyage is outside India, there was uncertainty with regard to the manner and basis of determination of the period of stay in India for crew members of such ships who are Indian citizens. Therefore, Sec. 6 has been amended by SO 2240(E) dt 17.8.15 stating that the period of stay in India shall begin with the dates of entry and signing off as per the Continuous Discharge Certificate in respect of the voyage.

RNOR

To mitigate the shock of an NRI suddenly becoming a Resident, after returning to India permanently there is a transitional status of RNOR

An RNOR is an individual who —

(a) has been an NRI in 9 out of the 10 previous years preceding that year, or

(b) has, during the 7 previous years preceding that year, been in India for a period of, or periods amounting in all to 729 days or less.

If a Resident person is not an RNOR he is an ROR.

Consequently, those returning after being NRIs for 5 continuous years or less, immediately become Residents. Those returning after 6 years may become RNORs for one year whereas others, including those after being NRIs, for say, 25 years may become RNOR for 2 years at the most.

However, in rare cases a person can become an RNOR for 3 years.

Miscellaneous

1. A person can be treated as a Resident of two or more countries at the same time.
2. India includes the territorial waters. Thus a person in a yacht moored around the shores of India would be staying in India.
3. Indian ships operating beyond the Indian territorial waters are treated as not in India.

Taxability Depends on Status

ROR: The total income of a person who is a Resident includes all income from whatever source derived which —

(a) is received or is deemed to be received in India in such year by or on behalf of such person; or
(b) accrues or arises or is deemed to accrue or arise to him in India during such year; or
(c) accrues or arises to him outside India during such year.

Many NRIs go in for cumulative deposits under the wrong impression that the tax becomes applicable in India only when the interest is actually received. Sec. 5(2) leaves no room for any doubt or ambiguity, that if an effective and final conclusion can be drawn, on the issue of accrual of income to a Non-resident, the actual date of receipt is inconsequential — *Smt. Trishla Jain* v *Income-tax Commissioner [ITR 43 to 48 of 1991]*.

RNOR: Tax liability of an RNOR is the same as that of an NRI. In other words, his forex income is not taxable in India. There is only one exception. In the case of RNOR, income received and accrued outside India from a business controlled in or a profession set up in India continues to be taxable in India.

NRI: On the other hand, an NRI is not liable to tax on income accruing or arising outside India, even if it is remitted to India. As per Sec. 5, he is liable to pay tax only in respect of income received or deemed to be received in India or which accrues or arises or is deemed to accrue or arise in India by or on behalf of such person.

Income "received or deemed to be received" in India has a strange and illogical aspect. You may be taken unawares if and when it bites. The receipt of income refers to the very first occasion when the recipient gets the money under his control. Once an amount is received as income abroad, any remittance or transmission of the amount to any other place, including India, does not result in receipt of income at other place. The position will remain the same if income is received outside India by an agent of the assessee who later on remits it to India. The same income cannot be received by the same person twice, once outside India and once within India — *Keshav Mills Ltd. v CIT (1953) 23ITR230 (SC).*

Many employees request their employers to remit their salaries directly to their accounts in India. If you are one such an employee, take immediate corrective action.

Similarly, income which "accrues or arises or is deemed to accrue or arise in India" has stranger effect. In the case of *Trishla Jain v CIT (310ITR274)*, decided by the Punjab & Haryana High Court, some NRIs had purchased debentures issued by Oswal Agro Mills Ltd., an Indian company. Interest was payable on July 1 and December 31 of every year. The assessee declared the interest in his return for the FY 1987-88 in which he received the interest. The ITO took the view that the interest income was assessable on accrual basis in FY 1986-87. This was upheld by CIT (Appeals) and also by the Tribunal. The High Court concluded that there is no room for any doubt or ambiguity that the actual date of receipt is inconsequential. Income of a Non-resident has to be included in the previous year on accrual basis, i.e., as and when such income arises (or is deemed to have arisen) to the assessee, in a specific, definite and crystallized manner.

Residential Status under FEMA

This is very complicated. It varies from Rule to Rule. The complication gets further confounded because the definition as per ITA is different from that of FEMA. Normally —

Sec. 2(*u*) of FEMA defines a "person" to include —

(a) an individual,
(b) an HUF,
(c) a company,
(d) a firm,
(e) an AOP or BOI, whether incorporated or not,
(f) every artificial juridical person, not falling within any of the preceding sub-clauses, and
(g) any agency, office or branch owned or controlled by such a person.

Sec. 2(*v*) defines a person *Resident* to mean —

1. A person residing in India for more than 182 days during the course of the *preceding* FY but does not include:
   (A) A person who has gone out of India or who stays outside India, in either case, for the following 3 purposes —
      (a) for or on taking up employment outside India, or
      (b) for carrying on outside India a business or vocation ,or
      (c) for any other purpose, in such circumstances as would indicate his intention to stay outside India for an uncertain period.
   (B) A person who has come to or stay in India, in either case, otherwise than the following 3 purposes:
      (a) for or on taking up employment in India, or
      (b) for carrying on in India a business or vocation in India, or
      (c) for any purpose, in such circumstances as would indicate his intention to stay in India for an uncertain period.
2. Any person or body corporate registered or incorporated in India.

3. An office, branch or agency in India owned or controlled by a person Resident outside India.
4. An office, branch or agency outside India owned or controlled by a person Resident.

A person *Resident Outside India* (ROI) means a person who is not a Resident.

Comments

This is important. ITA deals with previous year and FEMA with *preceding* year. What is the effect?

Note carefully that the definition for ITA begins by stating — "An individual is treated as a Resident for the FY...". In other words, one cannot be a Resident for part of the year and a Non-resident for the rest of the year. That is not so for FEMA. The person becomes an NRI from day-1 when he leaves Indian shores and becomes a Resident from day-1 when he returns to India permanently.

Since for ITA the status gets crystallise only when the year is over, the status depends upon previous year. This is the reason why FEMA definition depends upon preceding year. This is also the reason why ITA requires stay in India of "182 days or more" whereas FEMA requires "more than 182 days"!

Yes, very complicated indeed.

Take the case of a crew member of a foreign ship or airline who, because of requirements of his job is regularly forced to stay in hotels in India for more than 182 days every year. Can he be treated as a Resident? Such a person is not *residing* in India but is only present in India and *staying* in a hotel. Therefore he continues to be an ROI.

There are two exceptions to the rules related with ROI —

1. A student going abroad is treated as an ROI.
2. There is a third status of *Resident but not Permanently* Resident related with deputies.

Both these subjects are covered in subsequent Chapters.

Person of Indian Origin (PIO)

FEMA defines a PIO to mean —

A citizen of any country other than Bangladesh or Pakistan, if—

(a) He at any time held an Indian passport, or

(b) He or either of his parents or any of his grand parents was a citizen of India by virtue of the Constitution of India or Citizenship Act, 1955.

(c) The person is a spouse of an Indian citizen or of a person referred to in (a) or (b) above.

PIO includes an "Overseas Citizen of India" cardholder within the meaning of Sec. 7(A) of the Citizenship Act, 1955.

The definition of PIO differs from Rule to Rule.

These provisions related with "Deposits" and "Remittance of Assets" where the citizens (or an incorporated entity) of Bangladesh or Pakistan are excluded. This exclusion is expanded to citizens of Sri Lanka for the provisions related with "Investment in Firm or Proprietary Concern in India" or "Purchase shares or convertible debentures or preference shares of an Indian company" and further citizens of Afghanistan, China, Iran, Nepal or Bhutan for Rule related with "Acquisition and Transfer of Immovable Property in India".

Circular AP (DIR) 11 dt 13.9.04 has lifted the restriction imposed on investment in Indian companies by Sri Lankan citizens. Accordingly, persons Resident outside India (other than a citizen of Bangladesh or Pakistan) including citizens of Sri Lanka are eligible to purchase shares or convertible debentures of an Indian company under Foreign Direct Investment (FDI) subject to the specified terms and conditions. Moreover, as per notification GSR 713(E), dt 23.10.07 a person who is a citizen of Bangladesh or an entity incorporated in Bangladesh may, with the prior approval of the Foreign Investment Promotion Board of the Government of India, purchase shares and convertible debentures of an Indian company under FDI.

For ITA, Explanation to Sec. 115C states that a person shall be deemed to be of Indian origin if he, or either of his parents or any of his grand parents, was born in undivided India.

What if such a person was born in divided India? Well, any person born in any place which was part of undivided India can be treated as born in undivided India even if the person was born after 15.7.47.

Sec. 2(25A) of ITA proclaims that India includes, for the purpose of Residentship, Dadra and Nagar Haveli, Goa, Daman and Diu, and Pondicherry in respect of any period. Even when these parts were not a part of India, still, by a fiction of law, these territories will be deemed to have been part of India and the question of residence will have to be decided on the basis of this fiction.

FEMA depends upon the Constitution of India or Citizenship Act. This may result in the same person being treated as PIO for ITA and not for FEMA and *vice versa.*

These small differences result in large confusions.

Borderline Cases — One More Difference

Where a person is in India only for a part of a day, the calculation of physical presence in India in respect of such broken period should be made on an hourly basis. A total of 24 hours of stay spread over a number of days is to be counted as being equivalent to the stay of one day — *Walkie* v *IRC [1952] 1AER92.*

Yet another case law, *223ITR462 (AAR) New Delhi* has a different view. The dates of arrival and departure have to be taken into account for calculating the period of stay in India, even if for some hours on these dates the person was in India on these dates, however short the period may be. The same view is reiterated by *P. 7 of 1995, In re (1997) 90Taxman62.*

These rulings may be applied even in the case of ITA where data is not available to calculate the period of stay of an individual in India in terms of hours.

The latest one decided on 29.6.12 is [2012] 24taxmann.com193 (Mumbai — *Tribench F) Income Tax Officer (IT)-1(1) v Fausta C. Cordeiro*. In this case, Commissioner (Appeals) found that the assessee generally arrived late in night after completing his work abroad and attended to work next day and generally left early in morning so as to attend work again after arriving at destination. It was held that such days of arrival were to be excluded and by doing so assessee's staying was less than 180 days in India and not 187 as claimed by the ITO. Therefore, the date of arrival was to be excluded as it was not a complete day.

RBI has not yet taken any decision related with residential status of a trust. It is reported that the following internal guidelines are issued by it:

1. Appointment of a Non-resident as a trustee in a trust in India does not require any approval under FEMA.
2. Revenue income of a trust for Non-resident beneficiaries, can be remitted outside India after payment of tax, subject to compliance with other provisions of FEMA.
3. Any trust in which an NRI is a beneficiary or a trustee, cannot enter into prohibited activities.

3

~

Students Studying Abroad

Good news for students studying abroad. Through Circular 45 dt 8.12.03, RBI has declared that for the purpose of FEMA, students will be treated as NRIs as soon as they go abroad for studies.

A student is a non-resident alien in the USA who is temporarily in the country on "F", "J", "M" or "Q" visa and is not engaged in any activities that are prohibited by US immigration laws. If a non-resident alien receives a grant from outside sources, then it is not taxable in the USA. Students are, in reality, not dependent for a dominant part of their expenses on remittances from their households in India. Often they undertake certain employments.

Normally, the terms of a scholarship or fellowship grant specify that the amount or a part of it is to be used for tuition, enrolment fees, books and cost of supplies and equipment belonging to the institution that the student uses. This portion is not taxable but the portion representing payment for teaching, research or any service is taxable in the USA. It may also be taxable in India depending upon the residential status of the student as defined by ITA. Relief can be claimed from such tax under Article 21 of DTAA between India and the USA.

This benefit, in most cases, entitles a student to a refund of all or part of the money withheld. This can be exercised by filing a non-resident tax return in India. It is necessary to attach a covering note from the educational institution declaring that the whole or part of the scholarship or fellowship is an educational award and not money paid for personal services.

The greatest advantage lies in the fact that as non-residents, they will be eligible to receive remittances from India —

(a) up to US$ 1 million per FY out of sale proceeds of assets / balances in their NRO account maintained with an Authorised Dealer bank in India, and

(b) up to US$ 250,000 per FY under the Liberalized Remittance Scheme.

All other facilities available to NRIs under FEMA are equally applicable to the students. Educational and other loans availed of by them as residents in India will continue to be available.

We will be dealing with these facilities later in this book.

Students can open and maintain NRE, FCNR and NRO accounts in India. In the case of students proceeding to Russia and other Republics of CIS countries entire exchange admissible can be availed in the form of currency notes.

We strongly feel that the ITA definition of NRI should have been changed simultaneously. A student does not go abroad for the purpose of employment. Therefore during the very first year of his going abroad, the clause "365 days out of the preceding 4 FYs AND 60 days in the FY" will sink its teeth into him and treat him as a Resident for ITA unless he is in India for less than 60 days.

Consequently, those who desired to send some money to their family members in India were forced to take recourse to the illegal hawala route. We are afraid that they will resume doing so.

Foreign Students in India

Anyone who had come to India for study or training and has completed it, may remit the balance in his accounts, provided such balance represents funds derived out of remittances received from abroad or rupee proceeds of forex brought and sold to an AD or out of stipend / scholarship received from the government or any organisation in India.

Students and Insurance

Foreign universities particularly in US and UK insist on students taking medical insurance and additional risk cover for mental or nervous disorders, alcoholism and drug dependency, pregnancy, sports injuries, cancer, child care, etc., for as much as US$ 2,50,000. The average premium for this is around US$ 900.

Indian insures offer such covers as per the specific needs of various universities at around US$ 350. Many US universities allow a student taking over from India. National Health Scheme in UK does not allow such waiver for treatment in government hospitals. Students can buy risk cover from India using UK private institutions.

ICICI Lombard insures students for US$ 100,000 for travelling. The premiums vary. For students going to the US or Canada the annual premium starts from ₹6,600 for the Bronze Plan and could go up to as high as ₹17,000 for the Gold Plus Plan. For UK or Europe, the premium is lower — at nearly ₹9,500 for the Gold Plus Plan. This plan offers medical cover worth US$ 50,000-250,000, in addition to covering dental treatment for US$ 250, baggage loss up to US$ 1,000, among various other accidents.

Bajaj Allianz's Student Companion Policy offers 3 different plans — Standard, Silver and Gold. Medical cover ranges between US$ 50,000 and US$ 200,000; baggage loss up to US$ 1,000 and personal liability cover up to US$ 100,000, compassionate visit up to US$ 7,500 and sponsor protection up to US$ 10,000.

Tata AIG offers similar cover, in addition to baggage loss up to US$ 1,000; personal liability cover up to US$ 100,000; study interruption up to US$ 7,500; compassionate visit up to US$ 7,000; bail bond up to US$ 5,000 and sponsor protection up to US$ 10,000.

Since the premiums are very volatile, get the latest costs of insurance, whenever needed.

Compassionate visit cover comprises of a round-trip economy class air ticket and accommodation expenses for an immediate family member if the student is hospitalised for 7 consecutive days. The student can visit his/her parents if either of them is critically ill.

4

~

Not Permanently Resident

A person with a foreign passport, Resident for employment of specific duration, irrespective of its duration, or for non-specific duration not longer than 3 years, is defined by FEMA as a "Person not Permanently Resident" (= Expatriate).

Such a person has the following privileges and restrictions:

1. He can own a normal Resident bank account and not NRI-related NRO, NRE or FCNR accounts. While leaving India after employment, he can re-designate his Resident account as NRO to enable him receive his legitimate dues. The debit to the account should be only for the purpose of repatriation abroad subject to the US$ 1 million per FY under the general facility for NRIs discussed in Chapter *Forex Remittances — NRIs*.
2. He may possess forex, without any limit, in the form of currency notes, bank notes and travellers cheques, only provided he had acquired, held or owned it when he was an ROI and had brought it into India through legal channels, including baggage. It is absolutely necessary to fill the Currency Declaration Form (CDF) only if the total forex brought through baggage is above US$ 10,000. Nonetheless, it is advisable for him to file CDF even if the amount is less than this limit. Similarly, for each subsequent inward remittance he should obtain an Encashment Certificate Form (ECF). Moreover, he should get Form-BCI from the banks while purchasing DDs, MTs, TTs, etc. This then will he be able to repatriate unspent forex without any hassles.
3. He may purchase or sell foreign securities out of his forex resources abroad.
4. He can hold an insurance policy issued by an insurer outside India only if he pays the premium out of his foreign resources.

5. As per Notification FEMA 328/RB-2014 dt 30.12.14, a citizen of a foreign state, Resident, being (i) an employee of a foreign company or (ii) a citizen of India employed by a foreign company on deputation to its office, branch, subsidiary, joint venture or group company in India may open, hold and maintain a forex account with a bank outside India and receive his whole salary for the services rendered in India, by credit to such account, provided that income tax is paid thereon. "Company" shall include a "Limited Liability Partnership" (LLP).
6. Any salary payable for rest or leave period which is both preceded or succeeded by service in India and forms part of the service contract is also regarded as income earned in India. The same rule is applicable to a citizen of India, employed by a foreign company on deputation outside India.
7. No tax is payable in India if the conditions relating to short stay exemption under the relevant tax treaty are met with. For example, under the Indo-US tax treaty, if the US Resident is deputed to India for less than 183 days in an FY and the salary is paid by the US company, such employee would be taxable only in US even on salary relating to work carried out in India.
8. ADs can allow a citizen of a foreign state other than Pakistan to remit for maintenance of his close relatives abroad, amount up to his net salary after deduction of taxes, contribution to PF, etc. The same facility is extended to a citizen of India, who is on deputation to India of a foreign company. A problem arises when the expatriate comes to India along with his family but still has to meet his personal liabilities abroad. Repatriation options for him then become limited. Moreover, remittance of only his salary and not other income in India for meeting his other liabilities is a concern.
9. AP (DIR) Circular dt 22.1.15 has clarified that the facility of remittance of salary outside India available to an employee of a company, including an LLP shall also be available to an employee deputed to a group company in India. Salary includes earnings from stage shows and earnings from model-

ling assignments and acting assignments, etc. An individual who has remitted his entire earnings and salary and wishes to further remit "other income" may approach RBI through his AD.

10. An entity in India may remit an amount being its contribution towards the provident, superannuation, pension fund in respect of an expatriate staff (= a person whose funds are maintained outside India by his principal employer outside India) in its employment who is a Resident but not Permanently Resident.
11. In case the employee is tax equalised (his Indian tax liability is borne by the employer in India), the employer can pay whole of his salary outside India. TDS is applicable on salary even if the employer is not Resident. If any refund becomes due to the employee, after he has already left India and has no bank account in India by the time the assessment orders are passed, the refund can be issued in favour of the Indian employer as the tax has been borne by him — Circular 707, dt 11.7.95.
12. Indian tax is levied for services rendered in India even if the employer is outside India and the salary is paid outside India.
13. A deputy in India surely continues to earn non-employment income (such as dividends, interest on deposits, etc.) on his investments outside India. Subsequent transfer of the funds from his bank account outside India to his bank account in India will be tax neutral. However, such income directly remitted to the bank account in India is likely to be taxable in India. Take care!
14. Most of the deputies outside India earn some side income by way of moonlighting assignments. Such incomes are taxable in India if the individual is a Resident as per ITA definition.
15. When an expatriate comes to India as an employee of an Indian company, as opposed to his continuing on the foreign company payroll, keeping his salary outside India is riddled with problems. Indian companies can reimburse the expatriate's salary since it is a current account transaction. It in-

volves a cost to the foreign company. A re-look at these regulations is needed.

16. Unfortunately, AAR has held on the application made by Caterpillar, a US Company, that the salaries of the non-resident technicians paid in the US by the parent company for work carried out in India would be taxable in India. However, reimbursement of living expenses paid to non-resident technicians in India, by the Indian subsidiary or joint venture company would be exempt u/s 10(14). Very confusing indeed!

Miscellaneous

A foreign national is not permitted to take up employment in India unless he holds an Employment Visa. If he does not, his employment income received in India cannot be remitted abroad. If the period of engagement of such a person is up to 3 months, any other valid visa such as business, tourist, etc., will do.

Generally, extension of a visa is granted by the appropriate Indian Embassy/Indian Consulate abroad. Although an employment visa can be extended by the Ministry of Home Affairs, it is a time-consuming process. A business visa is normally not extended. The foreign national has to go back to his home country and apply to the Indian Embassy there to obtain an employment visa.

Upon arrival in India for employment purposes, one should apply for allotment of a Permanent Account Number (PAN).

While leaving India, at immigration, authorities may require a no objection certificate from the Indian tax authorities. If one does not have such a certificate he can furnish an undertaking, in the prescribed form, from the employer to the effect that the tax payable by employee, if any, shall be paid by the employer.

Registration for Foreigners

As per the provisions of the Registration of Foreigners Rules, 1939, any foreign national visiting India, who either has valid visa for more than 180 days or intending to stay for more than 180 days must register within 14 days of arrival with the "Foreigners Regional Registration Office" with the following documents — (a) Form A; (b) Certificate from employer about Indian employment; (c) 4 photographs; (d) Original passport and Visa (returned after verification); and Proof of residence.

Thereafter, a "Residential permit" will be issued to the foreigner.

Children below 16 years of age are exempt from registration if they have entered on PIO or OCI card.

No fee is charged for registration but a penalty in Indian currency equivalent to US$ 30 is charged for late registration unless the delay is condoned.

To Sum

The considerations which should be kept in mind are — (i) where salary should be delivered; (ii) if salary is to be paid outside India, would it be charged back to the Indian entity; (iii) current exchange control regulations for delivering salary; corporate tax implications (permanent establishment exposure), withholding tax, the transfer pricing regulations and service tax implications.

It is necessary to put in place a proper secondment structure. It is hoped that the authorities will smoothen and streamline the Indian tax and also the DTAA provisions to eliminate these hardships.

5

~

Deputies — Hardships and Confusion

Thankfully, students are treated as NRIs. The authorities should have extended similar benefit to deputies, namely employees of Indian companies sent on secondments, placed abroad or created yet another special category like "Not Permanently Resident". The tax provisions on the income of such deputies are riddled with a lot of confusion and resultant hardships and litigations.

Hardship-1: Residential Status

Some ITOs claim that a deputee cannot be considered as having gone abroad to take up an employment since he is already employed in India. Therefore "60 days" cannot be replaced by "182 days" in the rule for all deputies.

In the case of *ITR 218 AR, 2006 British Gas (I) (P) Ltd.* v *CIT*, the Indian company had deputed its employees to its group companies, including British Gas, UK. The Indian company also paid salary in India and recovered it from the UK company by raising a debit note. The employees were also given per diem by the UK company to meet their additional cost of living. Both the salary received in India and the allowances received in UK were taxed in UK since the employees were Tax Residents in UK. The AAR held that as per the Indo-UK DTAA agreement, since the employees are drawing their salary in respect of the employment being exercised in UK, the salary shall be taxable only in UK. Consequently, the Indian company need not apply TDS.

It is pertinent to note the particular statement in the verdict has a universal application — "An individual need not be an unemployed person who leaves India for employment outside India."

Hardship-2: Tax on Salary Received in India

1. Income which is not attributable to services rendered in India is not taxable in India — Supreme Court for *Sedco Forex Drilling International Inc (Civil Appeal No. 351-355 of 2005 and Others).* We strongly feel that this decision covers not only the salary received abroad even when the employee is a full-fledged Resident but also the salary received in India because both such salaries are paid for services not rendered in India.
2. U/s 9(1*ii*) salary payable for services rendered in India shall be regarded as income earned in India, even if paid outside India. It is not permissible to infer the corollary, viz., that in each and every case where services are rendered outside India, salary cannot be deemed to accrue or arise in India — *Capt. A. L. Fernandes* v *ITO [2002] 81ITD203 (Mum) (TM).*
3. A Japanese deputee worked in India for 273 days during the FY. Since he was not a "Resident" in India in any of nine out of ten previous years he was an RNOR. Tribunal held that where provisions of ITA were more beneficial to assessee, same should have been preferred over DTAA, and, thus income earned by assessee outside India could not be taxed in India.

On appeal, the High Court decided the case in favour of the assessee since he was an RNOR. Further it was held that Tribunal was right in holding that the rent-free accommodation provided by the Indian company to the assessee, was not a perquisite in the hands of the assessee u/s 17(2). Hence, the assessee was entitled to the benefit of the exemption provided by Section 10(14) — *CIT v Sakakibara Yutaka [2012] 25taxmann.com557 (HC Delhi).*

Hardship-3: Per Diem Allowance

Living allowance paid in addition to the regular salary to cover expenses incurred wholly, necessarily and exclusively in performance of office duties to the employees of Indian company who are on deputation are exempt from tax u/s 10(*14*)(*i*). Department wanted to tax any savings effected out of such allowances.

The ITAT held that it is not open to the revenue to call for the details of expenses actually incurred unless the specific allowances are disproportionately high compared to the salary received by him or unreasonable with reference to the nature of the duties performed by the taxpayer. It also held that ROIs coming to India and Indians going abroad are to be considered on same footing in respect of exemption u/s 10(14i) — *CIT v Sakakibara Yutaka [2012] 25taxmann.com557 (HC Delhi).*

U/s 9(1iii) salary payable by the government to a citizen of India for services rendered outside India is deemed to have accrued or arisen in India irrespective of the place where it is paid.

Sec. 10(7) exempts any allowance or perquisite paid or allowed outside India. As per CBDT Circular 8/2005 dt 29.8.05 the per diem allowance is exempt from tax u/s 10(14). Moreover, as per *[2011] 15taxmann.com328 (Kolkata — Trib)*, where, in addition to regular salaries and benefits in India, living allowance is given to employees of Indian company who are temporarily deployed in USA to work for Indian company, living allowance will be exempt.

Hardship-4: Salary Received Abroad

A deputy would face tax in India on "Residence" basis and in the overseas country on "Source" basis.

The employee can claim a short stay exemption (less than 183 days during the FY) on salary paid by the Indian employer under the "Dependent Personal Services", if the DTAA or the domestic tax laws of the host country have such a provision. If the employee is fully taxable abroad, he can claim credit for taxes paid abroad against his Indian tax liability for the same income.

Hardship-5: TDS at Lower Rate

Several banks in India give the benefit of DTAA while applying TDS on NRO deposits. Can the same benefit be extended by an employer taking into consideration the credit for foreign taxes to reduce the TDS on salary? Logical jurisprudence clearly gives the answer in the affirmative. However, unless the CBDT issues a clarification, the employers apply TDS to be on the safe side.

Hardship-6: Employer Pays Tax

Many Indian employers pick up the Indian tax liability of a foreign deputy and pay him net of tax salary. In such cases a multiplier effect comes into play. For clarity suppose the tax payable is ₹10,000. Since the employer pays this tax, it is considered as additional salary and charged to tax @ 30.9% which works out at ₹3,090 and this is also paid by the employer. Now, this ₹3,090 is an additional salary, etc., etc., *ad infinitum*. Finally, the employer ends up paying ₹4,472 as tax!

HC Uttarakhand in the case of *DIT (International Taxation), Delhi-II v Sedco Forex International Drilling Inc* taxmann.com 238 observed that perquisites not provided by way of tax paid by employer on salaries/remuneration of employees would constitute non-monetary benefits and, as such, same would be exempted u/s 10(10CC).

ITOs often take the stance that salary costs reimbursed by the Indian company under the secondment agreement are in the nature of technical service fees, warranting a withholding tax in India. Bangalore Tribunal has held that due consideration should be placed on the substance of the secondment agreement, which clearly proves that the real and economic employer of the seconded employee is the Indian company, even though he is on the payroll of the foreign company. Consequently, the services are not technical in nature.

Incidentally, as per Rule 26, for TDS on salary payable in foreign currency, the value in rupees of such salary shall be calculated at its "Telegraphic transfer buying rate" as on the date on which TDS is required to be applied.

If any refund becomes due to the employee after he has already left India and has no bank account in India by the time the assessment orders are passed, the refund can be issued to the employer as the tax has been borne by it [Circular 707 dt 11.07.1995].

Hardship-7: Foreign Taxes

Payment of foreign taxes by the Indian employer also has same problems. Fortunately, it can be solved by giving a loan to the employee. The notional interest may be liable to tax in the hands of the employee. Consequently, as and when the employee receives the tax refund, he would need to repay it to his employer.

Hardship-8: Filing Tax Returns Abroad

The FY is April-March in India and January-December in most of the overseas countries. Refer Chapter *Income tax* for details.

Hardship-9: Returns of Spouses

Certain countries require spouses accompanying the employees to file overseas returns based on their stay abroad. Some others require joint filing which attract some tax advances. Since there is no such provision in India, the deputies are forced to forego the advantage. Yes, in the erstwhile states under the dominion of Portugal, viz., Goa, Daman, Diu, Dadra and Nagar Haveli system of "Community of Property" continues to prevail which is similar but not same.

The Worst Hardship-10: Social Security

When a deputy of an Indian company goes abroad on an assignment for a few years, he has to contribute to the Social Security System, if it is prevalent in that country. It does not benefit him in any way as in most countries the minimum duration of contribution for deriving any benefit is 10 years. When the deputy returns to India before this period, he loses this amount *in toto*. According to an estimate, Indian IT professionals in the US contribute close to $1 billion every year to the Scheme.

Possibly to counter this atrocity, India had, w.e.f. 1.11.08 made it mandatory for International Workers (IWs) to contribute to Employee Provident Fund and Employee Pension System, as for local workers. Previously, IWs were eligible to withdraw the accumulated EPF after the end of their employment in India. Now IWs can withdraw only after they have reached 58 years of age. The amount is taxable in India if the contributions are for less than 5 years unless such withdrawals are due to total incapacity to work or suffering from prescribed diseases or on grounds specified in the Social Security Agreement (SSA).

SSA is a reciprocal program that prevents double payment and equality of treatment with the host country workers to social security systems between countries. India has signed SSAs with 12 countries: Belgium, Germany, France, Switzerland, Luxembourg, Denmark, Korea, Netherlands, Hungary, Czech Republic, Finland and Norway. We may have missed some countries.

Generally, the PF office has to make payments to the IWs in their home countries. Now, w.e.f. 1.12.11, expatriates coming from SSA countries are allowed to withdraw on completion of the Indian assignment the amount in his bank account directly or through the employer. Moreover, the number of years of service in a SSA country will be combined with the services in India for determining pension eligibility. Expatriates and the employer can file a joint application in Form-19 which does not require any supporting documents. It is not clear whether provident fund contributions made prior to 1.12.11 can be withdrawn.

Government of India will no longer be contributing to the pension scheme of IWs. Currently, out of employer's contribution of 12%, ₹541 per month, viz., 8.33% of the salary (capped at ₹6,500) goes to the pension fund. The limit of ₹6,500 per month as indicated for domestic workers above is not applicable to IWs. This results in a bigger loss for the individuals from non-SSA countries. Even the individuals coming from SSA countries need to be careful as most SSAs only cover pension benefits but not EPF.

Now, huge amounts will get blocked in IWs EPF account for a very long time. Bad! Or is it really bad? Getting around 9% tax-free interest is a great boon.

It has been clarified that on reaching the superannuation age, the amount can be directly credited to a bank abroad. It will no longer be necessary for IWs to hold an Indian bank account to claim the PF withdrawal.

What follows is most scary. A new rule has come into effect from 1.4.11 whereby PF accounts inactive for more than 3 years will not earn any interest after this period. Contributions of employees from non-SSA countries will surely remain inoperative for more than 3 years in most of the cases.

Good Solutions

To bypass such hardships, many proactive companies in India have got their offices abroad incorporated in that country. Salaries paid from such offices are not taxable in India if the employee happens to be an NRI for tax purposes. The employee can claim exemption if all the following conditions are satisfied —

(a) The employee becomes an NRI from ITA point of view.
(b) The employer transfers his service to his subsidiary incorporated abroad.
(c) The subsidiary in turn places the candidate on the project work and pays him salary directly, without getting reimbursement from the Indian company.
(d) The Indian company stops paying any salary or per diem abroad.

TDS not Applied when Applicable

Where the employer defaults in applying withholding tax when payments are made to non-residents, any interest, royalty, fees for technical services or other sum chargeable is not allowed as an expense if the entity making the payment does not deduct tax in respect of such payments.

There was some doubt related with the quantum of disallowance arising out of the expression, "other sum chargeable". The Department has clarified vide Circular 3/2015 dt 12.2.15 that the exposure of the tax withholder in his own income tax assessment should not exceed the liability of the recipient of the income.

6

~

Income Tax

It is necessary for every NRI to have at least handshake knowledge of the various tax provisions not only related with NRIs but also those related with Residents. He should also have a good insight into the investment avenues to be able to handle Indian assets acquired before leaving the Indian shores and also to obtain more mileage from his investible forex funds. The following is an attempt in that direction.

Income Tax Rates

Income Tax Rates — Individuals & HUFs		
Net Taxable Income Slab ₹	Tax at Minimum* ₹	Marginal Rate %
Up to 2,50,000	Nil	Nil
2,50,001 – 5,00,000	Nil	5
5,00,001 – 10,00,000	12,500	20
Over 10,00,000	1,12,500	30
*The tax amount is increased by cess @4%. This cess is applicable on normal tax, surcharge, TDS, advance tax, excise, custom, etc.		

	₹	₹
Income	10,00,000	1,12,500
Addtional	2,20,000	66,000
Total	12,20,000	1,78,500
Cess @ 4%		**7,140**
Net Tax Payable		**1,90,955**

Example: Mr. Date, (senior citizenship advantages not available to NRIs) has earned a total income, after deductions u/ss 80C, 80D, etc., of ₹12,20,000. His tax liability is as worked out in the alongside table.

Tax on Rich & Super Rich — Surcharge

A surcharge is a tax on tax and is a close cousin of cess. It was first introduced by FA13 @10% of income tax on every individual, HUF, AOP, BOI, whether incorporated or not, and every artificial juridical person whose income exceeds ₹1 crore. This surcharge was increased at 12% by FA15 and further increased at 15% by FA16. FA17 has roped in assessees having income exceeding ₹50 lakh but not exceeding ₹1 crore. And now, the recent FA19(2) has introduced 2 more slabs — (i) 25 % on total income exceeding ₹2 crore but not exceeding ₹5 crore; and (ii) 37% on total income exceeding ₹5 crore.

All this essentially means that those persons who have income over ₹5 crore have to pay a whopping marginal tax @42.7440%!

A marginal relief is put in place ensuring that the total income over each threshold does not exceed the tax payable.

For clarity, have a good look at the following Table.

Surcharge Applicable to Super-Rich				*Tax Rate*	*30%*	
				Cess Rate	*4%*	
Income Slab	*Surcharge*	*Rate plus surcharge*	*Extra Income*	*Total Income*	*Tax on Total Income*	*Surcharge*
₹	%	%	₹	₹	₹	%
50 Lakh	10	34.32	1,35,309	51,35,309	13,53,093	1,35,309
1 Crore	15	35.80	4,41,754	1,04,41,754	29,45,026	4,41,754
2 Crore	25	39.00	15,70,946	2,15,70,946	62,83,784	15,70,946
5 Crore	37	42.74	61,64,933	5,61,64,933	1,66,61,980	61,64,933

Now compute Surcharge on Tax on Total Income. You will be surprised to find that the surcharge is exactly identical with extra income. This is the Break-even Point. When the extra income is below this level, the surcharge happens to be more than the extra income. This is when the marginal relief comes into play and the surcharge gets reduced to the level of extra income. We strongly feel that it is this rate of 42.7440% which has irked the market, the main reason for its tanking, in spite of the fact that all the rest of it is geared towards growth of the economy.

Explanation —
Suppose a person has income of ₹1 crore and 3 lakh. Surcharge applicable to him is 15%.

Tax on ₹1 crore and 3 lakh = 1,12,500 + 30% of ₹93,000,000 = 29,02,500. Surcharge thereon @15% = 4,35,375.

Total Tax on ₹1 crore and 3 lakh = 33,37,875

Consequently, on extra income of ₹3,00,000, the surcharge applicable is 4,35,375.

Marginal relief allows the assessee to pay surcharge of ₹3,00,000 only.

The marginal relief becomes nil when the extra income reaches the level of ₹4,41,754.

The total tax payable on income of ₹1 crore and 3 lakh with cess = (29,02,500 + 3,00,000)*1.04 = ₹33,30,600.

This surcharge is @12% in the case of co-operative societies, firms, local authorities and those persons who are subjected to AMT if their income exceeds ₹1 crore. For domestic companies, it is 7% for income between ₹1 crore and ₹10 crore and 12% if it exceeds ₹10 crore.

It is claimed that this extra tax is applicable only on rich and superrich. This is strictly not true. Unfortunately, this surcharge of 12% along with the cess of 4% is also applicable to DDT and taxable capital gains. Surcharge is applicable even to the following types of income earned even by those under ₹2.5 lakh.

Sec.	*Description*	*Basic Rate-%*	*Total Rate-%*
115O	Dividend Distribution Tax — Equities	15	17.4720
111A	STCG on Equity & Equity-based MFs	15	17.4720
112	Taxable LT Gains	20	23.2960
115R	Dividend of Debt-based MF Schemes	25	29.1200
115QA	Buy Back by Domestic Companies	20	23.2960
115TD	Defaulting Trust Registered u/s 12AA	30	34.9940
115TA	Securitisation Trusts — for Individuals	25	29.1200
	— for Others	30	34.9940
115BBDA	Dividend exceeding ₹10 lakh	10	11.6480

Consequently, the exchequer is slated to get more revenue from the poor you and me on surcharge applicable on income under the above-mentioned Sections rather than the super rich.

In all our further discussions we shall give the basic rate, unless it is necessary to give the total rate for clarity. Readers are requested to keep this aspect in mind.

The following provisions are applicable only to Residents —

(a) The tax threshold for "senior citizen" (over 60 years in age) is ₹3 lakh and for "very senior citizen" is ₹5 lakh.
(b) The tax rebate applicable u/s 87A to the tax zone of ₹2.5 lakh to ₹5 lakh.
(c) Tax @10% on dividend income in excess of ₹10 lakh u/s 115BBDA
(d) Deduction available to handicapped persons.

What is Indian Income

1. Salary paid in India including charges collected as payable for a service rendered in India.
2. Reimbursement by the government to a government employee or citizen of India for rendering any service outside India.
3. Dividend paid by an Indian company outside India to a Resident.
4. Interest payable by the government on all kinds of government securities and saving instruments like bonds.
5. Interest received from a Resident except if the borrower has borrowed money to pursue business activities outside India. This ensures positive cash flow into India.
6. Interest paid by a non-resident to a Resident except when the non-resident has used the money borrowed for business activities in India. This would be to boost investments in India.
7. Non-compete fee received or receivable in relation to not carrying out any profession will be chargeable to tax as an income from business or profession.

Commission paid to non-resident for services rendered outside India is not chargeable to tax in India — *[2011] 16taxmann.com219 (Mum. — ITAT).*

Where the amounts are paid for preparatory study in a foreign country to an NRI for services which are utilised in India, such amounts would be deemed to accrue or arise in India. There is no difference between fees for Engineering Services and amounts paid as living allowances and travel allowances — Authority for Advance Rulings in the case of *Steffen, Robertson & Kirsten Consulting Engineers & Scientists v. CIT (1998) 230 ITR 206.*

Royalty or Fees for Technical Services

Points 4, 5 and 6 above are applicable for income generated from royalties, copyrights and fees for technical services. U/s 115A in the case of an NRI taxpayer, where the total income includes any income by way of Royalty or Fees for Technical Services received under an agreement entered after 31.03.1976 and which is not effectively connected with permanent establishment of the NRI, the tax is payable on the gross amount of such income has been drastically reduced to 10% from @25% by FA15. This action is slated to increase the flow of technology to India.

Sec. 40(ai) stipulates that any interest, royalty, fees for technical services or other sum chargeable under this Act, either payable in India to an NRI (not being a company or a foreign company) or outside India shall not be allowed as a deduction if there has been a failure in TDS.

Income Exempt from Tax

Following types of income are not treated as taxable income —

Agricultural Income: Sec. 10(1)

This income is tax-free but is aggregated with the other income only for rate, if it exceeds ₹5,000. NRIs are not allowed to purchase any agricultural land or farm house but they can continue to hold on to it if acquired before becoming NRI or inherited after becoming NRI. See the example at end of this Chapter for meaning of aggregation for rate.

Life Insurance: Sec. 10(10D)

Sums received under a life insurance policy are completely tax-free. Exceptions are (i) Keyman Insurance of LIC or like products of other insurance companies and (ii) Pension or annuity.

High-premium minimum-risk life policies are similar to deposits or bonds. The premium or other payment made on an insurance policy, other than a contract for a deferred annuity, is limited to 10% of the actual capital sum assured for the exemption. U/s 10(10D), where premium paid in any of the years during the term of the policy, exceeds 10% of the actual capital sum assured, the maturity value received by the policy holder will be fully taxable. However, any sum received under such policy on the death of the policy holder shall continue to be exempt. In calculating the actual capital sum, no account shall be taken of (i) the value of any premiums agreed to be returned or (ii) bonuses received.

Diplomatic Personnel

Remuneration of a foreign citizen (includes a PIO) is exempt

1. U/s 10(6ii) working as an official of an embassy, high commission, legation, commission, consulate or trade representation of a foreign state or a member of the staff of such official if the corresponding Indian official in that foreign country enjoys a similar exemption. Such officers should not be engaged in any business or profession or employment in India otherwise than as members of such staff.
2. U/s 10(6vi) for services rendered to a foreign enterprise during his stay in India provided (i) the foreign enterprise is not engaged in any business or trade in India, (ii) his stay in India does not exceed aggregate period of 90 days in the FY and (iii) such remuneration is not liable to be deducted from income of the employer.

3. U/s 10(6xi) if the remuneration is received for training in an undertaking or office owned by (i) the government or (ii) a company owned by the Central or State Government or its subsidiary or (iii) a statutory corporation or (iv) a co-operative society, wholly financed by the Central or State Government.

Allowance or Perquisite Paid by Government: Sec. 10(7)

Any allowances or perquisites paid or allowed as such outside India by the Government to a citizen of India for rendering service outside India is exempt.

Co-operative Technical Programme: Sec. 10(8)

The remuneration of an individual serving in India, received directly or indirectly, from a foreign Government in connection with any co-operative technical assistance programme in accordance with an agreement entered into by the Central Government and a foreign Government, is exempt from tax.

Remuneration of Consultant: Sec. 10(8A & 8B)

Any remuneration or fee received by a consultant directly or indirectly out of the funds made available to an international organisation under a technical assistance grant agreement between it and the Government of a foreign State is exempt. — Sec. 10(8A).

Similarly, the remuneration received by an employee of the consultant is also exempt, provided the employee is either not a citizen of India or is an RNOR — Sec. 10(8B).

Family Member of Employee: Sec. 10(9)

Foreign income of any family member of an employee referred to in Sec. 10(*8*) or 10(*8A*) or 10(*8B*) referred to above, accompanying him to India is exempt if the family member is required to pay income tax (including social security tax) to the foreign Government.

Allowance Received from UNO

Staff Assessment is an amount appropriated by the UN for its own expenses. This money does not belong to the employee of the UN. U/s 2 of the UN (Privileges and Immunities) Act, 1947 (read with Sec. 18 of the Schedule thereto) the rest of the salary and emolument is exempt from tax in India.

Consequently any pension received by an ex-employee after his retirement is also exempt from tax — Circular 293 dt 10.2.81.

The exemption is limited only to the salary and pension received from UN. The rest of the income will be treated as normal income, on par with other incomes.

The salaries may have been structured by the UN after factoring in this appropriation of monthly staff assessment. Yes, Staff Assessment is tantamount to deduction at source. However, there are no tax concessions on the Indian income earned from the financial assets in India of the employee. The two are unconnected.

Dividend and Capital Gains

Both these matters are dealt with in detail in Chapter *Capital Gains*.

Deductions

Some specified deductions are available on income from some specified sources. Contribution made is deductible from gross total income for arriving at the total income on which tax is required to be computed.

Contributions to Specified Schemes: Sec. 80C

Contributions by an individual or HUF to specified schemes u/s 80C qualify for a deduction up to an aggregate ceiling of ₹1.5 lakh from gross total income. There are no ceilings on deductions u/s 80C for individual schemes, unless the Rules of the schemes provide for their own limits. These schemes are —

1. Contributions to (i) any life insurance company for life cover, (ii) LIC deferred annuity, and (iii) ULIP and Dhanaraksha in the name of spouse and all children, major or minor, married or otherwise (including married daughters), but not parents

dependent or not, are also eligible for the deduction. Same is the case for such instruments taken in the name of any member of HUF by an HUF.

Sums paid or deposited to effect or to keep in force a contract for a deferred annuity is eligible for deduction provided that such contract does not contain a provision for the exercise by the insured of an option to receive a cash payment in lieu of the payment of the annuity. If the premium payment exceeds 10% of the actual capital sum assured, only 10% will be eligible for deduction.

Where a taxpayer discontinues an LIC policy before premiums for two years have been paid, the deduction allowed during earlier years shall be withdrawn and shall be deemed to be the income of the year in which the policy is discontinued.

In the case of Life Annuity, the amount of annuity instalments will be treated as Income from Other Sources. In the case of Annuity Certain, the interest portion of the annuity instalment is treated as income. If Cash Option is exercised, the difference between the amount of cash option received and the total amount of premiums paid is treated as taxable income.

2. Equity-Linked Tax-Saving Schemes of MFs.
3. Payment by an individual or HUF towards cost of purchase or construction of a residential house (not necessarily self-occupied) in respect of—
   (a) Installment or part payment due under (i) any self-financing or other schemes of any development authority, housing board or other similar authority engaged in the construction and sale of house property on ownership basis or (ii) any company or co-operative society of which the assessee is a shareholder or member towards cost of house property allotted to him.
   (b) Repayment of housing loans from (i) Central or State Government, (ii) any bank including a co-operative bank, (iii) deposits in HLA of NHB, (iv) LIC, (v) a housing finance public limited company, (vi) any co-operative society engaged in providing long-term finance for construction or purchase of houses in India, (vii)

employer, if the employer is a public company, viii) PSU, (ix) university and its affiliated colleges, (ix) a local authority or (x) a co-operative society and (xi) an employer being an authority, board, corporation, or any other body established under a Central or State Act.

(c) Stamp duty, registration fee and other expenses incurred on transfer. This payment need not flow from borrowed funds.

These expenses shall not include:

(a) admission fee, cost of share or initial deposit,
(b) cost of any addition, alteration, renovation or repairs carried out after the issue of the completion certificate or the house is occupied by the assessee or it has been let out, and
(c) any expenditure where a deduction is separately allowed u/s 24.

Such a house is required to be held for a minimum period of 5 years from the end of the FY in which its possession was taken. If the house is sold earlier, aggregate deduction claimed shall be added to the normal income of the assessee for the year during which the house is sold. The same tenet is applicable when the assessee receives the money back whether by way of refund or otherwise.

4. Tuition fees paid, whether at the time of admission or thereafter, to any university, college, school or other educational institution situated within India for the purpose of full-time education of any two children of the individual. However, the eligible amount shall not include any payment towards any development fees or donation or payment of a similar nature.

   The concession is available to each of the parents, if eligible, even in respect of the same child, on their respective payments.
5. A 5-year term deposit of a scheduled bank eligible for deduction.

Limit on Deductions u/s 80D — Mediclaim

For obvious reasons, health insurance on self from an Indian insurer is not useful to NRIs. However, they can claim the deduction on such insurance taken for their family members in India.

FA18 raised the deduction of ₹30,000 to ₹50,000 for medical expenditure for senior citizens also if they are not covered by health insurance. In view of this, it is advisable not to cover your parents in your family policy if they are senior citizens. The premium for family policy depends on the age of the oldest member of the family besides the sum assured. Getting independent covers for each family member can sometimes be cheaper.

For non-seniors, this deduction covers health insurance premiums paid, along with expenses incurred on preventive health check-up, by an individual for himself and his family up to ₹25,000. A similar deduction is also available to HUF for any of its member.

In the case of single premium health insurance policies having cover of more than one year, FA18 has declared that the deduction shall be allowed on proportionate basis for the number of years for which health insurance cover is provided, subject to the specified monetary limit.

The premium is required to be paid in any mode other than cash, except for preventive check-ups.

Loan for Higher Education: Sec. 80E

Deduction of interest on loan taken by the student or his parents, the spouse, or his legal guardian for full time studies in all fields of studies (including vocational studies) pursued after Senior Secondary Examination from a bank or an approved financial and charitable institution is available for 8 successive years.

If someone takes a loan from his employer for higher studies, he will not be entitled to the deduction, unless the employer himself falls within the category of an approved source.

Donations: Sec. 80G

An assessee is entitled to a deduction of 50% and in some cases 100% of donations made to approved charitable purposes. Some of these donations attract a ceiling of 10% of the total income of the assessee, as reduced by the amount deductible under any other provision of Chapter VI-A.

Such donations must be in the form of money and not in kind, unless the donor is the manufacturer of the items donated — *(178ITR171 Saraswati Industrial Syndicate)*.

The FA17 amended this Section to provide that no deduction shall be allowed in respect of donation exceeding ₹2,000 unless such sum is paid by any mode other than cash.

Sec. 80GGB & GGC

Donations to electoral trusts or political parties by an Indian Company or by any person (other than local authority and artificial juridical person) are eligible for 100% deduction.

In order to discourage the cash transactions and to bring transparency in the source of funding to political parties, the FA17 introduced Electoral Bonds, redeemable in a short period of time. Anyone can buy these bonds through designated banks, without any limit and donate these to the political party of his choice, who, in turn, can encash these through any of the designated banks into the bank account of the party.

Sec. 13A has been amended to provide that no donations of ₹2,000 or more shall be received otherwise than by a banking transaction or through new electoral bonds which will be launched soon. In order to address the concern of anonymity of the donors, the political parties shall not be required to furnish the name and address of the donors who contribute by way of electoral bond.

Interest on Savings Bank Accounts: Sec. 80TTA

A deduction up to ₹10,000 is available in respect of any interest on a savings account of an individual or HUF (but not a firm, AOP or BOI) with a banking company or a co-operative society engaged in carrying on the business of banking (including a co-operative land mortgage bank or a co-operative land development bank.

The FA18 has inserted a new Sec. 80TTB to allow a deduction up to ₹50,000 on interest from deposits held by all senior citizens (but not HUFs and Partnership Firms) from the above-mentioned entities. Consequently, the deduction u/s 80TTA of ₹10,000 shall be available only to non-senior citizens and HUFs. Normally, the concept of senior citizens is not applicable to NRIs but it is applicable to RNORs.

TDS @30.9% is applicable on interest on NRO accounts. This gives an impression that where such interest is under ₹10,000 (raised to 40,000 by FA19), no TDS is applicable. Contradiction.

It is earnestly hoped that CBDT takes a corrective action.

Interest on Housing Loans Deductible u/s 24
Refer Chapter Immovable Property.

Advance Tax

All taxpayers are required to pay advance tax in spite of the fact that most of their income is subject to TDS.

If the tax payable for the year is ₹10,000 or more, advance tax is payable without having to submit any estimate or statement of income in 4 instalments → on or before (1) 15th June: 15%, (2) 15th September: 45% (3) 15th December: 75% and (4) 15th March 100%.

TDS is treated as advance tax paid. FA16 has clarified that a return which is otherwise valid would not be treated defective merely because self-assessment tax and interest payable in accordance with the provisions of Sec. 140A, has not been paid on or before the date of furnishing of the return.

Tax Returns

The FY is April-March in India and January-December in most of the overseas countries. Consequently, the deadline for filing the returns in those countries is earlier than that in India. Since some of the crucial data related with Indian tax is not available before this deadline, the NRIs as well as foreign deputies can experience delay in refund of the tax by the Department. This problem is not yet satisfactorily resolved. Some countries, including the USA grant an extension for filing the return on receiving such a request. There is also a facility to file a revised return within a stipulated time period.

The due date for furnishing the returns in India is 30th September for (i) companies and (ii) assessees as well as working partners of a firm whose accounts are required to be audited. For other assessees the date is 31st July.

NRIs are not required to disclose their overseas bank accounts in their tax returns, unless they are in the refund zone and they have no bank account in India. This particular portion is only meant to facilitate the Department pay the refund and can be left blank, if the NRI so desires.

The single page Form ITR-1 (SAHAJ) has been withdrawn for NRIs from this year. Most of them now have to file ITR-2.

A person of this category who files income tax return for the first time would not be subjected to any scrutiny in the first year unless there is specific information available with the Department. Good! This will surely attract many otherwise hesitant entities to enter the tax net.

FA17 has introduced a new Sec. 139AA requiring every person eligible to obtain Aadhaar number shall, on or after 1.7.17, quote it in the return of income furnished by him.. An NRI need not possess Aadhaar card but can obtain one when he is physically present in India.

Sec. 139(1) requires a person to furnish his return of income if his total income during the previous year without claiming any deductions under Chapter VI-A (Sec. 80C, 80D, etc.) and also the concession u/s 38 related with LTCG on equities and equity-based units of MFs exceeds the maximum amount which is not chargeable to tax. In other words, the return has to be filed even if these deductions and exemptions bring down the income chargeable to tax below the tax threshold.

Though NRIs are not mandatorily required to possess PAN, it is desirable to have one. This subject is covered in detail in Chapter, *PAN is PAIN.*

Sec. 288B requires any amount payable and the amount of refund due, to be rounded off to the nearest multiple of ₹10.

To be able to achieve the aspiration of being able to process the returns within 12 months from the end of the AY in which the income was first assessable, from FY 18-19 and onwards, FA17 has amended Sec. 139(5) to provide that the time for furnishing of revised return shall be available up to the end of the relevant AY or before the completion of assessment, whichever is earlier. Moreover, Sec. 234F requires a fee for delay in furnishing of return to be levied if the return is not filed within the specified due dates. The fee applicable shall be ₹5,000 if the return is furnished after the due date but on or before the 31st December of the AY and ₹10,000 in any other case. However, where the total income does not exceed ₹5 lakh, the fee amount shall not exceed ₹1,000.

Belated filing suffers from an embargo on carry forward of loss earned during the current year, from business (speculative or otherwise), capital loss and loss from owning and maintaining race horses. Moreover, belated tax returns cannot be revised. The ITO has no powers to condone such a lapse. Fortunately carried forward losses from the earlier years suffer no damage.

FA16 has clarified that a return which is otherwise valid would not be treated defective merely because self-assessment tax and interest payable in accordance with the provisions of Sec. 140A, has not been paid on or before the date of furnishing of the return.

Filing Returns through Representative Assessee

Sec. 163 defines such a person as any person in India —

(a) who is employed by or on behalf of the NRI; or
(b) who has any business connection with the NRI; or
(c) from or through whom the NRI is in receipt of any income whether directly or indirectly; or
(d) who is a trustee of the NRI; and
(e) any other person who has acquired by means of transfer a capital asset in India.

No person is to be treated as an agent of an NRI unless he has had an opportunity of being heard by the Assessing Officer as to his liability to be treated as such. An NRI may also appoint an authorised representative to act as his agent.

E-verification

U/s 140, NRIs having Indian incorporated banks internet banking facility would be able to e-verify their returns/claims, etc. by available logging through their internet banking account. If such facility is not availed by them, they can authorise by registering an Indian resident as their agent through their e-Filing account to perform their tasks.

On-line Payment of Income Tax

e-Tax Payment facilitates payment of direct taxes online by taxpayers. To avail of this facility you are required to have a Netbanking/Debit card of the selected Bank.

All that is required is to log on to www.incometaxindia.gov.in or http://tin.tin.nsdl.com and follow the instructions. After payment, account holders would be able to generate the taxpayers' counterfoil containing the Challan Identification Number (CIN). Before undertaking e-payment, check whether your bank offers this facility.

Advance Ruling

With a view to promote ease of doing business, the Authority for Advance Ruling (AAR) for income tax, central excise, customs duty and service tax shall be merged.

National Company Law Tribunal will be the single adjudicating authority for all corporal default cases. Company Law Board, Board for Industrial and Financial Resolution are dissolved. Insolvency and Bankruptcy Code which was cleared in May 2016, will also come under the purview of this tribunal.

Applications will not be entertained for (i) determination of fair market value of property, (ii) any transaction which is designed *prima facie* for avoidance of income tax and (iii) matter already pending before any income-tax authority, tribunal or court.

The application cannot be rejected merely because the Appellate Tribunal, in another case, has decided a similar issue in favour of the revenue — *Burmah Castrol Plc (2008) 174 Taxman 95* (AAR — New Delhi).

U/s 245S, the advance ruling shall be binding only on the applicant and on the Department in respect of the specific transaction, unless there is a change in law or facts of the case. Application for advance ruling cannot be admitted if applicant has already filed return of income — *[2011] 16 taxmann.com 195* (AAR — New Delhi).

Annual Information Returns

U/s 285BA read with Rule 114E, the transactions of all persons, including NRIs undertaking any one of the following 7 specified financial transactions, equal to or over specified financial limits are required to be reported to the Department through Annual Information Return (AIR) —

1. Cash deposits in a year in any bank SB account	10 lakh
2. Payments in a year credit card	2 lakh
3. Purchase of units of a Mutual Fund	2 lakh
4. Acquisition of bonds or debentures	5 lakh
5. Purchase of shares	1 lakh
6. Purchase or sale of immovable property	30 lakh
7. Purchase of RBI bonds	5 lakh

Take care.

How to Compute Tax

The example of computation of tax elucidates the method of computing tax. Note that if there were no agricultural income the tax on normal income of ₹3,50,000 would be only ₹5,000. The agricultural income takes the tax to ₹20,000. Agricultural income is really not totally tax-free. This is in addition to the agricultural tax charged by the State Governments.

Computation of Tax

	₹	₹	₹
Business Income	4,17,000	4,17,000	
House Property			
Self Occupied	NIL		
Property Given on Rent	1,60,000		
Less: Interest on Loan	1,30,000	30,000	
Capital Gains STCG on debt MF		11,000	
Other Sources			
Interest on SB Deposits	52,000		
Less: Deduction u.s 80TTA	10,000	42,000	
Total Gross Income		5,00,000	
Deductions			
Equity Linked Saving Scheme	1,30,000		
Housing Loan Repayment	50,000		
Total / Limited to	1,80,000	1,50,000	
Taxable Income		**3,50,000**	
Agricultural income			
Non-agricultural Income	3,50,000		
Add: Agricultural Income	3,00,000		
TOTAL Income	6,50,000		
Tax on ₹6,50,000		42,500	
Agricultural Income	3,00,000		
Add: Threshold	2,50,000		
Total / Tax thereon	5,50,000	22,500	20,000
Long-term Capital Gains			
Total Sale Proceeds	1,50,000		
Less: Indexed Cost	90,000		
LTCG		60,000	
Less: Contribution to Sec. 54EC		50,000	
Taxable LTCG /Tax thereon @20%		10,000	2,000
Total Tax			22,000
Add Cess @ 4%			880
Tax Accrued			22,880
Less : Advance tax Paid		4,000	
TDS		16,070	20,070
Tax Payable			2,810

7

~

Wealth & Gift Tax

FA15 has abolished the wealth tax. Good! FA13 has brought it back by way of Surcharge. Bad!!

Wealth tax was levied only on "unproductive assets" and therefore investments in shares, debentures, MFs, Banks, etc., were exempt from wealth tax. Moreover, wealth tax was charged @1% of the amount by which the net wealth exceeded ₹30 lakh. The authorities realised that the cost of collection is not worth the effort.

The other reason presented was that this action is to counter-balance the hike on surcharge charged to super rich (income over ₹1 crore) @15%.

Consequently, the exchequer is slated to get more revenue from the poor you and me through these rather than the super rich through surcharge. A direct outcome of this provision is that the stated intention of the government to increase the investment in financial assets rather than physical assets (gold, real estate, etc.) will surely take a beating.

Yes, wealth tax is abolished but the Income Tax Return Form has been suitably modified to capture the information relating to the relevant assets. Consequently, we will have to give these details. And God forbid, if the value these assets was over ₹30 lakh (which was chargeable to wealth tax) in the past. Take care!

Gift is Income

FA98 had deleted Gift Tax Act (GTA) which charged gift tax to the donor. Good! FA04 amended Sec. 56 of Income Tax Act (ITA) and treated it as income of the donee. Bad!!

Accordingly, if an individual or an HUF receives from any person any sum of money and/or some specified assets without any or with some inadequate consideration, the aggregate value of which exceeds ₹50,000, the whole of such amount will be treated as Income from Other Sources of the donee. If it does not exceed ₹50,000, it will not be treated as income.

The specified assets are — 1. Cash 2. Land and building. 3. Shares and securities. 4. Jewellery and bullion. 5. Archaeological collections. 6. Drawings, paintings, sculptures or any work of art.

Movable property and immovable property will be considered at its Fair Market Value (FMV) and stamp duty value respectively. If it is received with inadequate consideration, the difference between the FMV or stamp duty and the inadequate consideration shall be taxed as the income, if it exceeds ₹50,000.

Gifts received from following sources are exempt from the tax —

(a) any relative; or
(b) on the occasion of the marriage of the individual; or
(c) under a Will or by way of inheritance; or
(d) in contemplation of death of the payer;
(e) from any local authority;
(f) from any fund or foundation or university or other educational institution or hospital or other medical institution or any trust or institution referred to in Sec. 10(23); and
(g) from any charitable trust or institution registered u/s 12A or 12AA.
(h) from an individual by a trust created or established solely for the benefit of relative of the individual.

For ITA "relative" means (differs from FEMA definition for which refer Chapter *General Provisions*) —

(i) spouse of the individual;
(ii) brother or sister of the individual;
(iii) brother or sister of spouse of the individual;
(iv) brother or sister of either parents of the individual;
(v) any lineal ascendant or descendant of the individual;
(vi) any lineal ascendant or descendant of the spouse of the individual; and

(vii) spouse of the persons referred in clauses (ii) to (vi).

Definition of relative is a paradox. Suppose I am your mother's brother. In that case, I am your relative but you are not my relative since you are my sister's daughter. Yes, I am your relative but you are not my relative. Strange!.

More strangely, and for no particular reason, SCRA and Companies Act define "relative" separately and not consistent either with each other or with ITA.

FA17 has widened the scope of taxability to gifts to companies, firms, etc. However, this provision will not apply to money or property received from an individual by a trust created or established solely for the benefit of a relative of the individual.

The recent FA19(2) has plugged a loop hole, arising of the fact that gifts made by Residents to NRIs are being claimed to be non-taxable in India as the income does not accrue or arise in India. Now it has provided that income arising from any sum of money paid, or any property situate in India transferred, on or after 5.7.19 by a Resident to an NRI shall be deemed to accrue or arise in India. In a treaty situation, the relevant article of applicable DTAA shall continue to apply for such gifts as well.

Clubbing Provision

Yes, the GTA stands omitted but not the clubbing provisions which require income and wealth from assets transferred directly or indirectly without adequate consideration to minor children, the spouse (otherwise than in connection with an agreement to live apart) or daughter-in-law will continue to be deemed income and wealth of the transferor. Same is the case when assets are held by a person or an AOP for benefit of the assessee, the spouse, daughter-in-law and minor children.

Gifts to a daughter-in-law are clubbed but not gifts to a son-in-law. Male chauvinistic indeed!

The entire income of a minor is to be included in the income of that parent whose total income (excluding the income includible) is higher. Where the marriage of the parents does not subsist, income of the minor will be included in the income of that parent who maintains the minor child. Once the income is included in the hands of one of the parents based on these criteria, it shall continue to be included, even if these change, unless the AO is satisfied that it is necessary to do so. Where the income of an individual includes the income of his minor children, an exemption up to ₹1,500 in respect of each minor child can be claimed by the individual u/s 10(32).

Where a minor is admitted to the benefits of a partnership firm, the value of the interest of such minor in the firm shall be included in the net income of the parent of the minor.

A minor earning income by way of manual work or an activity involving application of his skill, talent or specialised knowledge and experience, is directly assessed in the hands of the child. Unfortunately, the income arising from all his investments suffer clubbing. More unfortunately, the provision related with the income of a physically or mentally handicapped minor child being directly assessed in the hands of the child is not applicable to NRIs.

Income on Income

The main advantage of gifts accrues from the fact that in the case of spouse or daughter-in-law, income on income is not clubbed. If the spouse has no other income, no tax is payable unless the interest on interest crosses the minimum tax threshold of ₹2.50 lakh. In other words, instead of investing in your own name it is better to give a gift, pay tax on the income arising from the original corpus gifted and keep on building a corpus for your spouse or daughter-in-law. Yes, it is cumbersome to keep track of what is clubbable and what is not but it may be worth the effort.

Some Useful Tips

1. NRIs cannot open a PPF account or opt for its post-maturity continuation in their own names.

   Contributions to PPF standing in the name of spouse or minor children attract clubbing. The interest is tax-free, whether clubbed or otherwise. However, if the spouse or minor child is a Resident, surely the NRI can contribute to their PPF accounts and claim deduction u/s 80C.

2. Income of minors up to ₹1,500 is free from clubbing. More the number of minors better is the benefit. Forget family planning.
3. Savings made by the wife out of household expenses given by her husband is a separate property of the wife. Any income arising therefrom is not aggregated with the income of the husband.
4. Give gifts to close Resident relatives to take advantage of higher interest obtainable from schemes not available to NRIs.
5. Before the GTA was abolished, aggregate gift over ₹30,000 per FY was taxable @30% and therefore, it was a wise strategy to give a gift up to ₹30,000 per year and build up a corpus for the children and spouse. Now that you can give need-based gifts without any limit there is no need to build a corpus and take the risk of the child running away (and worse, the spouse eloping) with your money.

Do not Purchase House in Wife's Name

Purchasing a house in the name of the wife by applying your own funds means that you are using her as a name-lender and this is a "benami transaction". This is illegal. It can be made legal by gifting the money to the wife to enable her purchase the property in her name. An alternative is to gift your house to her, but this will attract stamp duty and registration charges. It is also necessary for you to follow the procedure for gifting. The utility, if any, is lost because of the clubbing provisions.

Moreover, if you take a housing loan in your name, you would not be entitled to claim any tax benefits associated with the loan, because the house belongs to the wife. Further, once you have gifted any repatriable asset, whether cash or the house, you have lost the right to repatriate it.

In short, do not buy a house property (or any other asset) in the name of the wife. The tax concessions on housing loan can be availed only by the person who owns the house.

Power of Attorney (PoA)

The same tenet holds for buying housing properties through PoA. This system is quite prevalent in Delhi and Haryana and is slowly percolating to other parts of India. It has the advantage of avoiding the hefty stamp duty. We do not approve this route because — EMIs paid by a PoA holder are on behalf of the original allottee and therefore, the PoA holder cannot claim deduction of interest u/s 24 and capital repayment u/s 80C. The original allottee cannot claim these benefits because he has not incurred the costs.

Gift Procedure

To safeguard against any hassles, it is advisable to follow proper gift procedure. All that is required is an offer by the donor and acceptance thereof by the donee in black and white. The donee should request the donor for a gift and then the donor should remit the amount to the donee. Alternatively, the donor can offer the gift. In either case, it is necessary for the donee to accept the gift in writing (may be through a thank you note). Only then it would be considered as a gift in India. It is preferable to mention the relationship between the donor and the donee. It is better to prepare a gift deed and get it registered (with related stamp duty) but such a precaution is normally needed in the case of high-value gifts, particularly those of real estate.

Note that the Department has a right to inquire into the genuineness of the gift to ensure that it is not a payment made for any hawala or smuggling transaction or services rendered.

8

Bank Accounts

RBI does not involve itself directly in routine operations and has passed on its own responsibility to monitor and control to the ADs and kept the regulatory authority with itself.

Opening of accounts by individuals, entities of Pakistan nationality or ownership and entities of Bangladesh ownership requires prior RBI approval. All such requests may be referred to the Chief General Manager-in-Charge, Foreign Exchange Department, Foreign Investment Division, Reserve Bank of India, Central Office, Mumbai — 400 001. An Individual of Bangladesh nationality can open an NRO account subject to the individual holding a valid visa and valid residential permit issued by Foreigner Registration Office or Foreigner Regional Registration Office.

Common Features

Opening Accounts

Documents required to open any new account are Passport (Copy of Name, Address and Photo pages along with dates of issue and expiry page). If it is an Indian passport, copy of Visa and resident permit is also necessary. In case the place of birth is outside India, OCI card is required, irrespective of the nature of the passport along with as many as the following self-attested documents, either original or its notarised copy —

1. Electricity/Landline telephone bill, not over 3 months old.
2. Latest 3 months transaction of passbook with a cancelled cheque.
3. Banker's verification, only from a scheduled commercial Indian bank required on bank letterhead with bank employee name, signature, employee code and designation.
4. Driving licence with name, address and photo pages along with issue and expiry date pages.

5. In case of Merchant Navy NRI persons, Mariner's declaration or certified copy of CDC (Continuous Discharge Certificate) is to be submitted.

In rare cases where there is a difficulty in submitting such details, a person can open a Basic Savings Bank Deposit Account (BSBDA) which is available at all the scheduled commercial banks, including foreign banks having branches in India. It does not have a mandatory minimum balance. There is no cap on number of deposits but withdrawals are capped at four a month, including withdrawals through ATMs. A BSBDA holder is not eligible to open any other savings account. Anyone desiring opening such an account will do well to check carefully the rate (large amounts attract higher rates) and its structure which differs from bank to bank.

ADs can convert Indian Rupees into the designated forex at the clean TT selling rate and convert forex at clean TT buying rates ruling on the date.

Interest Rates

Banks are free to determine their interest rates on both savings and term deposits under NRE and NRO accounts but in no case, such rates should be higher than those on comparable domestic rupee deposits. Banks are allowed to offer interest rates without any ceiling on NRE deposits with maturity of 3 years and above. Anyone desiring opening an account will do well to carefully check the rate and structure of interest of different banks.

Interest is paid at quarterly or longer rests. In the case of SB, interest is calculated on daily basis and credited regularly whether the account is operative or not.

On deposits repayable in less than 3 months or where the terminal quarter is incomplete, interest is paid proportionately for the actual number of days reckoning the year at 365 days. Some banks reckon the year at 366 days in a leap year. While banks are free to adopt their methodology, they should intimate this to their prospects.

If an FD matures and the amount is left unclaimed, it attracts savings bank rate of interest.

Conversion of NRE into FCNR(B) and *vice versa* before maturity would be subject to the penal provisions. In the case of conversion of NRE or FCNR term deposits into RFC account, there is no penalty. If such a deposit has not run for a minimum of 1 year, the bank may, at its discretion, pay interest at their SB rate. A bank should allow premature withdrawal of a term deposit. It can determine its own penal interest. Interest on the deposit for the period that it has remained with the bank will be paid at the rate applicable to that period. No interest is payable where premature withdrawal takes place before completion of the minimum period prescribed. However, the bank, at its discretion, may disallow premature withdrawal of large deposits held by entities other than individuals and HUFs.

Joint Accounts

Notification FEMA 5(R)/2016-RB dt 1.4.16 allows NRIs to have Resident close relative/s on "former or survivor" basis though nomination facility is available. Such a joint holder shall operate the account as if he is a PoA holder during the life time of the NRI. Operations in the account by a PoA are restricted to withdrawals for permissible local payments or remittance to the account holder himself through normal banking channels. An easier structure in terms of a Letter of Authority (LoA) of banks can be used for allowing the LoA holder to withdraw funds for local payments.

Such a Resident joint or PoA/LoA holder—

(a) Can make all local payments in rupees including payments for eligible investments through NRO accounts.

(b) Can effect remittance outside India through normal banking channels, funds out of the balances in NRE and FCNR accounts to the NRI's account abroad provided specific powers for the purpose have been given to that effect, and

(c) Shall not make payment by way of gift to a Resident or transfer funds from one NRE / NRO account to another account of a different person.

While making remittances, the limits and conditions of repatriability will apply.

Similarly, a Resident can include NRI close relative as joint holder in his resident bank accounts including EEFC/RFC but only on "former or survivor" basis.

At the request of all the joint account holders, the bank may, at its discretion, allow deletion of existing or add the name of another person as a joint holder. In no case the term and the aggregate amount of the deposit should undergo any change. This should not be construed as premature withdrawal of the term deposit.

Change in Residential Status

On a change from Non-resident to Resident, NRE accounts should be redesignated as resident accounts and conversely, the funds held in these NRO and NRE accounts should be transferred to Resident accounts or the RFC accounts, at the option of the account holder.

Deceased Depositor

In the case of current account of a deceased individual depositor or sole proprietorship concern, interest should be paid from the date of death of the depositor, till the date of payment to the claimant at interest rate applicable to SB as on the date of payment.

In the case of an NRE, when the claimants are Residents, the deposit on maturity should be treated as a domestic rupee deposit and interest should be paid for the subsequent period at a rate applicable to a domestic deposit of similar maturity.

In the case of a term deposit standing in the name of (i) a deceased individual depositor, or (ii) two or more joint depositors, where one of the depositors has died, interest should be paid —

(a) At the contracted rate on the maturity of the deposit.

(b) If the deposit is claimed before maturity, interest should be paid at the applicable rate for the period elapsed prevailing on the date of placement of the deposit, without charging penalty.

(c) In the case of death after maturity, interest should be paid at a RFC SB rate operative on the date of maturity from the date of maturity till the date of payment.

(d) If on request, the bank agrees to split the amount of term deposit and issues two or more receipts, no penalty should be levied provided the period and aggregate amount of the deposit do not undergo any change.

(e) If the claimant is a Resident, the maturity proceeds may be converted into Indian rupees on the date of maturity and interest be paid for the subsequent period at the rate applicable to a deposit of similar maturity under the domestic deposit scheme.

(f) In the case of NRO, the amount due or payable to an ROI nominee shall be credited to his NRO account. If the nominee is a Resident, it shall be credited to his resident account.

(g) A Resident nominee can remit funds outside India for meeting the liabilities abroad of the deceased account holder.

Tax on Interest

The interest on NRE is tax-free u/s 10(4ii) of ITA. Schedule-II (10) of the FEMR states, "When an account holder becomes a person Resident, deposits may be allowed to continue till maturity at the contracted rate of interest, if so desired by him. However, such deposits shall be treated as resident deposits from the date of return of the account holder to India."

Sec. 10(15fa) of ITA exempts interest "by a scheduled bank to a non-resident or to a person who is not ordinarily resident within the meaning of Sec. 6(6) on deposits in forex . . . ." FCNR and RFC are the two accounts covered by this Section.

Consequently, from the date of returning to India permanently, both NRE and FCNR would be treated as resident accounts, even if they are not redesignated as such. These can run up to their maturity but the interest on NRE becomes taxable from the date of the return whereas the FCNR interest is tax-free as long as the holder remains an RNOR. Alternatively, both NRE and FCNR can be converted into RFC without any penalty. RFC interest is taxable in the hands of RNOR.

NRO and RFC interest suffers TDS @30.9%, without any threshold, even though interest on RFC is tax-free for RNORs and not for Residents and even though interest on Savings Bank account is deductible u/s 80TTA (Refer Chapter *Income Tax*).

Non-Resident External Account (NRE)

The account can be opened only by the NRI himself. The AD should obtain an undertaking from the NRI that he would intimate the AD when he becomes a Resident.

On fixed deposits, the rate of interest should not be higher than the one applicable to resident deposits of comparable maturity. The term of FD should be from one to three years. However, banks are allowed to accept NRE deposits above three years from their asset-liability point of view.

Renewal of Overdue Deposits

All aspects concerning renewal of overdue deposits may be decided by individual banks subject to the customers being notified of the terms and conditions of renewal including interest rates, at the time of acceptance of deposit. The policy should be non-discretionary and non-discriminatory.

Permitted Credits

- Remittances to India in any permitted currency through normal banking channels.
- Forex notes or coins tendered by account holder during his temporary visit to India, provided the amount is declared on a

Currency Declaration Form (CDF), where applicable, and tendered to the AD in person by the account holder himself.

- Cheques drawn on his forex account, travellers' cheques or bank drafts issued outside India payable in any permitted forex and even in INR for which reimbursement is receivable in forex. These should be deposited by the account holder in person during his temporary visit to India.
- Transfers from other NRE/FCNR accounts.
- Transfer from NRO up to US$ 1 million per FY. Refer Chapter, *Forex Remittances NRIs*.
- AP (DIR) Circular 21 dt 23.9.03 has allowed the balances in the EEFC and RFCD accounts to be transferred to his NRE account at the option of the account holder consequent upon a Resident becoming an NRI.
- Interest accruing on the funds held in the account.
- Maturity proceeds and interest/dividend on government securities and MFs.
- Refund of share/debenture subscriptions to new issues of Indian companies or portion thereof.
- Refund of application or earnest money made by the house building agencies on account of non-allotment of flat/plot, together with interest, if any (net of income tax payable thereon).
- Cancellation of deals for purchase of residential or commercial property.
- Demand draft or banker's cheque issued against encashment of forex supported by encashment certificate.
- Current income like rent, dividend, pension, interest, etc., provided the AD is satisfied that the credit represents current income of the NRI and income tax thereon has been deducted or paid or provided for.
- Sale proceeds of assets including immovable property acquired out of rupee or forex funds or by way of inheritance.

Permitted Debits

- Remittances outside India of current income like rent, dividend, pension, interest, etc., net of applicable taxes.
- Local disbursements.
- Transfer to NRE accounts of the account holder or any other person, if eligible.
- Investment in shares, securities, CPs, or immovable property.
- Any other transaction covered under general or special permission granted by the RBI.

ADs may at their discretion allow for a period of not more than two weeks, overdrawing in NRE SB accounts, up to a limit of ₹50,000 subject to the condition that such overdrawing together with the interest payable thereon are cleared within two weeks by inward remittances through normal banking channels or by transfer of funds from other NRE/FCNR accounts in India.

Foreign Currency Non-Resident Account

FCNR(A) scheme was introduced in 1975, where the forex risk was borne by the government of India. It was withdrawn in August 1994 in view of its quasi-fiscal costs to the government. The FCNR(B) was introduced w.e.f. 15.5.93.

AP (DIR) Circular 36 dt 19.10.11 has permitted opening of FCNR(B) deposits in any permitted forex which is freely convertible. This is indeed a good move since earlier, NRIs/PIOs from other countries had to convert their remittances into one of the six permissible currencies while depositing and repatriating. This incurred exchange / swap losses and also bank charges.

On deposits with maturities of 1 year to less than 3 years interest shall be paid within the ceiling rate of LIBOR/SWAP plus 200 basis points for the respective currency and corresponding maturity. On deposits with maturity of 3-5 years it will be plus 300 basis points. On floating rate deposits, interest shall be paid within the ceiling of SWAP rates for the respective currency/maturity plus 200 bps/ 300 bps as the case may be. For floating rate deposits, the interest reset period shall be six months.

The interest on the deposits should be paid on the basis of 360 days to a year and be calculated and paid at intervals of 180 days each and thereafter for the remaining actual number of days. The depositor has the option to receive the interest at maturity with compounding effect and also to get the interest credited to any NRI-related accounts, existing or to be opened afresh.

Overdue FCNR Deposits

Banks have discretion to renew an overdue deposit or a portion thereof provided the overdue period from the date of maturity till the date of renewal (both days inclusive) does not exceed 14 days. The interest rate on renewal should be the appropriate rate for the period of renewal as prevailing on the date of maturity or when the depositor seeks renewal, whichever is lower. If the overdue period exceeds 14 days and if the depositor renews a portion or whole amount as a fresh deposit, banks may fix their own interest rate for the overdue period. However, if the deposit is withdrawn before completion of minimum stipulated period after renewal, banks are free to withdraw the overdue interest paid.

Other Conditions

The terms and conditions as applicable to NRE deposits in respect of joint holdings, opening accounts during temporary visit, operation by PoA / LoA, debits / credits, loans, overdrafts, change of Residential status, repatriation of funds, transfer of EEFC/RFC balances, etc., shall apply *mutatis mutandis* to FCNR deposits. Moreover, as per AP (DIR) Circular 57 dt 18.5.07, remittance of the maturity proceeds of FCNR deposits to third parties outside India is permitted if the transaction is specifically authorised by the account holder and the AD is satisfied about its bona fides.

Inland Movement of Funds

Any inland movement of funds for opening these accounts as well as for repatriation outside India will be free of inland exchange or commission. RBI has now allowed remittance of the maturity proceeds of FCNR to third parties outside India, provided the transaction is specifically authorised by the account holder and the AD is satisfied about the bonafide of the transaction.

Withdrawal from FCNR

Such withdrawal faces 2 hurdles — 1. It is an FD from which cash payouts are not made as a rule. 2. The branches do not have any forex and will direct you to its HO. You may be able to withdraw cash up to a limited amount from your NRE account with the branch though you may have to collect the forex from their HO. However, traveller's cheques can be obtained without any limit.

Taxability of Interest in the Host Country

The interest on NRE and FCNR is free from Indian taxes in the hands of NRI. However, you will have to check on the taxability of this income in your host country. Refer *"FATCA and CRS"* in Chapter *DTAA*.

Non-Resident Ordinary Account (NRO)

This is the only so called "non-repatriable" account. In practice, it is repatriable — well, almost. Interest is remittable subject to tax compliance and corpus is also remittable up to US$ 1 million per FY under some conditions. Refer Chapter *Forex Remittances, NRIs*.

It is mandatory for a Resident to inform his bank within a reasonable time when he becomes an NRI as per FEMA. What is reasonable is not defined. In practice, the number of persons who fail to inform their banks is so large that the default is mostly overlooked, unless the authorities suspect foul play. On receipt of the information from the NRI, the bank will redesignate his accounts as NRO.

On the other hand, when an NRI becomes a Resident, his NRO account should be redesignated as resident account. Where the account holder is only on a temporary visit to India, the account can continue as NRO.

NRO can also be opened and maintained with ADs or some designated post offices in India as current, savings, RDs or FDs.

The minimum tenure of domestic and NRO term deposits, irrespective of its quantum of the deposit, is 7 days. Since the NRO accounts are designated in Indian rupees, the exchange risk on such deposits is borne by the depositors themselves.

W.e.f. 16.12.11 the interest rates on NRO are deregulated. At present it is between 4% to 6% p.a. Scheduled commercial banks have been advised to calculate interest on savings bank accounts on a daily product basis. Interest should be paid at quarterly or longer rests. Interest on savings bank accounts should be credited on regular basis whether the account is operative or not.

Conversion into $s into ₹s

As per AP (DIR) Circular 14 dt 17.10.07, requests for payment in cash by ROIs may be acceded to the extent of US$ 3,000 or its equivalent. For higher amounts, the money changers should make payments through account payee cheques or demand drafts.

Permissible Credits

- Remittances from abroad in freely convertible forex through normal banking channels.
- Freely convertible forex tendered by the account holder during his temporary visit to India or transfers from rupee accounts of non-resident banks. Forex exceeding US$ 5,000 or its equivalent in form of cash should be supported by Currency Declaration Form. Rupee funds should be supported by Encashment Certificate, if they represent funds brought from outside India.
- Transfer from rupee accounts of non-resident banks.

- Legitimate dues in India of the account holder such as rent, dividend, pension, interest, etc.
- Sale proceeds of assets including immovable property acquired out of rupee/forex funds or by way of legacy / inheritance.
- Gifts and/or loans from a close relative within the overall limit of US$ 75,000 per FY as permitted under the Liberalised Remittance Scheme (LRS). Refer Chapter, *Forex Availability — Residents* for details.

Permissible Debits

- All local payments in rupees including payments for investments subject to compliance with the relevant RBI regulations.
- Remittance outside India of current income like rent, dividend, pension, interest, etc., of the account holder net of taxes.
- Remittance up to US$ 1 million per FY for all bona fide purposes. (Refer Chapter *Forex Remittances — NRIs*).
- Loans to non-resident account holders and to third parties may be granted in Rupees by Authorized Dealer/bank against the security of fixed deposits subject to certain terms and conditions. (Refer Chapter, *Loans & Overdrafts for details.*)

Rank Foreigner Tourists

Even a foreign national of non-Indian origin visiting India can open NRO with funds remitted from outside India or by sale of forex brought by him to India when he is in India on holidays or short tour. The account can be freely operated by the account holder or the joint holder for bona fide transactions. At the time of his departure from India, the amount can be converted into forex provided the account has been maintained for a period not exceeding 6 months and the account has not been credited with any local funds, other than interest accrued thereon. For accounts maintained beyond this period, application for repatriation should be made on plain paper to the related RBI Regional Office.

Resident Forex Currency Account (RFC)

Any person who was an NRI returning only from External Group of countries and now has become a Resident is eligible to open a RFC account, mainly for transferring his NRE and FCNR balances and the proceeds of assets held outside India to this account. The forex received as (i) pension, superannuation or other monetary benefits from the employer outside India; (ii) received or acquired as gift or inheritance from a person resident outside India (iii) sale of his assets abroad or (iv) received as the proceeds of life insurance policy, claims, maturity, surrender values settled in forex from an insurance company may also be credited to this account.

The main aspect is that the funds in RFC account are free from all restrictions regarding utilisation of forex balances including any restriction on investment outside India.

RFC accounts can be maintained in the form of current or savings or term deposit accounts, where the account holder is an individual and in the form of current or term deposits in all other cases. No loans or overdrafts will be permitted in these accounts. If and when the account holder again becomes an NRI he can transfer the funds from his RFC to NRE. Such accounts can be held jointly with resident relative as joint holder on "former or survivor" basis. However, such a relative cannot operate the account during the life time of the account holder.

The interest is tax-free as long as you hold RNOR status. However, the interest rate unfortunately is quite low, varies between 2.5% and 3.5% depending upon the term and the bank and moreover, it is subject to TDS even when you are an RNOR.

Resident Forex Domestic Account (RFCD)

A Resident individual can use this Resident Forex Currency (Domestic) Account for crediting forex in the form of currency notes, bank notes and travellers cheques acquired by him —

- While on a visit to abroad, for services rendered abroad not arising from any business in or anything done in India.

- As honorarium, gift, services rendered or in settlement of any lawful obligation, whether earned in India or abroad, from any person not Resident.
- As unspent amount of forex received from an AD for travel abroad.
- Gift from a close relative.
- Forex received from life insurance policy of an Indian insurer.
- Earnings through export of goods or services, royalty, honorarium or any other legal means.
- Disinvestment proceeds received on conversion of shares to ADRs / GDRs under sponsored and approved ADR / GDR Scheme.
- Claims, maturity or surrender values settled in forex from an insurance company in India.

Debits to the account shall be for payment towards current or capital account transactions which are eligible for Residents. Balances may be credited to NRE/FCNR accounts, if and when the account holder becomes an NRI.

The account will be maintained as only current account and shall not bear any interest. Cheque facility is available. The funds held in these accounts shall not be lent or made available in any manner to any person or entity Resident not being a unit in Special Economic Zones.

The sum total of the accruals in the account during a calendar month should be converted into Rupees on or before the last day of the succeeding calendar month after adjusting for utilization of the balances for approved purposes or forward commitments.

Existing facility of retention of US$ 2,000 or its equivalent in forex by Residents continues provided that such forex is in the form of currency notes, bank notes and traveller's cheques.

EEFC Account

Exchange Earner's Foreign Currency Account is a facility provided to the forex earners, including exporters, to credit 100% their forex earnings to the account, thereby minimizing their transaction costs. The accruals in the account during a calendar month should be converted into Rupees on or before the last day of the succeeding calendar month after adjusting for utilisation of the balances for approved purposes or forward commitments of the account holders. These are essentially non-interest bearing current accounts.

Payment received through an international credit card for which reimbursement will be provided in forex may be regarded as a remittance through banking channels.

Permitted Credits

- Inward remittance through normal banking channels, other than remittances received on account of forex loan or investment received from abroad or received for meeting specific obligations by the account holder.
- Payments received in forex by a 100% Export Oriented Unit or a unit in Export Processing Zone, Software Technology Park or Electronic Hardware Technology Park for supply of goods to similar such units or to a unit in Domestic Tariff Area.
- Payments received in forex by a unit in the Domestic Tariff Area for supply of goods to a unit in the SEZ.
- Payment received by an exporter from an account maintained with an AD for counter trade. Counter trade is an arrangement involving adjustment of value of goods imported into India against value of goods exported from India.
- Advance remittance received by an exporter towards export of goods or services.
- Payment received for export of goods and services from India, out of funds representing repayment of State Credit in

US$ held in the account of Bank for Foreign Economic Affairs, Moscow, with an authorised dealer in India.

- Professional earnings including directors' fee, consultancy fee, lecture fee, honorarium and similar other earnings received by a professional by rendering services in his individual capacity.
- Re-credit of unutilised foreign currency earlier withdrawn from the account.
- Amount representing repayment by the account holder's importer customer in respect of trade related loan/advances granted by the exporter (subject to compliance with the extant guidelines) holding EEFC account.
- The disinvestment proceeds received by the resident account holder on conversion of shares held by him to ADRs/GDRs under the Sponsored ADR/GDR Scheme approved by the Foreign Investment Promotion Board.
- Interest earned in the account.

The claims settled in rupees by ECGC and insurance companies are not export realisation and therefore these are not eligible credits to EEFC.

Permitted Debits

- Payment outside India towards capital or current account transactions.
- Payment in forex towards cost of goods purchased from a 100% Export Oriented Unit or a Unit in an Export Processing Zone, or Software Technology Park or Electronic Hardware Technology Park.
- Payment of customs duty.
- Trade related loans or advances extended by an exporter holding such account to his importer customer outside India
- Payment in forex to a Resident for supply of goods and services including payments for air fare and hotel expenditure.

- Withdrawal in rupees is permitted. It cannot be re-credited to the account.
- Exporters can repay packing credit advances, whether availed of in Rupee or in forex from the account to the extent exports have actually taken place.
- Balances held in the account may be credited to NRE or FCNR (B) Accounts, if the account holder becomes an NRI.
- It is obvious that the utility of RFC, RFCD and EEFC has been much diluted ever since the Residents can legally purchase sufficient forex for bona fide reasons. Moreover, NRIs as well as Residents are allowed to continue to hold bank accounts and investments abroad.

Miscellaneous

Forex International Deposits (FCID)
Some banks in India having their overseas banking units accept FCIDs which are essentially FCNRs but are free from the FEMA regulations. Consequently, the rate of interest is higher and so is the flexibility for the term of the deposit. Since the interest is paid by an Indian bank, it is taxable in India with the associated TDS applicability and the DTAA provisions.

Duplicate Demand Draft
Issue of duplicate demand draft can be effected up to ₹5,000 even before obtaining non-payment advice from the drawee branch on the basis of adequate indemnity. The drawee office may merely be cautioned in this regard. If the draft is for more than ₹5,000, non-payment certificate should be called for from drawee office by telex / telegraph at applicant's cost and other formalities completed.

A duplicate demand draft should be issued within a fortnight from the receipt of such request. For delay in issuing duplicate draft beyond the stipulated period, banks should pay interest at the rate applicable for fixed deposit of corresponding maturity.

Forex Rupee Options

In terms of AP (DIR) Circular 108 dt 21.6.03 as a part of developing the derivative market in India and adding to the spectrum of hedge products available to Residents and NRIs for hedging currency exposures, forex rupee options are permitted subject to certain conditions.

Residents and Bank Accounts in Foreign Countries

A resident individual can open a foreign currency account with a bank outside India in the following cases:

1. A Resident student who has gone abroad for studies: On the student's return to India after completion of studies, the account will be deemed to have been opened under the Liberalised Remittance Scheme (LRS).
2. A Resident who is on a short visit to a foreign country: The balance in the account should be repatriated to India on return of the account holder to India.
3. A person going abroad to participate in an exhibition or trade fair for crediting the sale proceeds of goods: The balance should be repatriated to India within one month from the date of closure of the exhibition or trade fair.
4. The following persons for remitting or receiving their entire salary payable to them in India:
   (a) A foreign citizen Resident, who is an employee of a foreign company and is on deputation to the office / branch / subsidiary / JV / group company in India;
   (b) An Indian citizen who is an employee of the above entities; and
   (c) A foreign citizen who is a Resident and is employed with an Indian company.
5. For the purpose of sending remittances under the LRS, a resident nominee of an account held outside India has to close the account and bring back the proceeds to India through normal banking channels on the death of the account holder.

The general permission also applies to Residents for accounts abroad opened prior to 8.7.47.

Money Transfer Service Scheme (MTSS)

Master Circular 1/2012-13 dt 2.7.12 deals with MTSS which is a quick and easy way of transferring personal remittances from abroad to beneficiaries in India. Only inward (and not outward) personal remittances into India by individuals to individuals towards family maintenance and remittances favouring foreign tourists visiting India are permissible. Any remittances related with trade, purchase of property, investments or credit to NRE accounts shall not be made through this arrangement. MTSS envisages a tie-up between reputed money transfer companies abroad and agents in India who would disburse the funds to the beneficiaries in India at ongoing exchange rates.

A cap of US$ 2,500 exists on individual remittances under the scheme. Amounts up to ₹50,000 may be paid in cash to a beneficiary in India. Any amount over this limit shall be paid through an account payee cheque, demand draft, payment order, etc.

In order to avoid any inconvenience to foreign tourists, ADs may issue pre-paid instruments to them in terms of the instructions issued by Department of Payments and Settlement System, RBI, in exchange of foreign exchange tendered. Passport may be treated as a valid document for issuance of this instruments.

Facilities for NRIs on Repatriation Basis — Summary

1. Government dated securities/Treasury bills.
2. Units of domestic mutual funds.
3. Non-convertible Debentures of Indian companies.
4. Shares and convertible debentures of Indian companies through stock exchange under Portfolio Investment Scheme.
5. Shares and Convertible Debentures of Indian companies under the FDI scheme.

6. Perpetual debt instruments and debt capital instruments issued by banks in India.
7. Bonds issued by Public Sector Undertakings.
8. Shares in Public Sector Enterprises being disinvested by the Government of India.

Facilities for NRIs on Non-Repatriation Basis — Summary

1. The first 4 items listed above.
2. Units of Money Market Mutual Funds.
3. SEBI approved Exchange traded derivative contracts out of INR funds held in India on non-repatriable basis, subject to the limits prescribed by the SEBI.

Note: NRIs are not permitted to invest in small savings or Public Provident Fund (PPF) or RBI Savings Bonds.

9

~

Capital Gains

It hurts to pay tax on capital gains. A large part of these gains is due to the endemic inflation. In terms of real money value, the actual gains may be negative. Yet, tax is levied on these gains. To counter this atrocity, we have to examine carefully the various tax-saving devices and take as much shelter behind them as possible.

Definition: Capital Asset and Transfer

The term *capital asset* does not include personal effects such as wearing apparel, furniture, air conditioners, refrigerators, etc., held for personal use by the assessee. Even cars, scooters, cycles, motorcycles owned and used by the assessee are personal effects. Therefore, the sale of personal effects do not attract any capital gains tax.

We have a cute suggestion. A car used for personal purpose (depreciation is not charged), is not a capital asset. When it is sold, no capital gains, arise. The profit or loss cannot be brought to income tax.

It is obvious that all the returning NRIs will do well by bringing their cars with them and sell these in due course.

Agriculture

Sec. 2(14iii) defines capital asset and Sec. 2(1A) defines agricultural income. Accordingly, an agricultural land is one which is not situated within a certain distance from the local limits of any municipality, cantonment board, etc., having a certain amount of population according to the last preceding census. Accordingly, the distance, as measured aerially (as the crow flies) should not exceed

(a) 2 kilometres where population is between 10,000 and 1 lakh.

(b) 6 kilometres where population is between 1 and 10 lakh.
(c) 8 kilometres where population is more than 10 lakh.

Obviously, the provisions bring the income from the land within the fold of agricultural land if and only if it is located nearer to the less populated area.

Rural agricultural land is not a capital asset. Consequently, its sale would not attract provisions of capital gains tax. Looking at it from another angle, sale of all lands, agricultural or not, located in urban areas and non-agricultural land located in rural areas would attract the tax.

However, gains arising out of compulsory acquisition of such an agricultural land irrespective of its location, are exempt u/s 10(37).

Transactions not Regarded as Transfer

Following are some of the transactions related with NRIs which are not considered as transfer:

1. Sec. 47(i): Distribution of assets on partition of an HUF.
2. Sec. 47(iii): Assets transferred under a gift or a Will or an irrevocable trust.
3. Sec. 47(ix): Transfer of any work of art, archaeological, scientific or art collection, etc., to the government or a university or the National Museum, National Art Gallery, etc.
4. Sec. 47(x): Conversion of debentures, debenture stock or deposit certificates, preference shares of a company into its shares or debentures. FA17 has extended this neutrality to the conversion of a company into its equity share.
5. Sec. 47(vii): In the case of shares of companies, mergers and amalgamations are not treated as transfer ever since 1.4.67! Unfortunately, only merger of different schemes of MF was tax neutral. FA16 took corrective action by passing on the same benefit to different options within the same scheme. FA17 took additional corrective action to provide that the period of holding shall include the period for which the units in consolidating scheme were held by the assessee and the

cost of acquisition of the allotted units shall be the cost of units in the consolidating plan.

6. Sec. 47(viic): In the wake of permission to the Indian corporates by the RBI to issue rupee denominated Sovereign Gold bonds outside India, FA16 amended Sec. 48 to provide that tax on capital gains had to be paid if these bonds are sold or transferred before their redemption, but not on their redemption. This was confusing. FA17 has amended both these Sections w.r.e.f. FY 15-16 to provide that any transfer of such bonds by an NRI to another NRI is not regarded as transfer.
7. FA18 has inserted a new Sec. 47(viiaab) to provide that any transfer of a Bond or GDR referred to in Sec. 115C(1) or rupee denominated bond of an Indian company or derivative, made by an NRI on a recognised stock exchange located in any International Financial Service Centre and where the consideration is paid or payable in forex, shall not be regarded as transfer.
8. FA18 has inserted a new Sec. 43AA to provide that any gain or loss on a transaction arising from any change in forex rates shall be treated as income (or loss). Such transactions include those relating to monetary/non-monetary or translation of financial statements of foreign operations or forward exchange contracts or forex translation reserves.
9. As per Explanation-5 to Sec. 9(1i) any share or interest in a company or entity registered or incorporated outside India shall be deemed to be situated in India if the share or interest derives, directly or indirectly, its value substantially from the assets located in India. The meaning of "substantial value" was not clear. FA17 has inserted Explanation-6 to provide that a share or interest of a foreign entity shall be deemed to be deriving its value substantially from Indian assets (tangible or intangible) if the value of Indian assets as on the specified date exceeds ₹10 crore and represents at least 50% of the value of all the assets owned by the foreign entity. The liabilities (even if identifiable) will not be reduced from the asset values for reckoning the monetary limit.

10. Further exemption has been provided for shareholders holding non-controlling interest up to 5% of a foreign company, which derives value substantially from Indian assets. It has also exempted overseas amalgamations and demergers undertaken, subject to certain conditions, which results in transfer of another foreign company shares deriving, directly or indirectly, its value substantially from the share or shares of an Indian company exceeding the aforesaid thresholds.
11. CBDT Circular 4/2015 dt 26.3.15 has clarified that declaration of dividend by a foreign company outside India does not have the effect of transfer of any underlying assets located in India and therefore, the dividends declared and paid by a foreign company outside India in respect of shares which derive their value substantially from assets situated in India would not be deemed to be income accruing or arising in India by virtue of Explanation-5 to Sec. 9(1i).

Judicial Pronunciations Negated

1. The Supreme Court had held in the case of *B. C. Srinivasa Shetty, 128ITR294* that no tax is chargeable on transfer of capital assets in respect of which there is no cost of acquisition. This decision has been negated steadily by ordaining that the cost of acquisition should be taken as nil in the following cases
   (a) Goodwill of a business (not of a profession).
   (b) Trademark or brand name associated with the business.
   (c) Patent, copyright, formula, design, etc.
   (d) Right to carry on any business. FA16 has added one additional item to this list namely — "cost of acquisition" and "cost of improvement" of "right to carry on any profession".
   (e) Tenancy rights, Route permits, Loom hours, etc.
2. FA87 negated principles laid down *in Dhun Kapadia v CIT [1956] 63ITR651* in respect of cost of acquisition of rights and bonus shares and renunciation of the entitlement to apply for rights. The court had ruled that the capital gain can be

setoff against the capital loss on the old shares due to depreciation in their value on account of fall in their quotations on the issuance of rights.

3. *Vania Silk Mills (Pvt) Ltd. v CIT (1991) 59Taxman3 (SC)* had laid down the principle — Transfer presumes the existence of both the asset and the transferee. When the property is destroyed both these criteria are not satisfied. This was negated by inserting Sec. 45(1A) according to which, tax will be charged on any gains arising from money or other assets received under an insurance arising out of damage to, or destruction of any capital asset, as a result of (i) flood, typhoon, hurricane, cyclone, earthquake or other convulsion of nature or (ii) riot or civil disturbance or (iii) accidental fire or explosion or (iv) action by an enemy or action taken in combating an enemy (whether with or without a declaration of war).
4. FA12 has inserted Sec. 50D to counter *CIT v Mandharsinhji P. Jadeja (2005) 14Taxman110 (Guj)* by ordaining that where the actual purchase consideration is not attributable or determinable, the then existing FMV of the asset shall be deemed to be the full value of consideration.

Redevelopment of Flats

Fortunately, any compensation paid by a redeveloper to flat owner due to the hardship caused to the taxpayer (cost incurred is nil) continues to be held as non-taxable as per several court verdicts. The latest one (*2016 (8) TMI 1087 ITAT Mumbai*) involves Jitendra Kumar Soneja who had received a sum of ₹22 lakh as compensation from the redeveloper and ₹8.55 lakh for paying rent as he had to vacate his flat. The ITAT held that ₹22 lakh is received as a corpus fund, is a capital receipt and not taxable. Going a step further, ITAT stated that while the compensation was a capital receipt and not taxable, it would be reduced from the cost of acquisition of the flat. This would have a tax impact, in case the redeveloped flat was subsequently sold. However, as Soneja had incurred a rent expenditure of only ₹6.80 lakh as against ₹8.55 lakh, the balance of ₹1.75 lakh was held liable to tax.

Purchases in Cash

FA17 has amended Sec. 43 to provide that any cash payments in the nature of capital expenditure above ₹10,000 shall not be considered to determine actual cost of asset u/s 43(1). Moreover, no deductions shall be available u/s 35AD, including depreciation for such expenditure. It will be income chargeable to tax.

Capital Gains Tax: Sec. 112

A "Short-term capital asset" (ST) is a financial asset held for 36 months or less immediately preceding the date of transfer. The holding period is only 12 months for shares of a company, units of MFs, zero coupon bonds and listed scrips, bonds, debentures. An asset which is not ST is LT (Long-term).

The holding period is 24 months in the case of — (i) immovable property, being land or building or both and (ii) unlisted equity shares.

Sec. 112(1c) as amended by FA12 provided concessional tax rate of 10% on LTCG arising from the transfer of unlisted securities in the case of NRIs. The ambiguity as to its applicability to shares of a private company was clarified by FA16 stating that the share of company in which public are not substantially interested shall also be chargeable to tax @10%.

FA14 has taken away debt-based MF schemes from this concessional lower period of 12 months. The normal period of 36 months will be applicable.

Note the word "held" in this provision. The assessee need not be an owner of the property and can hold it as a lessee, as a mortgagee, under a hire purchase agreement, or on account of part performance of an agreement.

In the case of other financial assets like houses, jewellery, etc., STCG is taxed like any other income at the rates applicable to the assessee. LTCG is taken as a separate block, charged to tax at a flat rate of 20% with indexation benefit. The benefit of gap between the tax threshold and normal income is not available to NRIs.

Cost Inflation Indexation (CII)

Sec. 55 has been amended to allow the cost of acquisition of an asset acquired before 1.4.2001 to be taken as FMV as on 1.4.2001 and the cost of improvement shall include only those capital expenses which are incurred after 1.4.2001. Consequential amendment is also carried out in Sec. 48 so as to align the provisions relating to cost inflation index to this new base year.

Table-1: Cost Inflation Index

FY	*Inflation Index*	*Growth %*	*FY*	*Inflation Index*	*Growth %*
2001-02	100		2010-11	167	12.84
2002-03	105	5.00	2011-12	184	10.18
2003-04	109	3.81	2012-13	200	8.70
2004-05	113	3.67	2013-14	220	10.00
2005-06	117	3.54	2014-15	240	9.09
2006-07	122	4.27	2015-16	254	5.83
2007-08	129	5.74	2016-17	264	3.94
2008-09	137	6.20	2017-18	272	3.03
2009-10	148	8.03	2018-19	280	2.94
CII for 2019-20 may be declared in August 2019.					

Indexed cost is arrived at by multiplying the cost with the ratio of CIIs for the year of sale and that of acquisition.

LTCG is computed by deducting from the full value of the consideration (i) any expenditure (brokerage, stamp duty, etc.) incurred in connection with the transfer, (ii) indexed cost of acquisition and (iii) indexed cost of improvement.

For assets acquired prior to 1.4.2001 the option of substituting the fair market value (FMV) in place of original cost is possible. In other words, if the cost of acquisition is lower than FMV as on 1.4.2001, the assessee may adopt the FMV as his cost. If it is higher, he may adopt it as his cost of acquisition. The CII based on 2001-02 only will be taken into account, whatever is the choice for the cost.

An assessee has the right to take the FMV as on 1.4.2001 even for bonus shares allotted to him prior to that date. Same is true for other assets, normally required to be taken at nil value.

Tax & FA14 Amendments

Security Transaction Tax (STT)

STT is a minuscule amount of tax collected from the following transactions taking place in a recognised stock exchange in India:

(a) Purchase and sale of shares.
(b) Sale of equity-based MFs.
(c) Sale of Options in securities.
(d) Sale of Futures in securities.

STT is also charged on redemption of equity-based units of MFs, (but not on debt-based) directly with the fund house which had issued these units. The LTCG was exempt (note the past tense; discussed later) and STCG is taxed at a concessional rate of 15% only arising out of the sale transaction has suffered STT.

CTT is close cousin of STT for commodities.

There are two hidden bombs in this provision.

1. If the gains are exempt, the loss is also exempt and cannot be set off against any other ST or LT gain.
2. Tax on STCG @15% is beneficial only to those who are in 20% or 30% zone; not to 10%.

The requirement to have the deal in a recognised stock exchange in India applied only to sales and not purchases. Therefore, when bonus shares are sold in the market, the tax concessions apply. These used to attract heavy tax since their cost of acquisition was required to be taken as nil. Same is the case for IPOs and right issues but to a lesser extent. Those who have lost the record of cost and date of acquisition need not now worry.

10%-or-20% Option

In the case of listed shares and securities which are not sold on any recognised stock exchange in India, such as sale of non-dematted shares on between two persons, as well as Zero Coupon Bonds (alternatively termed as Deep Discount Bonds) which do not suffer any STT, LT gains is charged to tax @10% without indexation (= sale – cost = profit) or 20% with indexation (= sale – indexed cost), whichever is lower. ST gains are to be added to the normal income of the assessee and charged to tax at the rate applicable to his slab of income.

FA17 has introduced a new Sec. 50CA to provide that where consideration for transfer of share of a company (other than quoted share) is less than the FMV of such share determined in accordance with the prescribed manner, FMV shall be deemed to be the full value of consideration for the purposes of computing capital gains.

For Debt-based units of MFs houses, jewellery, etc., LTCG is taken as a separate block, charged to tax @20% with indexation and STCG is taxed like any other income at the rates applicable to the assessee.

No deduction under sections 80C to 80U is allowed from long-term capital gains.

Large Scale Amendments by FA18

In the case of capital gains arising out of shares and securities and equity-based units of MFs or a unit of business Trust sold on a Recognised Stock Exchange in India or repurchased directly from MFs, STT is payable and therefore —

(a) LTCG was exempt u/s 10(38).
(b) STCG was and continues to be taxed @15% flat, u/s 111A.

This exemption u/s 10(38) was misused by certain persons for declaring their unaccounted income as exempt LTCG by entering into sham transactions. To address this abuse, FA18 has implemented large-scale amendments by making Sec. 10(38) non-operative and introducing a new Sec. 112A. Consequently —

1. The LTCG will be computed without giving effect to the 1st proviso to Sec. 48 dealing with CII and also the 2nd proviso dealing with foreign currency in the case of NRIs.
2. Such LTCG shall be taxed @10% if STT has been paid on both acquisition and transfer. The requirement of STT being paid at the time of acquisition shall not apply to purchases made before 1.4.2004 when STT was introduced and some additional notified transactions as mentioned later.
3. The tax of 10% is applicable only on amount of capital gain exceeding ₹1 lakh.
4. The cost of acquisitions in respect of the long term capital asset acquired by the assessee before 1.2.2018 shall be deemed to be the higher of –
   (a) the actual cost of acquisition of such asset; and
   (b) the lower of (i) the "Fair Market Value" (FMV) of such asset; and (ii) the full value of consideration received or accruing on the transfer of such asset.
5. FMV for this new Section has been defined to mean –
   (a) In a case where the capital asset is listed on any recognised stock exchange, the highest price of the capital asset quoted on such exchange on 31.1.18. Where there is no trading in such asset on that date, the FMV shall be its highest price on a date immediately preceding date when it was traded.
   (b) In a case where the capital asset is a unit not listed on recognised stock exchange, its NAV on 31.1.18.
6. The FMV of shares which are unlisted on 31.1.18 but listed on date of transfer (on or after 1.4.18) shall be indexed cost of acquisition. This will also apply for unlisted shares which are substituted in tax neutral transfers (like amalgamation, demerger, gift, succession, etc.) for shares which are listed on date of transfer.

7. The benefit of deduction under chapter VI-A as well as the rebate u/s 87A and also the exemption u/s 54EC is not available on such capital gains.
8. The STCG arising from sale of equities of shares purchased after 1.4.18 can be set-off against other gains or carried forward for 8 years as per the normal terms and conditions.
9. However, gains arising from a transaction on a recognised stock exchange in any International Financial Services Centre and where the consideration is received or receivable in Forex, shall be eligible under this Section without payment of STT.
10. Sec. 115D has been amended to make all these changes applicable to FIIs, consequent to non-application of Sec. 10(38) to equities.
11. Notification S.O. 1789(E) dt 5.6.2017 protects genuine cases where the STT could not have been paid like acquisition of share in IPO, FPO, bonus or right issue by a listed company, acquisition by non-residents in accordance with FDI policy, acquisition under ESOP framed under SEBI Guidelines, transfer of shares approved by the Supreme Court, High Court, National Company Law Tribunal, SEBI, RBI in this behalf, any non-resident in accordance with foreign direct investment guidelines, acquisition from the Government, etc. New notification is expected to be released on similar lines.

This is an attempt to bring private deals between parties outside the market, shares of listed companies acquired through, preferential allotments, ESOPs, etc., under the normal capital gains net. Fortunately mergers and acquisitions are tax neutral.

Analysis

Very complicated indeed. For clarity, let us take the following example —

Let's say you had purchased Maruti shares on 13.10.17 @ ₹7,900/share. Irrespective of this rate, the FMV will be taken @

₹9,500 or thereabout, which was the highest price on 31.1.18. However, the date of purchase will remain 13.10.17 only.

The FMV will be ₹9,500 and not the rate as on 1.4.01 with one exception. If anytime after 13.10.18, you sell Maruti at say ₹8,500, you will be incurring a loss of ₹1,000. In this case, your FMV will be deemed to be ₹8,500 thereby bringing your loss at nil level. In other words, you cannot set it off against your other gains. On the other hand, if your sale price is, say ₹10,500, you will earn LTCG of ₹1,000 (without indexation) on which the tax will be @10% with associated surcharge and cess. This works out at ₹116.48. Then again, had you sold Maruti after 1.4.18 but before 13.10.17, you will have earned short-term capital gains which will be taxed @15%.

Listed securities, not sold on a Recognised Stock Exchange in India (or bought on or after 1.4.04), the LTCG are taxed @10% without indexation or 20% with indexation, whichever is lower. In his budget speech FM referred to the 10% rate on listed shares as a "concessional" rate and yet the tax rate on unlisted shares is more concessional. Strange!

This is a result of the tax legislation being so complicated that even the law makers appear to have lost their touch with reality.

We strongly feel that all these amendments would be rendered largely impotent in view of the fact that the Sensex on 31.1. 2018 was at a very high level of 35,965.02 at close. Realise that the FMV of individual stocks which you already own will be taken as its highest traded price during this date. Moreover, LTCG is still tax-free upto ₹1 lakh during the year. Since the market has fallen precariously after the announcement by the Budget to levy tax on such LTCG, it will take a while to regain this level. Till that happens, there would in effect no LTCG. Once again, that is not to say there would be no profit (since the profit would be sale value less your actual cost) — but computed LTCG would incorporate the above mentioned FMV and hence due to the high level of such FMV, the provision to tax LTCG is being rendered toothless to a large extent.

Finally, the best thing you can do is to pocket the tax-free LTCG up to ₹1 lakh every FY.

Business of Dealing in Shares

Where dealings in shares is a business of the person, all capital gains (or losses) are charged to tax under the head, "Profits and gains of business or profession". Sec. 36 provides that STT paid on transactions entered into in the course of the business shall be allowable as deduction.

Shares & FIIs

FIIs, other foreign companies as well as NRI individuals pay a concessional 10% tax on LTCG (without indexation) from transfer of unlisted securities which are covered under the SCRA. This reduced rate was not applicable to transfer of shares of private companies, as they are not governed by SCRA. FA16 has extended the coverage by amending Sec. 112(1ciii) to provide that LTCG arising on transfer of shares of a company not being a company in which public are substantially interested shall also be charged to tax @10%.

The benefit of lesser rate of tax conferred by Sec. 112(1) can be invoked by NR foreign company as well, when it sells listed Indian shares. The expression "before giving effect to 2nd proviso to Sec. 48" cannot be construed as a condition precedent for invoking the proviso to Sec. 112(1). Hence, the applicant foreign company is liable to pay tax at the lesser rate of 10% as per the proviso to Sec. 112(1) — Fujitsu Services Ltd., In re [AAR 800 of 2009].

Exchange Rate Risk

Protection provided by First Proviso to Sec. 48 has been deleted for NRIs, even if it results in a loss, because of the introduction of 10% tax on LTCG arising out of equities and equity-based MFs. However, it still is applicable on STCG arising from shares or debentures of an Indian company (private or public) acquired by utilising forex.

In such cases, capital gains shall be computed by deducting the cost of acquisition from the net value of the consideration received or accruing into the same foreign currency as was initially utilised for the purchase of shares or debentures. The capital gains so computed in such foreign currency shall be reconverted into Indian currency. Thus the NRI is protected against the exchange risk.

Indian corporates, vide RBI's notification dt 29.9.15, are permitted to issue rupee denominated bonds (popularly known as Masala Bonds) overseas to enable them to raise funds. To protect the interest of NRI investors from exchange rate fluctuations FA16 has provided that while computing capital gains u/s 48 at the time of redemption, full value of consideration received shall exclude any gain arising on account of appreciation of rupee.

What if the rupee depreciates? We wonder . . .

FA17 has amended Sec. 48 to provide relief in respect of such gains also to secondary holders. Moreover, Sec. 47 has been amended to provide that any transfer of such bonds by an NRI to another NRI shall not be regarded as transfer.

The method of conversion into foreign currency is specified by Rule 115A and is dealt with in Chapter *Tedious TDS*.

Sale Value for Stamp Duty — Sec. 50C

Where the consideration declared by the assessee for transfer of land or building or both, is less than the value adopted or assessed for stamp duty, the latter shall be deemed to be the full value of the consideration. If the assessee claims that this deemed value exceeds the fair market value (FMV) the ITO may ask a valuation officer of the Department to assess the FMV. If it turns out to be less than the value adopted for stamp duty, the ITO shall take the FMV to be the full value of consideration. Otherwise, the original duty shall prevail, subject to revision in any appeal.

This results in the buyer paying higher stamp duty and the seller paying higher tax on capital gains. Unfortunately, when the buyer sells the property at a later date, he is forced to adopt the original value declared by him and not the stamp duty valuation.

FA16 has amended this Section to stipulate that where the dates of the agreement registration for the transfer of a capital asset differ, the value adopted by the stamp valuation authority may be taken for the purposes of computing full value of consideration on the date of agreement if and only if the amount of consideration, or a part thereof, has been received through a bank account, on or before the date of the agreement for transfer.

Dates of Transfer & Registration Differ

Where the date of the agreement fixing the amount of consideration for the transfer of the immovable property and the date of registration are not the same, the stamp duty value may be taken as on the date of the agreement. This exception shall, however, apply only in a case where the amount of consideration, or a part thereof, has been paid by any mode other than cash on or before the date of the agreement.

Advance for Transfer of a Capital Asset

Amount confiscated by the seller cannot be treated as his capital gain, since no transfer of any capital asset has actually taken place. — *CIT* v *Sterling Investment Corp Ltd.* [1980] 123ITR441 (Bom).

Such forfeited amount was treated as a capital receipt not chargeable to tax during the year of forfeiture. This amount was reduced from the cost of acquisition of the property so that tax would get collected if and when the property gets actually sold. This provision was ingeniously used by some persons to convert their taxable earnings into capital receipts by entering into a sham agreement to sell a property to an accommodating party on the understanding that the earnest money will be forfeited as per the terms of the agreement.

To counter this situation, FA14 amended Sec. 56 to provide that any advance money taken against sale of an asset and forfeited because the negotiations did not result in transfer shall be chargeable to tax under the head "Income from Other Sources".

This has resulted in punishing the buyer in genuine cases where there was no such understanding. Even if such forfeiture is a pecuniary loss, he cannot claim it as a capital loss u/s 45 as he neither ever owned nor relinquished the capital asset in question. A CBDT clarification is necessary to avoid litigations.

FA12 has curtailed the practice of receiving a very high premium against the issue of shares.

Treatment of Losses

U/s 74 losses under the head "Capital Gains" cannot be set off against income under any other head. Though short-term loss can be set off against both STCG as well as LTCG, any LTCL shall be set off against LTCG only. If there are no sufficient gains during the year, the balance loss, ST or LT, can be carried forward for 8 successive years for similar set off.

Buy Back by Unlisted Companies

Buy back is a corporate action in which a company buys some of its shares from the existing shareholders at a price higher than market price. This is an indirect way of paying dividend without attracting DDT. Sec. 115QA provides for the levy of additional Income-tax @20% of the distributed income on account of buy-back of unlisted shares by the company.

This Section was introduced as an anti-abuse provision to check the practice of unlisted companies resorting to buy-back of shares instead of payment of dividends as the tax rate for capitals gains was lower than that of DDT. However, instances of similar tax arbitrage have now come to notice in case of listed shares as well, whereby the listed companies are also indulging in such practice of resorting to buy-back of shares, instead of payment of dividends.

In order to curb such tax avoidance even by the listed companies, Sec. 115QA is extended to all companies including companies listed on recognised stock exchange w.e.f. 5.7.19.

As additional income-tax has been levied at the level of company, the consequential income arising in the hands of shareholders has been exempted u/s 10(34A) not only to unlisted but also to listed companies.

Dividend Distribution Tax (DDT)

U/s 10(34), dividend received from a domestic company and u/s 10(35) income distributed by any MF, is tax-free. However, this dividend suffers DDT @15%, payable by the company before distributing the dividend to its stakeholders. With the surcharge of 15% (raised from 12% by FA16), and educational cess of 4%, the effective rate works out at 17.4720% (= 15 × 1.12 × 1.04).

In other words, if the company desires to pay ₹100 as dividend, it can pay ₹82.5280 to the shareholder and pay ₹17.4720 to the exchequer.

This DDT is in addition to the normal income tax payable by the entity giving dividends on its own profits.

In the case of MFs, the equity-based schemes are exempt from this DDT u/s 115R(2). For individuals & HUFs, on all debt-based funds of MFs, DDT rate is 25%. (= 29.1200%). For all other categories of taxpayers, the rate is 30% (= 34.9400%).

Many investors feel that this is an atrocity. We do not. As a matter of fact, we are thankful to the FM for raising the rate on DDT. Surprised? Well, here are our reasons.

Dividends suffer DDT; growth does not. Yes, growth attracts tax on capital gains. But in the case of MFs, it works out at almost nothing. Let us examine this aspect carefully.

This was also the situation when the DDT was introduced way back in FY99. We had placed this very solution of opting for growth and not dividend before our readers at that time. Our success was perhaps limited to only those elite readers who understood our message with clarity.

Way back in 2003, we were appointed by UTI to design their "UTI Bond Fund". We had structured the scheme without the (or dividend reinvestment) option. "Give the investors what is good for them" we told UTI, "and not what they want". UTI accepted the suggestion and launched the scheme with aplomb. Unfortunately, in due course, UTI was forced to introduce dividend option because it found that there were a large number of investors who shunned the scheme only because they did not understand (in spite of huge amount spent on investor education) that they can, opt for "Systematic Withdrawal Plan" at the frequency they desire.

Mr. Arun Jaitley deserves kudos for punishing the investors if they opt for dividend option in MF schemes by —

(a) deleting the option of 10% which was useless in any case,
(b) raising the period from 1 year to 3 years for entitling it to be LT, and
(c) raising the DDT rates on dividends paid.

Sec. 54EC Bonds

This offers exemption if the capital gains are reinvested within 6 months in Bonds issued by National Highway Authority of India (NHAI), Rural Electrification Corporation (REC) and some other notified Bonds which are redeemable after 3 years. Unfortunately, the limit on such contributions of ₹50 lakh. The investment can be made during the FY when the CG occurs and the subsequent FY but within the stipulated period of 6 months.

FA18 has inflicted 2 major changes diluting the advantage—

1. The exemption has been restricted only to LTCG arising from land or building or both. In other words, Sec. 54EC cannot be used any more for LTCG arising from shares and securities, Bonds, precious metals and ornaments, archaeological collections, drawings, paintings, sculptures, any work of art, stock-

in-trade, etc. Moreover, this exemption is no more available for LTCG arising out of Sec. 54F on any asset other than land.

2. The lock-in period of such Bonds has been increased from 3 years to 5 years.

The Bonds are non-transferable, non-negotiable and cannot be offered as a security for any loan or advance. The present interest rate is 5.25% fully taxable. There is no TDS.

Deposits in the Bonds are riddled with 2 problems. The 1st one is that the date of allotment is the last date of the month during which the subscription is received, irrespective of the date when the company encashes your cheque. The 2nd one is that the face value of one Bond is ₹10,000. Consequently, if you have earned LTCG of ₹83,000 you can either purchase Bonds worth ₹80,000 and pay tax on ₹3,000 or purchase Bonds worth ₹90,000 and pay no tax. What should you do?

For arriving at the answer to this question, let us first find out whether it is worth buying the Bonds even if you have earned a round figure of LTCG worth ₹10,000. Suppose you are in 31.2% tax bracket. If you buy the bonds, you earn a low rate of 5.25% taxable (=3.61% after-tax) rate of interest. The maturity value of this after a term of 5 years works out at ₹11,941.26.

Now, suppose you decide to pay tax applicable to LTCG @23.30% comprising of the base rate of 20%, the surcharge of 12% and cess of 4%. Your take home happens to be ₹7,670.40. you will have to earn an after-tax rate of 9.26% after-tax (=13.45% taxable) rate to get a maturity value of ₹11,941.61.

If you are in the 31.2% tax zone, you may decide to pay tax on the capital gains and invest the remaining amount in any other equally safe avenue offering an interest rate of 13.45% of more.

This computation requires a little fine tuning taking into consideration that the annual interest received from the Bonds can be invested in the other avenue. The most accurate rates works out at 14.12% for 31.2% zone, 13.08% for 20.4% zone and 12.29% for 10.4% zone.

Now, we take up the case where the amount of capital gain is odd, such as 83,000. Without taking you through the rigmarole of the computation, if the recent RBI Savings Bonds offering taxable rate of 7.75% as a benchmark, you should buy Bonds worth ₹80,000 and pay tax on ₹3,000. If the odd amount is higher, go ahead with Bonds worth ₹90,000.

All said and done, if you have a good appetite for taking risk, you may consider choosing the avenue of direct investment in listed shares or indirect investment therein through MFs.

It is important to note the following court verdicts —

1. Investment made prior to the date of transfer out of earnest money or advance received is eligible for exemption u/s 54EC — *[2012] 28taxmann.com274 Bombay (HC) Mrs. Parveen P. Bharucha v DCIT Circle 2 Pune.*
2. For claim of exemption u/s 54EC, source of investment of fund is immaterial. *IAC v Jayantilal C. Patel (HUF) [1988] 26ITD1 (Ahd).* Surely, this verdict can be extrapolated to Sec. 54EC.
3. As per the language of Sec. 54EC, there is no requirement that investment should be in name of assessee. The only condition is that the sale proceeds of capital assets must be invested in certain specified bonds — *ITO v Smt Saraswati Ramanathan [2009] 116ITD234 (Delhi).*
4. Although as per Sec. 50, the profit arising from the transfer of a depreciable asset (industrial building) shall be a gain arising from the transfer of short-term capital asset, irrespective of the period of holding, but it nowhere says that the depreciable asset shall be treated as short-term capital asset. Sec. 54EC is an independent provision not controlled by Sec. 50 which is restricted only to the mode of computation of capital gain u/ss 48 and 49 and this fiction cannot be extended beyond that for denying the benefit otherwise available to the assessee u/s 54EC, if the other requisite conditions of the Section are satisfied — *Sudha S. Trivedi v ITO [ITA 6040 & 6186/Mum./2007].*

5. The time-limit of 6 months for investment in Bonds is to be reckoned from date of receipt of part or full payments and not from date of transfer as defined u/s 53A of the Transfer of Property Act — *[2012] 18 taxmann.com 304 Kolkata — Trib.* Moreover, this period should be reckoned from the end of the month in which the transfer takes place — *[2012] 17 taxmann.com 159 Mum.*
6. Where purchase of specified conversion of investment into stocks or bonds just a few days beyond period of six months was under a bona fide mistake, the exemption can be denied but penalty u/s 271(1c) cannot be levied *[2014] 45 taxmann.com 180 Punjab & Haryana.*
7. Bona fide realignment of interest by way of effecting family arrangements among the family members does not amount to transfer — *CIT v A L Ramanathan (2000) 245ITR494 (Mad).*

Sec. 54 & 54F

The ITA provides other opportunities for saving tax on long-term capital gains such as by way of Sec. 54 & Sec. 54F. Sec. 54 gives exemption from tax on capital gains arising out of sale (or transfer) of a residential house, self-occupied or not, provided the assessee has purchased within 1 year before or 2 years after the date of sale or has constructed within 3 years after that date, a residential house. If only a part of the LTCG is used, the exemption would be pro-rata and the excess will be taxed.

Two points are worthy of careful note —

1. For construction, there is no restriction on commencement date. It could have begun even more than 20 years before the sale.
2. The assessee need not apply the amount from the sale proceeds for purchasing another residential house. He can take a loan for the purchase or construction and use the sale proceeds for investment elsewhere, if it is beneficial for him to do so.

Sec. 54F deals with capital gains arising out of assets other than residential houses. The stipulations are essentially the same but with 3 differences —

1. The assessee should not be an owner of more than one residential property on the date of transfer.
2. Sec. 54F requires reinvestment of the net consideration (sale value less expenses) whereas Sec. 54 is content with reinvestment of only the amount of capital gains.
3. In the case of Sec. 54, the assessee is required not to sell the new house within 3 years. If this condition is not satisfied, the cost of the new asset is to be reduced by the amount of long-term capital gains exempted from tax on the original asset and the difference between its sale price and such reduced cost will be chargeable as short-term capital gain earned during the year in which the new asset is sold.

Sec. 54F also requires the assessee not to sell the new house within 3 years. In addition, he is expected not to purchase within 1 year or construct within 3 years, another residential house. If any of these conditions are not satisfied, the capital gain originally exempted shall be treated as long-term capital gain of the year in which the house is sold or another house is purchased or constructed.

This penalty is different from that of Sec. 54 and creates confusion. We do not comprehend the wisdom of imposing different punishments for the same offence.

"A" House is "One" House

Sec. 54 stated ". . . where, . . . the capital gains arises from the transfer of a long-term capital asset being . . . a residential house, and the assessee has . . . purchased a residential house, then . . . "

There were a flood of litigations revolving around the meaning of "purchased a residential house" and the judiciary pronouncements were contradictory and inconsistent with one another.

Additional flood arose because of faulty language used in the legislation which made it possible to claim the benefit even on a house purchased abroad.

FA14 has settled both the problems at one stroke by replacing the phrase "purchased a residential house" with "purchased one residential house in India".

Hereunder are some difficulties arising out of these amendments.

Difficulty-1: An assessee sells two houses, either on the same date or different dates. Can he buy one large house and claim deduction for both the houses together?

The amendment has replaced the word "a" associated with purchase of new house by the word "one". The word "a" associated with transfer of a long-term capital asset has not been replaced.

It appears that for claiming exemption arising from transfer of "a" house, the assessee has to purchase one house. If he sells yet another "a" house, he has to buy another one house.

This is illogical and we would continue to be guided by *DCIT Central Circle-32 v Ranjit Vithaldas [2012] 23taxmann.com 226 ITAT Mumbai Bench "A"* — If two flats are sold even in different years and capital gains from both flats is invested in one residential house, exemption will be available for each flat sold provided the time-limit for construction or purchase of new house is satisfied.

Difficulty-2: If "a" is "one" it is also not "half". Can an assessee purchase the new house jointly with his wife who has also contributed a share of the cost?

ITO v Rasiklal N. Satra (280ITR243 dt 19.9.05) — Ownership of a residential house, means ownership to the exclusion of all others. Therefore, where a house is jointly owned by two or more persons, none of them can be said to be the owner of that house.

Difficulty-3: U/s 80C(xviii) deduction on repayment of capital amount of housing loan is available — "for the purposes of purchase or construction of 'a' residential house property . . ."

Does this mean that if a person has taken two houses financed through housing loans, he cannot claim deduction on instalments towards part payment of the loan against only one house? Strangely, the interest paid on the same loans can be claimed as deduction even against more than one house!

CBDT clarification is required.

Capital Gains Accounts Scheme, 1988 (CGAS)

For ascertaining that the assessee really intends to purchase a new residential house within the stipulated time, all scheduled banks have a special bank account designated as CGAS. The amount deposited in such accounts before the last date of furnishing returns of income or actual date, if earlier, along with the amount already utilised, is deemed to be the amount utilised for the purpose.

This means that the assessee can utilise this amount for any purpose whatsoever during intervening period — *ACIT v Smt Uma Budhia (2004) 141Taxman39 (Kol.).*

If the amount is not utilised wholly or partly for the stipulated purpose, then, the amount of capital gains related with the unutilised portion of the deposit in CGAS shall be charged as the capital gains of the year in which the period expires.

Circular 743 dt 6.5.96 states that when the account holder expires, the unutilised amount in CGAS account is not taxable in the hands of the legal heirs or nominees as the unutilised portion of the deposit does not partake the character of income in their hands but is only a part of the estate devolving upon them.

10

~

Foreign Investment in India

> There are two kinds of investors — those who don't know where the market is headed, and those who don't know that they don't know. Then again, there is a third type — the investment professional, who indeed knows that he or she doesn't know, but whose livelihood depends upon appearing to know.
>
> — Bernstein William in his book *The Intelligent Asset Allocator.*

Investment in India, particularly in shares, is known to be more rewarding than elsewhere in the global markets since the returns are significantly high and safe. It has become higher and safer particularly under the aegis of the Modi Government. The economic health of the industries at large has improved considerably because of the policy of liberalisation and globalisation. Therefore, NRIs should invest in India (= Make in India) not only for their own benefit but also to boost the economy of their motherland.

FPI and FDI Merged

With an objective of simplifying the procedures, Foreign Portfolio Investments (FPI) and Foreign Direct Investments (FDI) have been merged together in respect of all the applicable terms and conditions along with composite sectoral caps. "Total foreign investment" in an Indian company will be the sum total of direct and indirect foreign investments. Consequently, Portfolio Investments up to aggregate foreign investment level of 49% or sectoral/statutory cap, whichever is lower, will not be subject to any Government approval or compliance, provided such investment does not result in change in ownership. Other foreign investments will be subject to conditions of government approval and compliance of sectoral conditions as laid down in the FDI policy and the related FEMA Regulations.

Since 90% of such investments come through automatic route FA17 has taken a further logical step by abolishing Foreign Investment Promotion Board (FIPB) to eliminate the regulatory hurdles and moreover, strategic areas like defense, telecom etc., will still need clearances.

This is yet another positive step to further liberalise FDI policy framework and attracting investments.

NRI individuals and registered FIIs/FPIs can invest or trade in the capital of Indian companies listed on recognised Indian Stock Exchanges only through a registered broker.

ROIs cannot purchase, hold, receive as a gift or by any other means shares of Financial Services Sectors which cover Banks, NBFC, Insurance, ARCs, Stock Exchanges, Clearing Corporations, Depositories, Commodity Exchanges, etc., without approval of RBI.

An NRI or a non-resident entity can invest in India, subject to the FDI Policy except in prohibited sectors and activities. In the case of Bangladesh and Pakistan, its citizen or an entity incorporated in these countries, can invest only under the Government route. Such a permission is not given to sectors / activities in defence, space and atomic energy and sectors/activities prohibited for foreign investment. RBI Circular (DIR) 1 dt 13.9.04 has lifted the restriction on dealing in Indian shares by Sri Lankan citizens.

NRIs resident in Nepal and Bhutan as well as citizens of Nepal and Bhutan are permitted to invest in the capital of Indian companies on repatriation basis, only if the amount of consideration for such investment shall be paid only by way of inward remittance in free forex through normal banking channels.

A.P. (DIR) Circular 22 dt 28.8.14 allows NRIs to invest, both on repatriation and non-repatriation basis, in non-convertible / redeemable preference shares or debentures as above.

An NRI can purchase shares, debentures, units of MFs, dated central and state government securities (other than bearer securities), treasury bills, units of domestic MFs, bonds issued by a PSU in India and shares in public sector enterprises being disinvested by the Government of India through stock exchanges, either directly or through a Resident trustworthy person, including stock broker as his agent in India.

Portfolio Investment Scheme (PIS)

Notification FEMA 361/2016-RBI dt 15.2.16 has defined an NRI to mean an individual NRI or a PIO with an OCI card. Under PIS, an NRI may acquire securities or units on a Stock Exchange in India on repatriation or non-repatriation basis, subject to the terms and conditions specified in Schedule-3 or Schedule-4 respectively. In the case of these Schedules, the term "share" also includes convertible preference shares, convertible debentures and warrants of an Indian company or units of an investment vehicle, including REITs, InvIts, AIFs, etc.

General Provisions

An NRI should operate only through one AD.

The bank shall ensure that amounts due to sale proceeds of shares acquired by modes other than PIS, such as underlying shares acquired on conversion of ADRs/GDRs, shares purchased outside India from other NRIs, shares acquired under private arrangement, shares purchased while he was a Resident, do not get credited or debited to his PIS accounts.

The system provides the facility to freeze the DP accounts for any debits or credits or both debits and credits.

The NRI shall operate on delivery basis for shares purchased and sold. In other words, short selling (sale without having the scrip in his godown) or day-trading is not permitted.

Schedule-3: Repatriable

An NRI may purchase or sell shares, convertible preference shares, convertible debentures and warrants of an Indian company or units of an investment vehicle and warrants of an Indian company or units of an investment vehicle, on repatriation basis, under PIS through a designated AD branch within a limit of 5% of paid-up value on individual basis. Additionally, the limit is 10% on the aggregate paid-up value of these instruments of any company purchased by all NRIs on repatriation basis.

This limit of 10% may be raised to 24% if a special resolution to that effect is passed by the General Body of the Indian company.

The NRI investor should take delivery of the shares / convertible preference shares / convertible debentures / warrants and units purchased and give delivery of the same when sold.

The investment shall be subject to the provisions of the FDI policy and Schedule 1 of these Regulations in respect of sectoral caps wherever applicable.

All this limit business need not bother you. RBI monitors this limit assiduously on a case-by-case basis and puts the scrip on "Caution List" when the trigger limit is very near the cap. Thereafter it grants permission on first-come first-served basis. When the limit is reached, such shares are kept on banned-for-purchase list.

An NRI may open a designated NRE account with an AD, for routing the receipt and payment for transactions relating to sale and purchase of shares under this Schedule. The designated account will be called an NRE-PIS Account (alternatively called as PINS). Any NRI or a PIO can have only one PINS account in India separately and exclusively for PINS purposes. Transactions relating to their personal banking as well as on account of transactions relating to shares acquired other than under PINS including IPOs should be routed in his savings bank account.

PINS account is applicable only for NRIs and not for Residents. It is only for trading in Indian markets and not in any other foreign markets. It is applicable only for equity trades and not for Mutual fund investments.

Following transactions are not allowed or are not covered under PINS:

1. Sale of shares, which were not bought under PINS. Like: Gifts, subscription to IPOs or shares bought as resident Indian, or received in bonus. If an NRI has bought some shares under PINS, and has gifted those shares to another NRI, these shares received as gift cannot be sold under PINS.
2. Fresh subscription for the IPOs as an NRI
3. Investment in Mutual Funds.

The designated branch shall ensure that sale proceeds of securities or units which have been acquired by modes other than PIS such as underlying shares acquired on conversion of ADRs / GDRs, shares / convertible preference shares / convertible debentures / warrants acquired under FDI Scheme or purchased outside India from other NRIs or acquired under private arrangement from residents / non-residents or purchased while Resident, do not get credited in the PINS Account and *vice versa*.

Permitted Credits to NRE (PIS) are —

(a) Inward remittances in forex through normal banking channels,

(b) Transfer from the NRI's other NRE or FCNR accounts maintained with AD in India,

(c) Net sale proceeds (after payment of applicable taxes) of shares sold on stock exchange through registered broker, and

(d) Dividend or income earned.

Permitted Debits to NRE (PIS) are —

(a) Outward remittances of dividend or income earned.

(b) Amounts paid for purchase of shares on stock exchanges through registered broker under PIS,

(c) Any charges on account of sale / purchase of securities or units under the Scheme, and (d)Remittances outside India or transfer to NRE / FCNR (B) accounts of the NRI or any other person eligible to maintain such account.

Schedule-4: Non-Repatriable

Such transactions should take place only through NRO (PIS) account of the NRI.

Mostly the shares held prior to becoming an NRI or out of Indian assets earned or received thereafter, are non-repatriable. NRIs can invest in SEBI approved Exchange Traded Derivative Contracts on non-repatriable basis, subject to the limits prescribed.

An NRI, including a company, a trust and a partnership firm incorporated outside India and owned and controlled by non-resident Indians, may acquire and hold, on non-repatriation basis, equity shares, convertible preference shares, convertible debenture, warrants or units, without any limit, either on the stock exchange or outside it. This will be deemed to be domestic investment at par with the investment made by residents.

An NRI may contribute, on non-repatriation basis, to the capital of a partnership firm, a proprietary firm or a Limited Liability Partnership without any limit.

The consideration for investment under this Schedule shall be paid by way of inward remittance through normal banking channel from abroad or out of funds held in NRE / FCNR / NRO account maintained with a bank in India.

The sale/maturity proceeds (net of applicable taxes) of the securities or units acquired under this Schedule shall be credited only to NRO account irrespective of whether the consideration for acquisition was paid by direct remittances from abroad or the type of account maintained in India.

Trading Account

Trading account is used to place-execute the order over respective stock exchange. NRIs can transact over registered Indian stock exchange National Stock Exchange (NSE) & Bombay Stock Exchange (BSE) through the trading account

Demat account can be held jointly or singly as per the preference of the customer.

Nomination facility is provided on the Demat accounts.

Demat account helps to maintain the transaction details such as the date of purchase; cost of the transaction; selling price of the transaction, etc.

Transfer of Shares

General permission has been granted to non-resident entities and NRIs for acquisition of shares by way of transfer subject to:

(a) An ROI (other than NRI and erstwhile OCB) may transfer by way of sale or gift, the shares to any ROI (including NRIs). Government approval is not required for transfer of shares in the investee company from one non-resident to another non-resident in sectors which are under automatic route. Approvals of Government or RBI will be required for transfer of stake from one non-resident to another non-resident in sectors which are under Government or RBI approval route.

(b) NRIs may transfer by way of sale or gift the shares held by them to another NRI.

(c) An ROI can transfer any security to a person resident in India by way of gift.

(d) An ROI can sell the shares of an Indian company on a recognized Stock Exchange in India through a stock broker registered with stock exchange or a merchant banker registered with SEBI.

(e) A person Resident can transfer by way of sale, shares (including transfer of subscriber's shares), of an Indian company under private arrangement to a person resident outside India.

(f) General permission is also available for transfer of shares by way of sale under private arrangement by an ROI to a person Resident.

(g) Such general permissions also cover transfer of shares by a non-resident to an Indian company under buy back and / or capital reduction scheme of the company.

The sale consideration in respect of equity instruments purchased by an ROI remitted into India through normal banking channels shall be subjected to a Know Your Customer (KYC) check by the remittance receiving AD Category-I bank. If the remittance receiving AD is different from the AD handling the transfer transaction, the KYC check should be carried out by the remittance receiving bank and the KYC report be submitted by the customer to the AD carrying out the transaction.

An ROI including NRI investor who has already acquired and continues to hold the control in accordance with the SEBI (Substantial Acquisition of Shares and Takeover) Regulations can acquire shares of a listed Indian company on the stock exchange through a registered broker under FDI provided that the original and resultant investments are in line with the extant FDI policy and FEMA regulations in respect of sectoral cap, entry route, mode of payment, reporting requirement, documentation, etc.

Depository Receipts (DRs)

FCCBs / DRs may be issued in accordance with the Scheme for issue of Foreign Currency Convertible Bonds and Ordinary Shares (Through Depository Receipt Mechanism) Scheme, 1993 and DR Scheme 2014 respectively.

DRs can be issued against the securities of listed or unlisted and private or public companies against underlying securities which can be debt instruments, shares, units, etc. DRs can also be issued by shareholders without involving the company, through the so-called unsponsored DR route. DRs can be freely held and transferred by both Residents and Non-residents. Since the tax benefits were intended to be provided in respect of sponsored DRs and listed companies only, the definition of DR has been changed to mean depository receipts issued to NRIs against (i) ordinary shares of issuing company listed on a recognised stock exchange in India or (ii) FCCBs of issuing company.

Therefore, the benefits u/ss 115(AC), 47 and 49(2ABB) would not be available in respect of DRs issued other than under sponsored issuance of a listed company. Accordingly (i) the gains arising on transfer of such non-sponsored issues to NRIs outside India, would not be exempt from capital gains and, (ii) on conversion of these DRs into the underlying shares, the provision of Sec. 49(2ABB) shall not apply and the cost of acquisition of such underlying shares on conversion of DR shall be the cost at which the DR had been acquired by the investor.

The process of conversion of DRs into the underlying shares involves the non-resident holding the DRs in the overseas market giving instruction to his foreign broker who then delivers the DRs to the foreign depository delivering the underlying shares into a demat account of the foreign investor in India. The foreign depository thereafter cancels the DRs and issues an instruction to its local custodian in India who delivers the shares to the specified "DR type" demat account and informs the foreign depository of the completion of the process. The foreign investor may choose to hold the underlying shares or sell them in India either on exchange through a SEBI registered broker or through private arrangement.

There are no end-use restrictions except for a ban on deployment or investment of such funds in real estate or the stock market. There is no monetary limit on raising of DRs.

The DR proceeds can be utilised for the first stage acquisition of shares in the disinvestment process of PSUs and also in the mandatory second stage offer to the public.

An eligible person can issue or transfer eligible securities to a foreign depository, for the purpose of converting the securities so purchased into DRs. The aggregate of eligible securities, issued or transferred to foreign depositories, along with eligible securities already held by the ROI, shall not exceed the prescribed limit. The pricing of such securities should not be at a price less than that applicable to domestic investors.

DRs listed on Stock Exchanges in the US are referred to as American Depository Receipts (ADRs) and other markets, like Singapore, Luxembourg, London, etc., are Global Depository Receipts (GDRs). In the Indian context, DRs are treated as FDI.

Limited Two-way Fungibility

A SEBI-registered stock broker in India can purchase shares of an Indian company from the market for conversion into DR as required by overseas investors. Re-issuance of DRs would be permitted to the extent of DRs which have been redeemed into underlying shares and sold in Indian market.

Summary: Cases where Prior RBI Permission is Required

1. Transfer of capital instruments from resident to non-residents by way of sale where:
    (a) Transfer is at a price which falls outside the pricing guidelines specified by the RBI from time to time.
    (b) Transfer of capital instruments by the non-resident acquirer involving deferment of payment of the amount of consideration. Further, in case approval is granted for a transaction, the same should be reported in Form FC-TRS, to an AD Category-I bank for necessary due diligence, within 60 days from the date of receipt of the full and final amount of consideration.
2. Transfer of any capital instrument, by way of gift by a person Resident to a person resident outside India who is a close relative. The gift should not exceed 5% of the paid-up capital of the Indian company and each series of debentures / MF scheme.
3. The value of capital instruments to be transferred together with any capital instruments already transferred by the transferor, as gift, to an ROI should not exceed the rupee equivalent of US$ 50,000 during the FY.

4. Transfer of shares from NRI to NRI.

Indian Depository Receipts (IDR)

An Indian company can also sponsor an issue of IDRs where the company offers its Resident shareholders a choice to submit their shares to the company enabling it to issue IDRs abroad on the back of such shares. The proceeds of the issue are distributed amongst those Residents who offered their rupee denominated shares for conversion. The proceeds can be credited to their RFCD account in India. Moreover, where a Resident has since become an NRI, the sale proceeds can be credited to his foreign currency accounts abroad or in India.

Moreover, companies Resident outside India, with prior approval of sectoral regulator, can issue IDRs denominated in Indian Rupees, through any domestic depository to Residents, NRIs and also SEBI registered FIIs. For raising funds through issuances of IDRs by financial and banking companies having presence in India, either through a branch or subsidiary, prior approval of the sectoral regulators is necessary.

There is an overall cap of US$ 5 billion for raising capital through IDRs. This cap is akin to the cap imposed on FIIs for investment in debt securities.

The FEMA Regulations shall not be applicable to Residents for investing in IDRs and subsequent transfer arising out of transaction on a recognized stock exchange in India.

To encourage greater foreign participation in the Indian capital market and to retain the domestic liquidity, SEBI has allowed partial fungibility to the extent of redemption of IDRs into underlying equity shares and re-conversion of equity shares of a foreign issuer (which has already listed their IDRs) into IDRs up to 25% of the IDRs originally issued. IDRs shall not be redeemed into underlying equity shares before the expiry of 1 year.

Residents, other than Indian Companies and MFs can hold the underlying shares only for sale within 30 days from the date of conversion of the IDRs into underlying shares.

Incidentally, gains arising on redemptions of IDR into the underlying equity shares, if not specifically exempt, would lead to the holder being subjected to tax, making any redemption unattractive — a point for CBDT to note.

Miscellaneous Provisions

Transfer of sale of not listed or thinly traded shares under private arrangement are subject to guidelines related with fixing of price, collection of proceeds, documentation, etc.

A Resident can sell shares (including subscriber's shares), of an Indian company under private arrangement to an ROI, unless the shares are of an Indian company engaged in financial sector.

Companies incorporated in India can borrow in rupees by way of issue of Non-Convertible Debentures (NCDs) to NRIs on non-repatriation or repatriation basis.

RBI ADMA Circular 27 dt 31.8.99 has granted general permission to Indian Proprietorship Concerns, Firms and Companies for issue of CPs to NRIs on non-repatriable, non-transferable basis.

Dividend and Interest

U/s 9(1v) interest payable by the following entities is taxable in India —

(a) The Government, or

(b) A Resident, except where the interest is payable in respect of any debt incurred or moneys borrowed and used for business or profession carried on outside India or for earning any income from any source outside India.

(c) An NRI, where the interest is payable on any debt incurred or moneys borrowed and used for business or profession in India.

Investment in Partnership Firm / Proprietary Concern

An NRI (other than a citizen of Bangladesh, Pakistan or Sri Lanka) can contribute capital of a firm or a proprietary concern in India or any association of persons in India on non-repatriation basis.

Offshore Funds of Foreign MFs

India-dedicated offshore funds invest in the shares of Indian companies but are priced in a foreign currency. Such funds offer a lot of advantages to overseas investors —

1. Currency risk is absent.
2. Any income earned either through dividends or capital gains from offshore funds registered in Mauritius and other extremely tax-friendly regimes will not be taxed in India.
3. Offshore funds have a lower expense ratio of around 1.75% against 2% on domestic funds, thanks to over-regulation.

Yes, there are some problems —

1. Some offshore funds are priced on a weekly basis limiting the entry and exit facilities to once a week, causing liquidity problems.
2. Usual currency risk also exists for funds which maintain their portfolios in rupees but the NAV is marked to market in US$.
3. The time involved for the fund to sell the underlying investments in India can cause delays.
4. The shares redeemed on any valuation day may be limited to 10% of the total number of shares prior to the valuation day.

Exchange Traded Derivatives Contracts

FIIs and NRIs may invest out of Rupee funds held in India on non-repatriation basis in such contracts subject to the limits prescribed by SEBI. Accordingly, the position limits for FIIs and NRIs shall be the same as the client level position limits.

For Index-based contracts, there is a disclosure requirement for any person or persons acting in concert who together own 15% or more, of the open interest of all derivative contracts on a particular underlying index. For stock option and single stock futures contracts, the gross open position across all derivative contracts on a particular underlying security of an NRI shall not exceed the higher of (i) 1% of the free float market capitalisation in terms of number of shares, or (ii) 5% of the open interest in the derivative contracts on a particular underlying stock in terms of number of contracts.

These position limits would be applicable on the combined position in all derivative contracts on an underlying stock at an exchange.

An NRI is required to notify to the Exchange the names of the Clearing Member/s through whom he would clear his derivative trades. The exchange would then assign a unique client code to the NRI and monitor his position limits.

Alternative Investment Funds (AIFs)

These are privately-pooled investment vehicles, which collect funds from Indian and foreign investors and are primarily established in India. AIFs can be set up as a trust, company, limited liability partnership or any other body corporate. Similarly, the investment by AIFs can be in entities which can be a company, firm, etc., including another AIF.

In order to regulate AIFs, in May 2012, SEBI had categorised the funds into 3 categories:

Category-I: Funds which invest in start-ups, early stage ventures, social ventures include certain Venture Capital Funds (VCF) and Venture Capital Companies (VCC).

Category-II: Funds including PEs or debt which do not fall in Category-I and Category-III which generally are not leveraged.

Category-III: AIFs which employ diverse or complex trading strategies including leveraging and dealings in listed or unlisted derivatives.

Since the distinction between FPI and FDI has been done away with, the present separate caps for both would be merged into one for the purpose of AIFs.

To bring about clarity in taxation in the hands of the AIFs as well as their unit holders, a new Sec. 115-UA has been inserted by FA15 providing a special tax regime of a pass-through tax status to Category-I and Category-II AIFs. Consequently —

1. Any income (other than "Profits and Gains from Business") earned by the AIF shall be chargeable to tax in the hands of the unit holder. Such income shall be completely exempt from tax in the hands of AIF.
2. The income in the nature of "profits and gains of business or profession" shall be taxable in the hands of AIF. Such income shall be completely exempt in the hands of unit holder.
3. The income paid or credited by the AIF to the unit holder shall be deemed to be of the same nature and in the same proportion in the hands of the unit holder as it had accrued to or received by the AIF.
4. The income paid by an investment fund to its unit holders shall not be subject to DDT.
5. Where any income (other than business income, which is taxable at AIF level) is payable to a unit holder by an AIF, the fund shall deduct income tax @10%.
6. The income received by the AIF is exempt from the TDS requirement u/s 197A(1F).
7. If in any year, AIF incurs a loss, whether business loss or otherwise, such loss shall not be passed through to the unit holders but would be carried over at AIF level to be set off against income of the next year in accordance with the provisions relating to carry-forward and setoff of losses.
8. FA16 has extended DTAA benefits by allowing for rate in force being applicable for withholding tax purposes in respect of distribution by Category-I and II Alternate Investment Funds to the non-resident investors. It is also provided that the investors may seek certificate of lower deduction or nil deduction of tax.

The AIF is required to provide the details of various components of income to the prescribed tax authority and the unit holders.

The existing pass-through regime for VCF and VCC u/s 115-U, which is somewhat different from the proposed regime for AIF will continue to be applied to existing VCFs and VCCs which are registered under SEBI (VCF) Regulations, 1996.

The remaining VCFs and VCCs, being part of Category-I AIFs, shall mandatorily have to follow the new regime.

Now that there is enough clarity in respect of this new tax regime, it will surely bring in considerable growth in long-term foreign investment and Private Equity investment in India.

NRI Director of Indian Companies
RBI permission is not required for appointment as a director or to continue as a director of Indian companies, unless the sitting fees, commission, travel fare, etc., are to be paid to him in forex. For seeking RBI permission, there is no prescribed form. Only the Memorandum and Articles of Association and proof of directorship, is required to be submitted.

For Dividend Stripping, see Chapter *Mutual Funds*.

FDI Related Policies

Before closing, a loud and clear message. India is inviting you to "Make in India" and towards this goal, the government has taken several steps to make such a move very attractive to you by smoothening and streamlining the tax structure as well as the procedures as follows:

- Foreign investment will be allowed in the insurance and pension sectors in the automatic route up to 49% subject to the extant guidelines on Indian management and control to be verified by the Regulators.
- 100% FDI in Asset Reconstruction Companies (ARCs) will be permitted through automatic route. Foreign Portfolio Investors (FPIs) will be allowed up to 100% of each tranche in securities receipts issued by ARCs subject to sectoral caps.

- Investment limit for foreign entities in Indian stock exchanges will be enhanced from 5% to 15% on par with domestic institutions. This will enhance global competitiveness of Indian stock exchanges and accelerate adoption of best-in-class technology and global market practices.
- The existing 24% limit for investment by FPIs in Central Public Sector Enterprises, other than Banks, listed in stock exchanges, will be increased to 49% to obviate the need for prior approval of Government for increasing the FPI investment.
- The basket of eligible FDI instruments will be expanded to include hybrid instruments subject to certain conditions.
- FDI will be allowed beyond the 18 specified NBFC activities in the automatic route in other activities which are regulated by financial sector regulators.
- With a view to promote "Make in India" and following the practices in advanced countries, foreign investors will be accorded Residency Status subject to certain conditions. Currently, these investors are granted business visa only up to 5 years at a time.

International Financial Services Centre in India

- The companies located in international financial services centre shall not be liable to dividend distribution tax.
- MAT shall be charged at the rate of 9%.
- The transaction in foreign currency of sale of equity share or units of equity oriented funds or units of a business trust taking place on a recognised stock exchange established in international financial services centre shall not be liable to STT. Similarly, transaction in foreign currency of sale of commodity derivatives shall not be liable to CTT.
- LTCG shall be exempt from tax.

Deepening of Corporate Bond Market

- LIC of India will set up a dedicated fund to provide credit enhancement to infrastructure projects. The fund will help in raising the credit rating of bonds floated by infrastructure companies and facilitate investment from long term investors.
- RBI will issue guidelines to encourage large borrowers to access a certain portion of their financing needs through market mechanism instead of the banks.
- Investment basket of foreign portfolio investors will be expanded to include unlisted debt securities and pass through securities issued by securitisation SPVs.
- For developing an enabling eco system for the private placement market in corporate bonds, an electronic auction platform will be introduced by SEBI for primary debt offer.
- A complete information repository for corporate bonds, covering both primary and secondary market segments will be developed jointly by RBI and SEBI.

A framework for an electronic platform for repo market in corporate bonds will be developed by RBI.

11

~

Employees' Stock Options

Notification FEMA 344/2015 RB dt 11.6.15 has redefined ESOP to mean the option given to the directors, officers or employees of a company or of its holding company or joint venture or wholly owned overseas subsidiary / subsidiaries, if any, which gives such directors, officers or employees, the benefit or right to purchase, or to subscribe for, the shares of the company at a future date at a pre-determined price. "Sweat Equity Shares" means such equity shares as issued by a company to its directors or employees at a discount or for consideration other than cash, for providing their know-how or making available rights in the nature of intellectual property rights or value additions, by whatever name called.

An Indian company may issue ESOP and / or sweat equity to its own employees / directors or those of its holding company or joint venture or wholly owned overseas subsidiary who are resident outside India, provided such shares are in compliance with the sectoral cap applicable. Citizen of Bangladesh / Pakistan shall require prior approval of the Foreign Investment Promotion Board.

The equities should be issued within 180 days from the date of receipt of the inward remittance or by debit to the NRE/FCNR account. Transgression without prior permission of RBI, attracts penalty, unless the amount is refunded within this period.

Residents and Foreign Shares

Under AP (DIR) Circular 16 dt 15.12.01, a Resident employee or a director of an Indian office, branch, subsidiary or a JV (based on the foreign shareholding in the JV) of a foreign company can acquire foreign securities under ESOP without any monetary limit provided (i) annual return is submitted by the Indian company to RBI through the AD giving details of remittances, beneficiaries, etc., and (ii) the ESOP is offered globally on uniform basis.

AP (DIR) Circular 30 dt 5.4.06 permits AD banks to allow remittances without any monetary limit for acquiring shares under ESOP irrespective of whether it is offered directly by the issuing company or indirectly through a trust, SPV, or a Step Down Subsidiary, etc.

General permission is granted to foreign companies for repurchasing the shares issued to Residents under any ESOP provided:

(i) The shares were issued in accordance with the Rules and Regulations framed under FEMA and the shares are being re-purchased in terms of the initial offer document, and
(ii) The proceeds thereof are repatriated to India not later than 90 days from the date of their sale.

A Resident who has acquired or holds such foreign securities, may transfer them by way of pledge for obtaining fund-based or non-fund-based facilities in India from an AD.

ADR-GDR of Knowledge-based Indian Companies

RBI may permit an Indian company engaged in the field of software to allow its resident employees, including working directors, to purchase foreign securities under a GDR-linked ESOP, provided the consideration for purchase does not exceed US$ 50,000 or its equivalent in a block of 5 calendar years.

Cashless ESOP

Under Cashless ESOP issued by a company outside India, the employees can hold stock options and shares granted by the parent organisation without any restrictions on its monetary value, provided it does not involve any remittance from India. However, the employees are bound to sell the shares immediately on the date of exercise. The difference between the sale consideration and the exercise price needs to be promptly repatriated to

India. This scheme does not involve any cash outflow and therefore the RBI does not control the implementation of cashless ESOP.

Do cashless ESOP permit acquisition of stock options by employee of subsidiaries, branches, JVs of foreign corporations or is it restricted to employees of the parent corporations working in India? Can these be continued to be held post-retirement or on termination of employment? What about the legal heirs? Clarity is required.

JVs/WOS

RBI permits purchase of shares of a JV/WOS abroad of the Indian promoter company which is engaged in the fields of software, by its employees / directors provided —

(a) The purchase consideration does not exceed US$ 10,000 per employee in a block of 5 calendar years.
(b) The shares so acquired do not exceed 5% of the paid-up capital of the JV or WOS outside India, and
(c) After allotment of such shares, the percentage of shares held by the Indian promoter company, together with shares allotted to its employees is not less than the percentage of shares held by the Indian promoter company prior to such allotment.
(d) Proceeds from sale of shares so acquired have to be repatriated to India. In most cases, foreign companies with a stake of more than 51% are listed. So employees are given ESOPs on the local shares.

The period of holding in such a case shall be reckoned from the date on which a request for redemption is made by the assessee. Sec 49(2ABB) has been inserted to provide that the cost of acquisition of shares acquired by a non-resident on redemption of GDRs shall be the price of such shares as prevailing on any recognized stock exchange on the date on which a request for redemption is made by the assessee.

The proceeds so raised have to be kept abroad till actually required in India. Pending repatriation or utilisation of the proceeds, the Indian company can invest the funds in —

(a) Deposits with or Certificate of Deposit or other instruments offered by banks who have been rated by Standard & Poor, Fitch, IBCA, Moody's, etc., and such rating should not be below the eligible rating stipulated by RBI. Current eligibility is at AA-
(b) Deposits with branches of ADs outside India, and
(c) Treasury bills and other monetary instruments with a maturity or unexpired maturity of one year or less.

Foreign ESOPs

Several multinational companies listed on an overseas stock exchange have issued stock options to employees of their Indian subsidiaries. Possibly the new Rule has meticulously avoided the words "listed in India" following "recognised stock exchange" to rope in such companies. However, the good work is undone by defining a "recognised stock exchange" to have the same meaning assigned to it in Sec. 2(f) of the Securities Contracts (Regulation) Act, 1956. This raises some queries. Is FBT payable or not on such ESOPs and if payable, would these have to be treated as "unlisted"? Can a merchant banker situated abroad do the valuation by registering itself with SEBI? Unless these issues are addressed with clarity, we are in for a large number of litigations. Indian companies listed abroad, also carry these question marks.

Since the sale does not take place in a recognised stock exchange in India, the LTCG gets taxed @20% with indexation benefits and STCG at rates applicable to the assessee.

If the employee does not have enough funds to exercise the option, he may use the "cashless exercise" also known as "flipping the option" by effecting the sale and purchase on the same day and pay the cost of acquisition out of the sale proceeds.

Such a transaction gives rise to short-term capital gains. A bit of aggression on the employee's part can prevent this from happening. The employee should exercise the option by paying for the shares through a loan, if necessary, one year before effecting the sale. Of course, the cost benefit analysis of the tax saved *vis-a-vis* the interest paid on the loan will have to be carried out.

Where shares, debentures or warrants, are allotted by a company, directly or indirectly, to its employees under ESOP and such shares are transferred by the employee by way of gift or irrevocable transfer, the market value on the date of such transfer shall be deemed to be the full value of the consideration. Such gift would attract provisions of capital gains.

The industry was clamouring for a roll back in FBT which essentially is an expenditure tax. Instead, a fresh item that basically encourages employees to stick to the job and put in that much extra effort has been effectively discouraged.

One step forward, one step backward.

ESOP and Income Tax

FA09 has abolished Fringe Benefit Tax (FBT) under which ESOP was taxed as a perk. Yes, FBT has been abolished but Rule-3 has not been correspondingly amended. This means that beginning from FY 09-10, all the employees, irrespective of the type of the employer, will be taxed on all the fringe benefits.

Accordingly, where the share is listed on a recognised stock exchange, its value shall be the average of the opening price and closing price on that date. If it is listed on more than one recognised stock exchange, the value shall be governed by the exchange which records the highest volume of trading in the share. Where the exchange quotes both "buy" and "sell" prices, the "sell" prices of the first and the last settlement would be taken into account. If there is no trading on that date, the "sell" price quoted nearest to immediately preceding such date shall be the value.

In the case of non-listed shares, the value shall be determined by a category-I merchant banker registered with SEBI. To avoid multiple valuations depending upon the vesting dates of different employees, the valuation done earlier, not exceeding 180 days, can be taken for the purpose. Thus, the company may have to ask for valuation from the merchant banker, at the most twice in one year.

Sec. 115ACA inserted by the FA99 is applicable to a Resident employee of an Indian company, including its Indian and foreign subsidiaries, engaged in the specified knowledge based industry such as Information Technology. It taxed @10% the Residents deriving income by way of dividends or LTCG arising from DRs purchased either directly or under its ESOP.

12

~

Mutual Funds

There are only two investment avenues, besides Banks, where retail NRI can invest freely with repatriation benefits. One is the share market. Those who do not have time, energy and inclination to track the markets in India may invest through MFs. As a matter of fact, even those who have time should invest through MFs, because an individual can never compete with the team of researchers the MFs employ.

All the MFs have the twin objectives of mobilising the savings of the masses in order to channelise them into productive corporate investments, and providing facilities to persons of even modest means of owning indirectly, equity shares, company bonds, debentures and government securities. An MF is a financial intermediary between investors and the markets (stock and debt). It protects the investor against capital risk by giving him the benefit of its professional expertise in investment management. MF's constant supervision on the portfolio, which it holds on behalf of the investor and the diversification of large funds over a large portfolio throughout the spectrum of industries, is of great value to the investor.

Before investing in MFs, you will do well to check whether your host country (particularly USA and Canada) allows you to invest in Indian MF schemes.

STT and DDT

The matter related with Securities Transaction Tax and Dividend Distribution Tax is covered in Chapter *Capital Gains*.

Dividend & Bonus Stripping for Shares & Units

The 4 conditions applicable for Sec. 94(7) to be operational are —

1. The purchase of shares or units is within 3 months before the record date for dividends.
2. The sale of shares is within 3 months after the record date for dividends or bonuses. In the case of units this period is 9 months.
3. The dividend is tax-free.
4. The transaction results in a loss.

If all these conditions are simultaneously satisfied, loss arising to the taxpayer on the sale, to the extent it does not exceed the dividend, has to be ignored.

Sec. 94(8) deals with bonus stripping, only of MFs and not equities. The stipulation for its applicability is identical with that of dividend stripping with one difference. The loss, if any will also be ignored for the purposes of computing the income chargeable to tax. However, the amount of loss so ignored shall be deemed to be the cost of purchase or acquisition of the bonus units.

This is indeed very unkind to the MF industry.

Which Scheme to Opt For

All MFs normally offer 3 schemes — Equity-based, Balanced and Debt-based, each with three options, Dividend paying, Dividend reinvestment and Pure-growth. Thus there are nine options.

We do not like the balanced scheme since the investor can choose his own ratio, by going in separately for the Equity-based and Debt-based scheme. We also do not like the dividend paying or dividend reinvestment plan since it attracts DDT. This leaves us with only 2 options — (i) debt-based growth and (ii) equity-based growth even after the recent FA18 has diluted the advantage.

Similarly, we do not like any specific sector-based schemes. For instance at this particular juncture, the IT and pharma sectors are facing some problems with US policies but much as the fund manager would like to shift, even partly, he cannot do so.

Mark to Market

Strange but true, interest rates and prices of fixed income instruments have an inverse relationship. In other words, when the overall interest rates in the economy rise, the prices of fixed income earning instruments fall and *vice versa.*

To illustrate, let us assume that the current NAV of the MF is ₹10 and its corpus is ₹1,000 crore. This means that if the fund sells all the assets of the scheme and distributes the money on equitable basis to all the unit holders, they will receive ₹10 per unit. Now suppose, the interest rate falls from 6.0% to 5.4%. Immediately thereafter you wish to invest ₹1 lakh in the scheme. Realise that the entire corpus of the fund stands invested at an average return of 6.0%. If the Fund sells the units to you at its current NAV of ₹10, you will be allotted 10,000 units. This will benefit you immensely. You will be a partner in sharing the benefit of the higher returns of 6.0%, though the fund will be forced to invest your ₹1 lakh at the lower rate of 5.4%.

This is injustice to the existing investors. Therefore, comes the "mark to market" concept. The fund raises its NAV to ₹11.11. You will be allotted only 9,000 units and not 10,000. The returns on 9,000 units @ 6.0% would be identical with the returns on 10,000 units @ 5.4%.

Consequently, NAV rises when the interest falls and *vice versa.*

Capital Assured Schemes

The retail investor wants some kind of guarantee, any guarantee. In the past, in their effort to garner as many investors in their fold, the MFs chose the simple way out by giving some assurance or the other, instead of launching on educating the investor. The way the MFs tried to take advantage of this weakness for assurance and their analytical ignorance is manifest from the fact that for one of their schemes, UTI assured respectable dividends but not the capital. All such MFs faced bad problems when the market went into a prolonged bear phase. The parents of the MFs had to rescue their children by funding the deficit.

In spite of all this, there are still many investors who have fallen in love with some assurance without realising that the decision-oriented criteria should only be the brand image, the parentage and the ability of fund manager of the MF and not any assurance.

The MFs have discovered a way to guarantee capital and also derive some benefit from the share market. The idea is simple yet effective. Invest the entire capital in fixed income schemes and invest the interest received therefrom in equities. This way the capital remains intact while participating in equity upside, if any.

Numbers being easier to understand, let us assume that you have investible funds of ₹5 lakh. Here is what you do. Out of ₹5 lakh invest around ₹2 lakh in a bank 10-yr cumulative FD which gives 9.5% interest. Invest the rest ₹3 lakh in an equity-based MF. This ₹2 lakh FD would grow to ₹5 lakh in 10 years. Now, no matter what happens to the money invested in the MFs, at the end of 10 years, you will certainly have ₹5 lakh which is what you originally started with. The market value of ₹3 lakh of equity-based MF is an additional icing on the cake.

For ease of understanding and not to compromise simplicity over accuracy, we have left out the tax angle.

Surely, the MFs have a vast field from which they can choose guaranteed returns, and this would be much higher than the market rate. Moreover, there are tax benefits for MFs and not for others.

No wonder they say, a steady job and an MF is still the best defence against social security.

Fixed Maturity Plan (FMP)

We never liked the close-ended schemes (having a fixed tenure) of MFs because —

1. At redemption scrips in large quantity had to be sold, even when the fundamentals scream for a "buy". This would spell disaster for the share market and consequently for the Indian economy.
2. At redemption the investor is forced willy-nilly to pay tax, if any, and reinvest the remaining funds, possibly in similar schemes and possibly in those launched by the same MF. This is a national waste. Longer the term, lesser is this wastage.

   Open-ended funds have the longest term.
3. At present, the debt market is experiencing an upward pressure on the interest rates causing concerns about the rate risk.

The MFs have discovered a new product, Fixed Maturity Plan (FMP) with varying terms of maturity. These invest in instruments that mature at the same time their scheme term ends. So a 90-day FMP will invest in debt instruments that mature within 90 days. Holding the underlying instruments up to their maturity effectively eliminates the interest rate risk as the value of the instruments at their redemption is known at the time of investment itself. At this particular juncture, it is possible to pick up papers which give a little higher than 10%!!

The MF declares a dividend which is tax-free a day or two in advance of the date of maturity.

Yes, for the short-term FMP, there is this tax arbitrage. For growth FMP schemes with a term of over one year, there is the concessional tax on long-term capital gains. Moreover, the benefit of double indexation can be pocketed.

Double indexation is a neat trick where you hold an investment for a little more than one year but get the benefit of the index multiple of two years. Let us take an example for clarity.

An FMP of a term of 370 days is launched on 29.3.10, i.e. FY 09-10 and the date of maturity is 3.4.11, i.e., FY 11-12. Let us assume you have invested ₹1,00,000 and it has grown by 8.0% to ₹1,08,000. The CII for FY 09-10 was 632 and it was 785 for FY 11-12. The indexed cost is ₹1,24,209 (= 1,00,000*785/632). The capital gains work out at a loss of ₹16,209 (= 1,08,000 – 1,24,209)! This loss is available for set off.

Sadly the retail investor requires guarantee; not double indexation.

To protect the MFs against any unreasonable run on close-ended schemes as happened during the 3rd quarter of 2008, SEBI has made it compulsory for all close-ended schemes (except ELSS) to be mandatorily listed. Now, the investor has an exit route only through the markets where he will have to pay a price for the distress sale.

Liquid Schemes

MF houses have taken advantage of the advancement of technology in designing this product which is better than Saving Bank Accounts. Alternatively termed as "Any Time Money", it allows instant withdrawals over telephones, SMS and also ATM cards issued by the fund houses. There is no exit load. The returns, though not assured, are around 8.0%, fully taxable. This is not much useful to NRIs because of the distance, but can serve as emergency fund for family members in India.

Equity-based MF Schemes

Equity-based schemes of MFs have evolved as the best parking place for all investible funds. These have become more attractive than ever before because of the various tax concessions discussed earlier.

The one and the only disadvantage is the risk factor. The fortunes of equity-based schemes are linked closely with the market and its associated volatility. One can get very good rewards but the possibility of losing one's shirt (and also, in some cases, more intimate garments) cannot be lost sight of.

At this particular juncture, the markets have been sliding down because of several external factors such as Chinese meltdown, Global depression, European misery, Oil prices, etc., etc. The markets all over the globe have crashed but the Indian market has crashed much less than all the others, thanks to the Modi factor. Indian GDP is slated to grow significantly, thanks to the Modi factor.

Perhaps this is the right time to go for equity-based.

Equity-Linked Saving Scheme (ELSS)

ELSS is a variant of equity-based schemes with a lock-in of 3 years, though all of them have one open-ended scheme and a few are with a term of 10 years. At least 80% of its corpus is statutorily required to be invested in equities, cumulative convertible preference shares and fully convertible debentures and bonds of companies. Investment may also be made in partly convertible debentures and bonds including those on rights basis subject to the condition that the non-convertible portion of the debentures shall be disinvested within 12 months. These restrictions enable the scheme to come under the umbrella of Sec. 80C within the overall general ceiling of ₹1,50,000.

ELSS, being equity-based is, in theory, highly risky. In practice, it is highly attractive. A savvy investor never has a short-term view. He looks at the macro levels. Since the fundamentals of most companies have become robust, the ELSS has beaten PPF by miles. Consequently, though past performance is not a guide for its future achievements, in practice, ELSS has become highly rewarding as can be seen from Table-1

Thanks to the mandatory 3-year lock-in (1 year if the investor expires), in funds invested, the fund managers have better freedom to play since he need not keep large funds liquid to meet repurchase demands.

Units can be transferred, assigned or pledged after 3 years.

Other Advantages

MFs schemes have become more flexible than flexibonds.

1. *Saving Bank Account*: Deposit and withdraw whenever you feel like. Banks permit issue of cheques to third parties whereas withdrawal slips (= self-cheques) are for MF schemes.

2. *Systematic Withdrawal Plan (SWP)*: You can give standing instructions to receive some amount of your choice at a periodicity of your choice — annual, 6-monthly, quarterly or even monthly! That is not all. You can ask for additional withdrawals whenever you need more funds. This becomes a pension plan.

ELSS Returns of All Exising Scheme

Mutual Fund Scheme	AUM ₹Crore	Growth 3 Yrs-%
Aditya Birla SL Tax Relief 96	8,599	13.7
Axis LT Equity Fund	1,851	14.3
Can Robeco Equity Tax Saver	947	14.2
DSP Tax Saver	5413	14.8
Franklin India Tax Shield	3,367	10.7
HDFC Tax Saver	7,405	13.6
ICICI Pru LT Equity	6,192	13.0
IDFC Tax Advantage -RP	1991	14.9
Invesco Tax Plan	834	14.0
Kotak Tax Saver — Regular	888	14.9
L&T Tax Advantage	3,337	13.4
Mirae Asset Tax Saver	1,839	20.9
Motilal Oswal LT Equity	1338	15.4
Reliance Tax Saver	10,695	8.7
SBI Magnum Tax Gain	7,012	10.3
Sundaram Diversified Eq	2,710	12.1
Tata India Tax Saving	1,769	14.6
UTI LT Equity Tax Saving	1,191	11.3
Weighted Average		**12.63**
Maximum		**20.9**
Minimum		**8.7**

3. *Systematic Investment Plan (SIP)*: You can make investments of an equal amount of money at regular intervals (monthly or quarterly) until you cancel the facility. You may either submit post-dated cheques covering a period of your choice or opt for the auto-debit facility. If you adopt this strategy, you will be averaging out the market movements and this is really a great advantage.

4. *One Plan Equals All:* Can be converted into Tax-free Savings Bonds, Children's Gift Growth Plan, Children's College and Career Fund, Marriage Endowment Plan, etc.

Repatriable DP Account

Normally, investments made by either direct remittance of forex from abroad or by applying NRE funds are repatriable and can be credited to NRE account. This is true in the case of investment in shares, MFs and immovable property in India. The income in India of an NRI from any source can be repatriated abroad after taxes are paid thereon.

However, in the case of shares, the transactions have to be carried out from a Repatriable DP account. In other words, an NRI is required to have, if need be, separate DP accounts, one repatriable and the other non-repatriable.

In the case of MFs, on redemption, MFs issue a certificate indicating that the original amount was invested through an NRE account or direct remittance from abroad.

Tax Neutrality on Merger of MF Schemes

In the USA, very strangely, the number of MF Schemes is much higher than the number of listed shares. India is moving in that direction mainly because of the uncanny attraction of the retail investor to NFOs (= IPOs). In spite of millions of rupees spent on the so-called "investor education" the investor brings money to the Fund only when it floats a new scheme. He refuses to look at the old schemes, even those which have performed very well.

The fund manager is forced to offer brand new schemes with regular ferocity for garnering funds for his house. A natural outcome of this situation is that every fund house has many schemes which are clones. Since long, it had become urgently necessary to merge some of such schemes for better governance. Unfortunately such mergers attracted provisions of capital gains and therefore any attempt in that direction by SEBI received lukewarm response.

Thankfully Sec. 47(viii) has now been inserted to provide tax neutrality when two or more schemes of equity oriented fund or of other than equity oriented fund get merged or consolidated.

Tax on Dividends and Capital Gains

This matter has been covered in Chapter *Capital Gains*.

13

~

Immovable Property

For most transactions in immovable property of an ROI, RBI has granted its general permission to ADs for administering and monitoring it. All situations not falling under the general permissions, including requests for acquisition of agricultural land by any ROI may be made to the Chief General Manager, RBI, Exchange Control Department, Central Office (External Payments Division), Amar Building, Fort, Mumbai 400001.

Rank Foreigners

Citizens of Pakistan, Bangladesh, Sri Lanka, Afghanistan, China, Iran, Nepal, Bhutan, Macau, Hong Kong and Democratic People's Republic of Korea, irrespective of their residential status, need RBI prior permission to acquire or transfer immovable property in India. For this purpose the term "citizen" shall include natural persons and legal entities. Thus prohibition shall not apply to an OCI. They can get it on lease, not exceeding 5 years. However, approvals, if any, required by other authorities such as the concerned State Government will have to be obtained. The visa should clearly indicate his intention to stay in India for an uncertain period to determine his residential status.

Foreign nationals of non-Indian origin who are ROI can inherit a property in India by way of inheritance (but not a gift) from a Resident. He needs to seek prior approval of RBI for selling or gifting an agricultural land, plantation property and farm houses held by him in India. He cannot even be a joint 2nd holder along with an NRI or a PIO. Such a person who has acquired immovable property in India by way of inheritance or have purchased it with the specific approval of the RBI cannot transfer it without prior permission of RBI.

Acquisition by a Long-Term Visa (LTV) holder

A citizen of Afghanistan, Bangladesh or Pakistan belonging to minority communities in those countries viz., Hindus, Sikhs, Jains, Buddhists, Parsis and Christians, who is residing in India and has been granted (LTV) may purchase only one residential immovable property in India for self-occupation and only one immovable property for self-employment.

The property should not be located in and around notified or cantonment areas. The person should submit a declaration to the Revenue Authority specifying the source of funds.

The property of such person may be attached / confiscated in the event of his/ her indulgence in anti-India activities.

A copy of the documents of the purchased property shall be submitted to the Deputy Commissioner of Police, Foreigners Registration Office, Foreigners Regional Registration Office and to the Ministry of Home Affairs Foreigners Division. Sale of the immovable property so acquired is permissible only after such person has acquired Indian citizenship. Prior sale requires approval of all these authorities.

Permanent Establishment

An ROI, including a foreign company, who has been permitted to establish a branch or office or any other place of business in India (excluding a liaison office) can acquire an immovable property in India which is necessary for or incidental to his business. The payment for acquiring such a property should be made by way of forex. A declaration, in Form-IPI is required to be filed with the RBI within 90 days of the acquisition of the property.

Such a property can be mortgaged with an AD as a security for other borrowings. On winding up of the business, the sale proceeds of such property can be repatriated only with the prior approval of RBI.

However, if the foreign company has established a Liaison Office, it cannot acquire immovable property. In such cases, Liaison Offices can take property by way of lease not exceeding 5 years.

Resident Holding Property Abroad

A Resident can hold, own, transfer or invest in any immovable property situated outside India if such property was acquired, held or owned by him when he/she

A Resident can purchase immovable property outside India

(i) out of forex held in his/ her Resident Foreign Currency (RFC) account or under the Liberalised Remittance Scheme (LRS).

(ii) jointly with a relative who is a person resident outside India, provided there is no outflow of funds from India.

These restrictions do not apply to the property held by a Resident who is a foreign national or if the property was acquired by a Resident on or before July 8, 1947 and continued to be held by him with the permission of RBI. The restrictions also do not apply to properties held on a lease not exceeding 5 years by a Resident.

External Commercial Borrowing by a Resident

An AD bank may permit a Resident or on behalf of the Resident to create charge on his immovable property in India in favour an overseas lender or security trustee, to secure an external commercial borrowing as per Regulations.

It can also create a mortgage on an immovable property in India owned by an NRI or an OCI, being a director of a company outside India, for a loan to be availed by the company from an overseas lender provided the funds shall be used by the borrowing company only for its core business purposes overseas. In the case of invocation of charge, the Indian bank shall sell the immovable property to an eligible acquirer and remit the sale proceeds to the overseas lender.

NRI or an OCI and not a PIO can

(a) Purchase any immovable property in India.

(b) Get gift of immovable property in India from a Resident or from an NRI or an OCI who is a relative.

(c) Acquire immovable property in India by way of inheritance. If it is from an ROI who had acquired the property in accordance with the then existing foreign exchange law.

(d) Transfer immovable property to an NRI or an OCI. If it is a gift, the transferee should be a relative.

(e) Transfer any immovable property in India to a resident.

The last two items may include agricultural land or plantation property or farm house if the individual was in possession of it or has inherited it subsequently.

A rank foreigner who is a spouse of an NRI or an OCI may acquire one immovable property (other than agricultural land/ farm house/ plantation property), jointly with the spouse. The marriage should have been registered and subsisted for a continuous period of not less than two years immediately preceding the acquisition of such property.

Mortgaging property to party abroad requires RBI's prior approval.

The payment of purchase price should be made out of funds received in India through normal banking channels by way of inward remittance from any place outside India or funds held in any non-resident account maintained in India and no other mode such as traveller's cheque, foreign currency notes, etc. No payment can be made outside India.

Repatriation of Sale Proceeds

Repatriation of sale proceeds of residential property purchased by NRI/PIO is permitted to the extent of the amount paid for acquisition of immovable property in forex. Such repatriation is restricted to not more than 2 such properties. There is no restriction on repatriation of number of commercial properties. The balance amount, if any, can be credited to the NRO account and can be remitted under US$ one million facility.

Where the funds were raised by way of loans from ADs or housing finance institutions, repatriation is allowed to the extent of such a loan was repaid in forex.

Repatriation of amounts representing the refund of application or earnest money, purchase consideration made by the house building agencies, seller on account of non-allotment of the property, cancellation of bookings or deals, together with interest (net of income tax payable) may be allowed by the AD provided the original payment was made in forex.

Note that the right to repatriate is acquired by a person who was an NRI/PIO at the time of acquisition and who is an NRI/PIO at the time of the sale. The residential status between these two periods is immaterial.

If the sale takes place on or before the expiry of 2 years, provisions of STCG and if after 3 years LTCG will be attracted.

The remittance facility in respect of sale proceeds of immovable property is not available to citizens of Pakistan, Bangladesh, Sri Lanka, China, Afghanistan, Iran, Nepal and Bhutan. The facility of remittance of sale proceeds of other financial assets is not available to citizens of Pakistan, Bangladesh, Nepal and Bhutan.

Commission to Agents

AP (DIR) Circular 76 dt 24.2.04 permits ADs to freely allow, without RBI permission, remittance by way of commission to agents abroad for sale of residential flats or commercial plots in India up to US$ 25,000 or 5% of the inward remittance, per transaction, whichever is higher.

Remittance of Rent

The rental income being a current account transaction is repatriable irrespective of whether the property was purchased through forex or otherwise, subject to tax compliance.

Where the house is purchased through housing finance and it is rented out, the entire rental income, even if it is more than the prescribed instalment, should be first applied towards repayment of the loan. If it is less than the prescribed instalment, the borrower should remit the amount to the extent of the shortfall from abroad or pay it out of his NRE or NRO accounts in India.

Cash Used During Transfer of Real Estate

Sec. 269SS and Sec. 269T have been amended to mandate that no person shall accept or repay from any person any loan or deposit or any sum of money, whether as advance or otherwise, in relation to transfer of an immovable property, otherwise than by an account payee cheque or account payee bank draft or by electronic clearing system, if the amount of such loan, deposit or specified advance is ₹20,000 or more. The specified advance means any sum of money in the nature of an advance, by whatever name called, whether or not the transfer of the immovable property takes place. Related penalties are contained in Secs 271D and 271E.

We were under the impression that almost all the transactions of real estate involve a large portion of black money and this fact is known to the lawmakers. Do they feel that this limit of ₹20,000 in the legislation will curb black money?

Tax Provisions

Self-occupied House

Sec. 23 provides for determination of the annual value of house property, subject to the deductions u/s 24. Annual value of a house or part of a house shall be taken as nil if it —

(a) is in the occupation of the owner for his own residence, or

(b) cannot be occupied by him because of his employment, business or profession at any other place and he has to reside at that place in a building not belonging to him. If the assessee has more than one self-occupied house, the annual value of only one of such houses, at his option, can be taken as nil.

(c) All the others will be deemed to have been let out. The option can change from year to year.

(d) The latest FA19(interim) has modified Sec. 23, 24 and 54 to exempt notional rent on 2nd residential house. Now one can have two separate self-occupied houses Moreover, the tax concession on LTCG if the gains are invested in purchasing or constructing one residential house within certain stipulated time frame has been extended to two residential houses for a tax payer having capital gains up to ₹2 crore. This benefit can be availed once in a life time.

Let-out Property

If the authorities find that the actual rent charged by the owner is quite low, a notional rent value is arrived at by taking into consideration municipal valuation, fair rent and standard rent prevalent in the area. The Gross Annual Value of the property is arrived at by deducting from this rent, the property taxes paid to any local authority during the year only if these are borne and actually paid by the owner. Moreover as per Sec. 25 the amount of such rent received subsequently by an assessee shall be deemed to be the income from house property of the FY in which such rent is received or realised, whether the assessee is the owner of the property or not in that FY. The normal standard deduction of 30% can be claimed on such rent.

Thereafter, Sec. 24 allows the following two further deductions:

1. A standard deduction of 30% of the annual value.
2. The interest payable on capital borrowed (inclusive of processing fee) for acquiring, constructing, repairing, renewing or reconstructing the property with a ceiling of ₹30,000 on self-occupied property. The limit of ₹2,00,000 is applicable on loans taken on or after 1.4.99 but only for acquiring or constructing. The lower limit of ₹30,000 continues to be ap-

plicable for loans taken for repairing, renewing or reconstructing. Complicated!

While raising the deductibility of interest up to ₹2 lakh, FA14 imposed two caveats —

1. The house should be completed within 5 years from the end of the year during which the loan is taken, and
2. This higher limit is applicable only for acquisition or construction but not for repairs, renewals or reconstruction.

There was (note the past tense) no limit on the deductibility of interest on loans taken for business, commercial or let-out properties. Sec. 71 relates to set-off of loss from one head against income from another. FA17 has inserted Sec. 71(3A) to provide that after setting off the loss incurred due to interest payable for the FY against the rent (or deemed rent) received from the property during the year, the remaining loss, if any, can be set-off against any other head of income with a cap of ₹2 lakh. The unabsorbed loss, if any, shall be allowed to be carried forward for set-off in subsequent years in accordance with the existing provisions of the Act.

Both the concessions, deduction for repayment of capital u/s 80C and of interest u/s 24 are allowed only when the income from house property becomes chargeable to tax. In other words, the construction should be complete, the flat should be ready for occupation and the municipal annual value is known. However, if the interest payable is for a period prior to the year in which the property was acquired or constructed, it shall be deducted in 5 equal annual instalments commencing from the year of purchase or construction. The ceilings are applicable to the aggregate of interest payable and the annual instalments distributed over 5 years taken together. Similar facility is not available for repayment of capital u/s 80C.

If the construction or acquisition is completed any time in a FY, the interest paid during the entire FY is deemed to be the normal interest though a part of the FY is pre-construction period.

There is no restriction on the source of the funds borrowed to claim the exemption of interest. It is only the tax deduction u/s 80C that requires the loan to be taken from specified sources.

Housing loan is cheap and the tax concessions make it cheaper. Therefore take as large a loan as possible for as long a period as possible, even if you have enough funds on hand.

Many NRIs treat purchase of a house as an investment offering hedge against inflation. When the market price of the property keeps pace with inflation you make payment against the original price with money that becomes cheaper and cheaper. Therefore, they buy a house and keep it under lock and key. In India, it is quite dangerous to give a house on rent. It is quite difficult to evict a non-cooperative tenant even if he stops paying rent. The judiciary is virtually non-existent.

Do not buy a house just because of the tax benefits. There are better methods to save the tax. Similarly, do not buy a house as an investment. You will be putting too many eggs in one basket. Buy it, only if you need it for your personal use. Giving it on rent is fraught with risks.

Housing Finance

The loans can be procured even to (i) purchase a piece of land, (ii) pay stamp duty and (iii) extend or improve an existing house. The security for the loan is always by way of creating equitable mortgage of the property in favour of the lender. Additionally, any existing or a new life insurance policy equal to the loan amount sanctioned should be assigned as collateral security.

The sanction is around 85% of the property cost and starts from a minimum of ₹25,000.

Equated Monthly Instalments (EMI) is the fixed amount, required to be paid by the borrower every month till the end of the loan tenure. It consists of part principal and part interest. At start, the component of interest is understandably high. As time passes, it reduces and the component towards repayment of capital correspondingly increases.

Housing loan in rupees availed of by NRIs from ADs or Housing Financial Institutions in India can be repaid by the close relatives in India of the borrower.

RBI has made it mandatory for banks not to charge any penalty if borrowers pay back home loans taken on floating interest rates before the end of their repayment schedule. If you are in a fixed interest rate regime, you might face a penalty, which, in some cases may run up to 2% of the outstanding balance.

Where a mortgage was created by the previous owner during his/her lifetime and the same is subsisting on the date of his / her death, the successor obtains only the mortgagor's interest in the property and by discharging the mortgage debt, he / she acquires the mortgagee's interest in the property and thus, the amount paid to clear off the mortgage is the cost of acquisition of the mortgagee's interest in the property which is deductible as the cost of acquisition u/s 48 of the Act. But, if the property is mortgaged by the assessee himself / herself, then the amount paid for discharge of the debt is not part of cost of acquisition — *V. S. M. R. Jagdishchandran v CIT [1997] 93Taxman389 (SC)* and *R. M.. Arunachalam v CIT [1997] 227ITR222 (SC)*.

The expenses incurred towards society charges can be deducted from the rent for determining the taxable income.

Funds Borrowed Abroad for Purchase of Property in India

Sec. 25 specifically prohibits deductibility under the head "Income from house property" of any annual charge or interest chargeable which is payable outside India on which tax has not been paid or deducted in India. What if the assessee treats this as his "business income?" ROIs are prohibited by FEMA from indulging in business of real property. What if the interest is paid out of the repatriable interest earned on NRE, FCNR accounts? Sec. 14A introduced by FA01 states that the total income can be computed without allowing any deduction in respect of expenditure incurred in relation to income which does not form part of the total income.

This is in line with the intent of the tax legislation. The rent has its nexus in India and therefore it is taxable in India. The interest paid outside India is forex, not taxed in India.

As far as the deduction on repayment of the loans is concerned, it is available only if the loan is taken from specific approved sources and these do not include loans taken abroad.

House Held Jointly with a Resident

An NRI can be owner of a house jointly with a Resident. But there are some precautions to be taken —

1. If he has paid his share of acquisition through forex, he should make direct payments to the builder. Sending drafts in the name of a friend or the joint holder may hamper repatriability when the house is eventually sold.
2. The share of each holder should be well defined and ascertainable for computing the amount of income from housing property, either notional or otherwise. The contribution of the funds should also be preferably in the proportion of the defined share.
3. Housing loans, if any, should be taken either strictly in individual names or jointly in the same ratio. This helps in arriving at the amount of tax concessions on housing finance.
4. No loans are easily given on houses in joint names because, in the case of default, a part of a house cannot be confiscated. It is possible that you yourself do not need a loan. In that case, you can stand as a co-obligant or a guarantor to the loan taken by the joint owner.

Do not Purchase House in Wife's Name
Refer Chapter Wealth & Gift Tax.

TDS on Sale of Property
This subject is covered in Chapter — *Tedious TDS.*

14

~

Special Provisions

NRIs enjoy the benefit of "Special Provisions" u/ss 115C to 115-I, dealing with tax on incomes from certain Forex Assets (FEA) which the assessee has acquired, purchased or subscribed to in convertible forex. These are:

1. Shares in an Indian company but not units of MFs.
4. Debentures (convertible as well as non-convertible) issued by an Indian company which is not a private company as defined in the Companies Act 1956.
5. Deposits with an Indian company which is not a private company as defined in the Companies Act 1956.
6. Securities of the Central Government as defined in Sec. 2(2) of the Public Debt Act 1944.

Any income which is derived from FEA is connoted as *investment income*. The definition of FEA does not include bank deposits! But mostly, these can be brought under the purview of the provisions through the above mentioned point-3, "deposits with an Indian company". All the banks (i) of which shares are listed in the stock market (e.g., SBI, HDFC Bank, ICICI Bank), (ii) which continue to be Indian companies (e.g., United Western Bank Ltd.) and (iii) nationalised banks which were originally incorporated as Indian companies before nationalisation are eligible for the concessions of special provisions.

None of the foreign banks, or co-operative banks are eligible for this facility, a point which dawns only when it is too late.

Salient Features

The NRI is given the option in respect of investment income to be governed either by the special or the general provisions of the ITA. This option can be exercised by expressing his desire through his return of income. He is free to decide for each FY as to whether he wants to opt for the special provisions or not.

If the individual opts for the special provisions, his total investment income, without taking any cognisance of the income threshold or deductions under Chapter VI-A, is taxed as a separate block at a flat rate of 20% and @10% on LTCG, unless exempt.

In case the assessee has other taxable income in addition to investment income, the other income will be taxed at the rates as per the general provisions, where the income threshold and Chapter-VIA are operative.

U/s 115G it is not necessary to furnish a return of income if the total income consists only of investment income or income by way of LTCG or both and TDS has been correctly applied and there is no additional tax liability. In practice, it is better to file returns to establish continuity.

In order to avoid delays in remitting the sale proceeds of FEA, Sec. 204(iia) authorises an AD to deduct tax if it is not a short-term gain and remit the balance to the NRI or credit it to his NRE account, without requiring any NOC from the Department.

U/s 115F, LTCG arising out of transfer of FEA is not charged to tax if the net consideration is reinvested in FEA within 6 months from the date of transfer. If part of the consideration is invested, proportionate deduction would be allowed. There is a lock-in of 3 years on the new asset acquired. If this new asset is transferred within that period, the exempted capital gains would be brought to tax as LTCG of the year in which the new asset is transferred.

Continuation of Special Provisions

When an NRI becomes a Resident, the Special Provisions continue to apply till the assets get eventually transferred.

To Be or Not to Be

Special provisions have lost almost all their sheen since, in the case of shares, the dividend is tax-free, LTCG is charged @10% with the associated grandfathering by the recent FA18 and short-term gains are taxed @15%. Only in very rare cases, it may be advantageous to opt for this Special Provision where the rate is 20%.

Good News

A. Sinha & Rao Ranvijay Singh (AAR 762 of 2007 dt 3.3.08) held, — NRO deposits shall be treated as FEA and interest thereon shall be treated as investment income u/s 115C(*c*) which is liable to be taxed @ 20%. The only conditions applicable are that the funds in the account should be made out of convertible forex and further that the account should be in a banking company which is not a private company as per Companies Act.

Some of the very enterprising ADs take advantage of "Special Provisions" to bring down the TDS rate at 20.6% (Refer Chapter *Tedious TDS*) provided the account balance represents deposits made only in forex.

15

~

Loans and Overdrafts

Any businessman knows for a fact that loans and overdrafts are excellent leveraging devices for boosting his bottom line. Most of the NRIs prefer to park their funds in India to obtain higher returns and opt for instruments having loan facility even if they have no need for it at the current juncture.

General Conditions

Use of credit card in India by an ROI shall not be deemed as borrowing or lending in rupees.

The rate of interest and margin on all loans may be decided by the ADs, subject to the latest RBI directives.

Funds borrowed either by a Resident or an ROI can be used for his personal requirements and/or own business but not for —

(i) Business related with the prohibited transactions such as chit fund, agriculture or plantation, TDRs, etc.

(ii) Any investment, whether by way of capital or otherwise, in any company, partnership firm, proprietorship concern, any entity whether incorporated or not, or for relending. Such investment includes purchase of immovable property or shares, debentures, bonds, etc., issued by companies in India, including margin trading or derivatives.

Loans can be granted against the security of NRE, FCNR and NRO term deposits but not SB. The term of the loan shall not exceed the balance maturity period of the deposit. The facility of premature withdrawal of NRE/FCNR deposits shall not be available where loans against such deposits are availed of.

Loans to Depositor and 3rd Party against NRE/FCNR

An AD or its overseas branch or correspondent can grant loans against security of the funds to the account holder or a third party in or outside India. Premature withdrawal of such deposits is not permitted.

Rupee loans may be granted by ADs provided —

- There is no direct or indirect forex consideration paid to the NRI depositor for agreeing to pledge his deposits.
- There is no transaction between the guarantor and the borrower involving forex until the guarantee is invoked or the loan is settled. If the guarantor is forced to discharge his guarantee, the NRI may enforce his claim against the Resident borrower. If the liability is discharged by payment out of rupee balances, the amount recovered becomes non-repatriable.
- A Resident, being a principal debtor can make payment to any ROI who has met his liability. The amount remitted or credited shall not exceed the rupee equivalent of the amount paid by the ROI guarantor against the invoked guarantee.

Forex loans in or outside India can be granted by ADs provided

- The document is executed by the deposit holder himself and not by his PoA or LoA holder.
- If the repayment is made by using the NRO account, the interest has to be charged at the full commercial rate in force.
- FEMR (Deposit) permits a branch outside India of an AD to give a forex loan against the security of NRE or FCNR deposit.

Loans to NRIs against Shares/Properties, Non-repatriable

An AD can grant a loan in India in rupees to NRIs on non-repatriable basis against the security of shares or other securities or immovable property in India.

Temporary Overdrawing

ADs may allow overdrawing in NRE SB account, up to ₹50,000. Such overdrawing together with the interest should be cleared within 2 weeks, out of inward remittances through normal banking channels or by transfer of funds from other NRE accounts.

Forex Borrowing by Residents from NRI Relatives

AP (DIR) Circular 24 dt 27.9.03 grants general permission to borrow up to US$ 2,50,000 or its equivalent on a repatriable basis by an individual Resident from his close NRI relative if—

(a) The loan shall be free of interest.

(b) The minimum maturity period of the loan shall be 1 year.

(c) The amount of loan is received by inward remittance in free forex through normal banking channels or by debit to the NRE account of the NRI.

AP (DIR) Circular 95 dt 21.3.12 allows the borrower to repay in installments, interest and other charges directly to NRE account of the lender concerned.

Rupee Loan or Gift to an NRI/PIO Close Relative

A resident individual is permitted to make a rupee loan or gift to a close relative NRI/PIO by way of crossed cheque or electronic transfer subject to:

(i) The loan is free of interest and its minimum maturity of the loan is one year.

(ii) The loan (or Gift) amount should be within the overall LRS limit of US$ 250,000 per FY.

(iii) The loan shall be utilised for meeting the borrower's personal requirements or for his own business in India. It shall not be utilised, either singly or in association with other person, for any of the activities in which investment by ROI is prohibited.

(iv) The loan (or Gift) should be on non-repatriable basis.

(v) Repayment of loan shall be made by way of inward remittances through normal banking channels or by debit to the NRO or NRE account of the borrower or out of the sale proceeds of the shares or securities or immovable property against which such loan was granted.

Borrowing in Rupees by Residents, Non-repatriable

A Resident individual, partnership or proprietorship firm, may borrow in rupees on repatriable or non-repatriable basis from an NRI subject to —

(a) The term of the loan does not exceed 3 years.
(b) The rate of interest does not exceed 2% over the bank rate.

Loans to NRI Employees

Indian companies are allowed to give term loans in rupees to their NRI/PIO staff for personal purposes, including purchase of housing property in India. The loan shall be granted in accordance with the Lender's Staff Welfare or Housing Loan Scheme. The amount shall be credited to the employee's NRO account. This facility is also available to employees of branches outside India for forex loans.

SEBI Circular CFD/DIL/3/2013, dt 17.1.13 states that listed entities are prohibited from framing any employee benefit schemes involving acquisition of own securities from the secondary market. This prevents such entities adopting a fraudulent and unfair trade practice of manipulating the price of the securities.

Loans for ESOP

ADs are allowed to grant Rupee term loans to their NRI / PIO employees for acquiring its shares under its ESOP subject to —

1. The loan should not exceed 90% of the purchase price of the shares or ₹20 lakh whichever is lower. Incidentally, these limits are also applicable to loans to Resident employees.
2. The amount shall be paid directly by the bank to the company and should not be credited to the borrowers' accounts in India.

Loans to Foreign National Employees

ADMA Circular 36 dt 11.9.97 has imposed a ceiling of ₹5 lakh on loans granted to foreign nationals, not permanently Resident, for personal purposes such as purchase of household articles, etc. The same ceiling is applicable to liaison offices of the companies. The terms and conditions should be the same as those applicable to its staff Resident.

Housing Finance

An AD or an approved housing finance institution may provide housing loan to an NRI with Indian passport (and not to PIOs) for acquiring a residential house in India. The loan is subject to:

- Term of the loan should not exceed 15 years.
- The quantum of loans, margin money and the period of repayment shall be at par with those applicable to Resident borrowers.
- The loan shall be fully secured by equitable mortgage of the property proposed to be acquired, and if necessary, also by a lien on the borrower's other assets in India. A Resident close relative may also be taken as a co-obligant or guarantor.
- Repayment by close relative in respect of loan in rupees availed by NRI was restricted to housing loans only. AP (DIR) Circular 19 dt 16.9.11 has granted general permission to Residents to repay loans availed by their NRI close relatives for any purpose.
- The amount should not be credited to borrower's NRE account.
- Where the property is rented out, the entire rental income, even if it is more than the prescribed instalments, should be adjusted towards repayment of the loan.
- Rate of interest shall conform with RBI and NHB directives.
- The flat shall be used by the NRI for self-occupation on return to India and not for any other purpose.

Where the land is owned jointly by an NRI borrower with a Resident close relative, the relative should be taken as a co-obligant or guarantor. In such cases the payment of margin money and repayment of the loan installments should be made by the NRI. The loans can also be given to Residents with NRI as a co-obligant.

An NRI requires prior approval of RBI for mortgaging an immovable property to a party abroad.

AP (DIR) Circular 95 dt 26.4.03 has extended the loan facility for repairs, renovation and improvement of residential accommodation owned in India by NRIs as well as PIOs.

Change in the Residential Status of the Borrower

An AD may (or may not) allow continuance of loan or overdraft of a Resident who subsequently becomes an ROI. In such cases, payment of interest and repayment of loan may be made by inward remittance or out of legitimate resources in India of the borrower.

If a rupee loan was granted by a Resident to another Resident and the lender subsequently becomes an NRI, the repayment of the loan by the Resident borrower should be made by credit to the NRO account of the lender.

Company Deposits

Circular AP (DIR) 89 dt 24.4.04 prohibits deposits by NRIs with persons other than ADs out of forex. However, an Indian proprietorship concern, firm, or a company (including a credit-rated NBFC registered with RBI) can accept deposits from NRIs on non-repatriation basis subject to —

- In the case of a company, the deposit may be accepted either under private arrangement or a public deposit scheme.
- The term of the deposit shall not exceed 3 years.
- For NBFCs the rate of interest shall be in conformity with RBI guidelines. For others it shall not exceed the rate prescribed under the Companies (Acceptance of Deposit) Rules.

- The amount received shall be only by debit to NRO account and should not arise from inward remittances or transfers from NRE.
- The interest earned on such deposits, being current income, is repatriable subject to tax compliance.
- The borrower shall not utilise the amount for relending (not applicable to NBFC) or for the prohibited activities for NRIs.

This happens to be most risky investment especially at the current juncture of unbridled scams.

16

~

Tedious TDS

During the process of liberalisation and globalisation, India has given the NRIs a plethora of investment opportunities, on repatriable and non-repatriable basis. However, the authors of legislation entrusted with implementing the vision have not done their home work properly. This has resulted in an NRI walking on the red carpet laid for him with "WELCOME" signs being entrapped.

Take the case of an NRI intending to purchase a residential property. He is told that — if the consideration is paid out of forex remitted through normal banking channels or the funds held in NRE, repatriation of the amount equivalent in forex paid for the acquisition is permissible when he sells the property for maximum two such properties. Even the properties purchased out of NRO funds (non-repatriable) can be remitted under the US$ one million facility. (Refer Chapter, *Forex Remittances — NRIs)*. Excellent!

When he actually buys it, he finds that u/s 195(1), he has to apply TDS on the capital gains incurred by the seller if the consideration is ₹50 lakh or over. How does he know what is the capital gain of the seller? Well, simple! He applies TDS on the entire sale consideration. This is harsh.

Another way is by way of the seller paying the tax on the capital gains incurred by him even before the due dates for paying the tax. Thereafter, the buyer makes an application to the AO to indicate the amount of TDS by his general or special order and on receiving such order applies the TDS indicated in the order. This is nicely explained in *Syed Aslam Hashmi v ITO [2012] 26taxmann.com6*.

The NRI faces a bigger difficulty if and when he sells this house in due course. It is he who has to apply TDS. U/s 203A, every person deducting or collecting tax is required to obtain Tax Deduction and Collection Account Number (TAN).

To reduce the compliance burden on such one-time transactions, FA15 allows submission of PAN in place of TAN for reporting of TDS from payment over a specified threshold made for acquisition of immovable property (other than rural agricultural land) from a Resident to a Resident u/s 194-IA This facility has now been extended to NRIs.

What if the NRI does not have a PAN? Fortunately FA16 has taken a corrective action by amending Sec. 206AA enabling the NRI to submit any other document that provides the required information.

The NRI seller has several options to save this tax on capital gains such as buying another house or investing in REC/NHAI Bonds. Can the ITO accept his intentions? The answer is in the negative. He can apply for a refund through filing of his tax returns for the year.

The benefit of (i) setting off the basic threshold against the capital gains and (ii) filing Form-15G or 15H for non-deduction of TDS are not available to NRIs. The only way of avoiding TDS for an NRI as provided u/s 195(2) is to request the ITO (Form-13) for issuing a certificate to the person who is responsible for applying TDS (Form-15AA) allowing them not to apply TDS or apply it at lesser rate. The moot question is — why should any AO issue any order unless he likes the face of the applicant?

Fortunately, this knotty problem has been addressed by the recent FA19(2) by amending Sec. 195(2) w.e.f.1.11.19. This states that a person responsible for paying any sum to an NRI can make an application to the AO to obtain a certificate/order indicating the amount of TDS to be applied. This process is manual. Modern technology will be used to reduce the time and manner related with the application form and also determination of appropriate TDS.

TDS Rates

Though, for ease of understanding, we have not mentioned the applicability of cess @ 4% on TDS, note that it is always applicable for NRIs but not for Residents. Yet another injustice.

What is the sanctity of having different rates for different incomes? (See Table-1). It behoves the Department to have a standard uniform rate, convenient for itself as well as the taxpayers. The TDS is not the final tax payable. Advance tax is a close relative of TDS. Moreover, the balance tax, if any, is paid along with filing of his tax returns.

Table-1: TDS Rates

Income Avenue	%
Investment income	20
LTCG from listed as well as unlisted shares	10
Income under Special Provisions	10
Other LTCG, unless exempt	20
STCG from listed shares & Equity-based Units of MFs	15
Interest on forex loans by Government or an Indian concern	20
Royalties & Fees for Technical Services	25
Winnings from lotteries, crossword, puzzle, horse race, etc.	30
On the whole of the other income	30

TDS Thresholds

TDS is not required to be applied if the payments do not exceed prescribed threshold limits — Refer Table-2. Readers are requested to take cognisance of these thresholds during our subsequent discussion.

Table-2: TDS Thresholds

Section	Nature of Payment	Threshold ₹
194B	Winnings from lottery or crossword puzzles	10,000
194BB	Winnings from horse races	10,000
194H	Commission or Brokerage	15,000
194-I	Rent	1,80,000
194J	Fees for professional or technical services	30,000
194M		

Since an RNOR is basically a Resident, the base rates and thresholds as applicable to Residents is applicable to him. Particular attention is drawn to interest received from bank deposits where the base rate is 10% and the threshold is ₹10,000 for Residents (₹50,000 for senior citizens) and the rate is 30% without any threshold for NRIs.

FA16 has allowed for TDS not to be applied upon self-certification, if the income of the payee is less than the maximum amount not chargeable to tax.

Because of technological advancements and availability of KYC of the depositor, it is now possible for a bank to add the interest paid to the depositor by all its branches put together. Therefore, FA15 requires the TDS to be applicable at bank level and not branch level. Moreover, since Recurring Deposits are same as Time Deposits, these also have been brought under the ambit of application of TDS. We are afraid that in the near future this provision will become applicable at the level of all the banks put together.

Non-Resident Entertainer

U/s 194E, TDS rate is 20% for payments made to an NRI:

(a) sportsman (including athlete), who is not a citizen of India, or

(b) sports association or institution, or

(c) entertainers (such as a theatre, radio or television artists and musicians) who are not citizen of India. The term, "entertainer" is not defined anywhere and this might lead to ambiguity and consequent litigations related with its scope and applicability.

Brokerage to Distributors

Explanation-I to Sec. 194H defines "commission or brokerage" to include any payment received or receivable, directly or indirectly, by a person acting on behalf of another person for services rendered (not being professional services) or for any services in the course of buying or selling of goods or in relation to any transaction relating to any asset, valuable article or thing, not being securities.

CBDT Circular 786 dt 7.2.2000 declares that commission and brokerage payable to an NRI agent for securing export business is not taxable in India.

In the case of MFs, some countries such as USA and Canada do not approve of investment in MFs, FDs and some other investment products in India. However, the taxability of such income depends upon DTAA. For instance, under Article 22 of DTAA between India and UAE, the payment of brokerage being in the nature of other income, it will not be taxable in India.

Royalties & Fees for Technical Services

The TDS is 10%, the same as the tax payable (See Chapter *Income Tax-Royalty or Fees for Technical Services*).

Salary Paid Outside India

Now a bombshell. Expatriate employees' salary for working in India is chargeable to tax in India, whether a part or the whole of the salary and allowances are received in or outside India. This issue was raised in *CIT* v *Eli Lilly & Co. (India) P Ltd.*, which was decided by the Supreme Court on 25.3.09. It held, "TDS had to be applied on the salary and allowances paid abroad, even if the Indian Company was unaware of the payments made abroad by the foreign employer of the expatriate. It is the duty of the Indian company to apply TDS even on salary and allowances paid abroad by the foreign company, particularly when no work stood performed for the foreign company and the total remuneration stood paid only on account of services rendered in India during the period in question."

Jewellery

FA12 has amended Sec. 206(*c*) to provide that the seller of bullion and jewellery shall, at the time of receipt of such amount in cash, collect tax @1% of sale consideration from every buyer of bullion and jewellery, if it exceeds ₹2,00,000. Payment by any other means does not attract this provision.

Buy-back of Unlisted Shares

Refer Chapter, *Capital Gains*.

DTAA

Refer Chapter, Double Taxation Avoidance Agreement.

Procedure for Refund of Tax

In the case of NRIs there are many circumstances where income does not either accrue or it accrues but the excess amount has been paid as TDS. This may happen where the contract is cancelled in part or full or change of law or because of a mistake. This warrants refund to the resident responsible for applying TDS but he could not do so because the refund is payable to the person who has earned the income and not to the deductor.

Circular 7/2007 dt 23.10.07 has solved this difficulty by allowing this amount to be refunded directly to the deductor.

The amount paid into the Government account in such cases to that extent, is no longer "tax". In view of this, no interest u/s 244A is admissible on such refunds. Similarly, no expenses related with amount representing TDS refunded is allowable.

Such a refund should be granted only after obtaining an undertaking that no certificate u/s 203 has been issued to the NRI. If it has been issued, the person claiming the refund should either retrieve it from the NRI or should indemnify the Department from any possible loss on account of a separate claim of refund for the same amount by the NRI. The refund should be granted only if the deductee has not filed return of income and the time for filing it has expired.

The limitation for making a claim of refund shall be 2 years from the end of the FY in which TDS is applied. However, all pending cases may also be considered.

Sec. 197A read with Rule 29C provides for furnishing declarations by only a Resident individual in Form-15G Form-15H (for senior citizen) in order to enable the payer to make the payment without TDS if the tax payable on the estimated total income is nil.

Can TDS be Avoided?

Yes, all individuals, including NRIs can apply to his ITO for deduction of income tax at a lower or nil rate. The ITO, after examining the veracity of the claim, may (or may not) issue an appropriate certificate on a plain paper to that effect within one month from the date of application (Instruction No. 1/2014, dt 15.1.14).

Almost always, this turns out to be a fruitless exercise. Firstly, for obvious reasons, it is difficult to convince the ITO and secondly, if the sanction is granted, it is applicable for only the current FY. Moreover such a certificate is interim or tentative or provisional in nature and would not bar the AO from initiating proceedings by changing of his opinion — *Areva T&D the Division Bench of the Delhi High Court*, held on 25.4.11.

This leaves only the avenue of filing returns and this is a smooth process. All that you have to do is to appoint an accountant in India specialising in the field of filing returns practicing in the area of your home town in India to do the job. All he requires is your NRO pass book entries and his fees are very nominal, possibly below ₹1,000.

We have two suggestions.

1. A large amount of your money in NRO account is repatriable and can be shifted over to your NRE account. The interest rates in NRO and NRE are mostly identical. NRE is tax-free without any limit and NRO is taxable.
2. Shift over from Bank FDs to MF schemes. The MFs are excellently tax efficient.

Forex Income: Conversion into Rupees

As per Rule 115, the rate of exchange for the calculation of the value in rupees of any forex income shall be the telegraphic transfer buying rate of such currency as on the specified date.

Telegraphic Transfer Buying Rate (TTBR) and Telegraphic Transfer Selling Rate (TTSR) are the SBI rates for buying and selling forex made available through a telegraphic transfer.

For following incomes, specified date means the last day of the month immediately preceding the month in which:

(a) Salary is due, or is paid in advance or in arrears.

(b) Interest on securities is due.

(c) Profits and gains from the business of operation of ships which is deemed to accrue or arise in India.

(d) Dividend is declared, distributed or paid by the company.

(e) Capital gains where the capital asset is transferred.

For following incomes, specified date means the last day of the previous year unless such income is received in, or brought into India by the assessee or on his behalf before the specified date in accordance with the provisions of FERA (now FEMA):

(a) Income from house property.

(b) Profits and gains of business or profession (other than from operation of ships).

(c) Income from other sources (other than dividends and interest on securities).

For capital gains arising from the transfer of shares or debentures of an Indian company, the rate of exchange shall be —

(a) For converting the cost of acquisition: Average of TTBR and TTSR of the forex initially utilised for purchase of the asset.

(b) For converting expenditure incurred in connection with its transfer: Average of the TTBR and TTSR.

(c) For converting full value of consideration received or accruing on its transfer: Average of the TTBR and TTSR.

(d) For reconverting capital gains computed in the forex initially utilised for its purchase into rupees: TTBR of such currency as on its date of its transfer.

However, where TDS is required to be applied on such incomes, the specified date would be the date on which the tax was required to be deducted and the exchange rate would be the TTBR of such currency on this date.

Uniform Rate of Exchange

In the case of capital assets acquired in forex, where the amount received in forex has to be converted into INR for determining the value of the acquisition and the consideration received for transfer of such a capital asset, it is the uniform rate of exchange which should be adopted for the purpose. It has been held by the Karnataka High Court, in the case of *Jaya Kumari and Dilhar Kumari v CIT [1991] 189ITR99*, that the exchange value prescribed in Rule 115 must necessarily be followed in computing the capital gains or loss, as the case may be. If the revenue takes the value of pound sterling as on 1-1-1954 (now 1-4-1981) as per Sec. 48 for the purpose of determining the acquisition value of the capital asset and the exchange rate of pound sterling as on the date of sale, it would be acting outside the scope of the Rules.

No TDS on Software

Notification 21/2012 SO 1323(e) dt 13.6.12 declares that w.e.f. 1.7.12 no TDS shall be made u/s 194J on payment by a resident transferor for acquisition of software where —

1. the software is acquired in a subsequent transfer and the transferor has transferred the software without any modification, and
2. tax has been deducted —
   (a) under Section 194J on payment for any previous transfer of such software; or

(b) u/s 195 on payment for any previous transfer of such software from a non-resident, and the transferee obtains a declaration from the transferor that the tax has been deducted either under clause (*iia or b*) along with the PAN of the transferor.

No TDS on Interest from Offshore Banking Units

U/s 197(A) interest paid by an offshore banking unit on interest paid on deposits made on or after 1.4.05 by an NRI or RNOR is not chargeable to tax u/s 10(15)(viii) and consequently, no TDS need be applied. CBDT Circular 26/2016 dt 4.7.16 has observed that any branch of a bank, Indian or foreign, located in Special Economic Zone is treated as an offshore bank.

Sec. 194LC & 194LD Rupee Denominated Bonds

As per Sec. 194LC, interest payable to an NRI on forex borrowings under a loan agreement entered into between 1.7.12 and 1.7.17 or by way of forex long-term bonds, including long-term infrastructure bonds issued between 1.10.14 and 1.7.17, suffer TDS at the concessional rate of 5%. Moreover, u/s 194LD, the benefit of this concessional rate was also available to FIIs and QFIs on their investments in Government securities and rupee denominated corporate bonds issued outside India.

The time limit for this concessional tax rate benefit has been extended up to 1.7.20, retrospectively from 1.4.16 in both the cases.

17

~

Before Leaving and After Returning

Any person, after becoming an NRI is required to inform the following institutions about change in his residential status:

(a) banks where he has savings or term deposits,
(b) companies where he has shareholding in physical form,
(c) DPs where he has demat accounts, and
(d) MFs whose units he holds.

The banks will redesignate the person's running accounts as NRO. Some banks close all such accounts and open new ones, causing the account holder untold inconveniences such as requirement to change his KYCs, ECSs, etc. The companies and DPs will inform RBI to enable it monitor the limit on shareholding of all NRIs put together and the MFs will monitor the TDS and repatriability of the funds.

In practice, most of the NRIs do not inform. Fortunately, many of them do not face any problems because the regulatory mechanism of the regulators is not yet in place. Obviously, a few are apprehended and we hope you are not one of them. Realise that nothing is gained by breaking this rule.

It is also necessary to file the tax returns with status as an NRI. If the Indian income is below the taxable threshold, there is no need to file the returns, and if these are to be filed, an NRI need not have a PAN. It is prudent to file the returns to maintain continuity and possess the card which you may need sometime.

Even after becoming an NRI, one is free to deal with all the investments and assets held prior to becoming an NRI any which way he desires. The only restriction is that, in theory, the original corpus is non-repatriable whereas in practice, it can be remitted under the one-million per FY facility. Income arising out of these assets is repatriable subject to tax compliance.

It is advisable to give a Power of Attorney (PoA) to a trustworthy Resident for ease of operations of bank accounts, investments and other financial transactions. All AD banks have their own Letter of Authority LoA) for the limited purpose of effecting local disbursements and withdrawals for household expenses. Note that all the Post Office Schemes, including PPF are not available for NRIs.

Returning NRI

A person who returns to India permanently, becomes a Resident from day-1 of his arrival and is required to take within a reasonable period, the following actions —

1. Inform the banks, MFs, DPs, etc. about the change in his status. Then these entities will redesignate these as Resident accounts.
2. The NRE and FCNR accounts can be closed either immediately or allowed to run up to their maturity. Such deposits are treated as Resident deposits from the date of return. The originally contracted rates of interest will continue to be applicable until the maturity of the accounts. The FCNR remains tax-free if and only if the returning NRI becomes an RNOR but the NRE becomes taxable from the day of his return, irrespective of the status. Premature withdrawals attract penal provisions.
3. There is also an option of transferring part or full balance to the credit of NRE and FCNR accounts to RFC account within a reasonable period from the date of the arrival in India. There is no penalty for such transfers.

If an NRI is on a short visit to India, the account may continue to be treated as non-resident account even during his stay in India.

If the required actions are not taken in a reasonable time, one would be violating FEMA. He would also lose the benefit of Special Provisions as discussed in a previous chapter. What is reasonable time is not indicated in the Act and there are many who do not inform for years on the grounds that they might decide to go abroad once again. Acceptance of such an intention by the AO would depend upon the rent received by him.

Keeping Assets Abroad

FEMA Sec. 6(4) permits an NRI returning to India permanently to continue to hold, own, transfer or invest in foreign currency, foreign security or any immovable property situated outside India, if such assets were acquired, held or owned by him when he was an ROI or inherited these from an ROI. The income and sale proceeds of assets held abroad need not be repatriated.

Similarly, Sec. 6(5) permits an ROI to hold, own, transfer or invest in Indian currency, security or any immovable property situated in India if such currency, security or property was acquired, held or owned by such person when he himself was a Resident or inherited these from a Resident.

This general permission will not apply in respect of any asset received after becoming a Resident by way of gift or inheritance from abroad. Similarly, the benefit is not available on earnings from employment secured subsequent to the return. If the ex-NRI wishes to retain such assets abroad or liquidate them and deposit the money in an RFC account, he has to apply for permission to RBI.

18

~

Forex Remittances — NRIs

Indian rupee has virtually become fully convertible. NRIs need no more hesitate to grab good investment opportunities in their motherland without any fear of not being able to repatriate the funds abroad, if and when needed. As a matter of fact, the convertibility has reached such a level that they can remit even their non-repatriable funds without much of a difficulty. These are the funds they owned before leaving India or inherited assets thereafter or invested their forex earnings in India on non-repatriable basis.

The procedure for tax compliance as discussed in Chapter *General Provisions* has to be followed for all the types of remittances.

Remittance of Current Income

Sec. 2(*j*) defines "current account transaction" to mean a transaction other than a capital account transaction and without prejudice to the generality of the foregoing it includes —

(a) Payments due in connection with foreign trade, other current business services and short-term banking and credit facilities in the ordinary course of business.

(b) Payments due as interest on loans and as net income from investments.

(c) Remittances for living expenses of parents, spouse and children residing abroad. and

(d) Expenses in connection with foreign travel, education and medical care of parents, spouse and children.

Remittance of current income of an NRI like rent, dividend, pension, interest, etc., is freely allowed. It can also be credited to NRO if he has such an account. It can also be credited to NRE provided the AD bank is satisfied that the credit represents current income and the procedure for tax compliance has been followed correctly.

Remittance up to US$ 1 million

ADs allow remittance of assets up to US$ 1 million per FY to —

1. A foreign national not being a PIO or a citizen of Nepal or Bhutan), if he or she —
   (a) has retired from employment in India;
   (b) has inherited the assets from a person [referred to in Sec. 65) of FEMA] resident outside India who, when he was Resident held, owned, transferred or invested in Indian currency, security or any immovable property situated in India or inherited it from a person who was a Resident; and
   (c) is a non-resident widow or widower and has inherited assets from the person's deceased spouse who was an Indian citizen Resident.
2. An NRI or a PIO,
   (a) out of balances held in NRO which may include sale proceeds of immovable property acquired by the NRI out of the resources in India, or by way of inheritance or gift;
   (b) out of assets acquired under a deed of settlement made by either of his/her parents or a relative. The settlement should take effect on the death of the settler. Any settlement without the settler retaining life interest may be reckoned as transfer by way of gift.

ADs also allow remittance of balance amount, held by a foreign student in a bank in India, after completion of studies or training in India. In case the remittance is made in more than one installment, all these should be made through the same AD.

Where the remittance is to be made from his NRO, the AD should obtain an undertaking from the account holder stating that the remittance is sought to be made out of the remitter's balances held in the account arising from legitimate receivables in India and not by borrowing from any other person or a transfer from any other NRO account. If such is found to be the case, the account holder will be liable for penal action.

ADs also allow Indian entities to remit their contribution towards PF, superannuation or pension fund in respect of their expatriate staff resident but "not permanently resident" in India.

Remittance of assets on hardship ground in excess of US$ 1 million in an FY would require RBI's prior approval.

It is necessary to produce documentary evidence in support of the acquisition, inheritance or legacy of assets by the remitter. Additionally, proof of tax compliance is also necessary.

This US$ 1 million facility is over and above the repatriation of the sale proceeds of immovable property purchased through forex (Refer Chapter *Immovable Property*).

AP (DIR) Circular 117 dt 7.5.12 has now permitted the transfer of such funds from his NRO account to NRE account within the overall ceiling of US$ one million per FY. The tax, if any, must be paid out of the sale proceeds. The rest of the amount can be remitted abroad or credited to NRE.

The remittance facility in respect of sale proceeds of immovable property is not available to citizens of Pakistan, Bangladesh, Sri Lanka, China, Afghanistan, Iran, Nepal and Bhutan. The facility of remittance of sale proceeds of other financial assets is not available to citizens of Pakistan, Bangladesh, Nepal and Bhutan.

For arriving at annual ceiling of remittance, sale proceeds of shares and immovable property owned or held by the citizen of foreign state on repatriation basis in accordance with the FEMR — Acquisition and Transfer of Immovable Property in India and also Transfer of Indian Security by an ROI shall not be included.

Surrendering Forex

An individual who is not a Resident should surrender forex due or accrued as remuneration for services rendered, whether in or outside India, or in settlement of any lawful obligation, or an income on assets held outside India, or as inheritance, settlement or gift within 7 days from the date of its receipt of and within 90 days in all other cases.

If such a person has acquired or purchased forex for any purpose mentioned in the declaration made by him to an AD and does not use it for such purpose or for any other permissible purpose shall surrender the unused portion thereof to an AD within 60 days from the date of its acquisition or purchase by him.

Where the forex acquired or purchased is for foreign travel, then, the unspent balance shall be surrendered within 90 days from the date of return of the traveller to India when the unspent forex is in the form of currency notes and coins and within 180 days when it is in the form of travellers cheques.

To Be or Not to Be

India is a great parking place for investible funds of NRIs. The money multiplies faster here. This opportunity should not be lost just because it has now become possible to convert rupees in forex and remit it abroad. The limit of US$ 1 million can be used every FY. Therefore, NRIs should indulge only in need-based remittances.

Other Issues

1. A foreigner who has come to India for study or training and has completed it may remit the balance in his account, representing funds derived out of remittances received from abroad or forex proceeds of FE sold to an AD or stipend or scholarship received.
2. Foreign nationals on temporary visit are allowed to take back the unspent amount of forex against Encashment Certificate or Bank Certificate in Form-ECF or Form-BCI respectively. Both the ECF and BCI are valid only for 3 months for reconversion of rupees into forex in all the cases, temporary visits or otherwise. Take care.

3. Rupee loans can be availed by foreign nationals or liaison offices of foreign companies only for personal purposes such as purchase of household articles up to a maximum of ₹5 lakh on the total borrowings of the depositor and his dependents from all the banks.
4. The RBI has, in a press release dt 2.5.03 clarified that foreign nationals, including PIOs, while in India, are free to pay charges towards booking airline and train tickets, hotels, hospitals, etc. either in Indian rupees or in equivalent forex.
5. Notification FEMA 5/2000-RB dt 3.5.2000 allows diplomatic missions, diplomatic personnel and non-diplomatic staff, who are the nationals of the concerned foreign countries and hold official passport of foreign embassies to hold deposits maintained in foreign currency accounts, subject to the conditions stipulated therein.
6. Notification GSR 90E) dt 18.9.07 permits ADs in India to effect remittance of assets of Indian companies under liquidation subject to compliance with the order issued by a court, Official Liquidator or the liquidator in the case of voluntary winding up.

Payment in Rupees

The following transactions are permitted by the RBI —

1. Requests for cash by foreign visitors or NRIs may be acceded up to US$ 3,000 or its equivalent.
2. Any person, to receive any payment in rupees —
   (a) By order or on behalf of a ROI during his stay in India out of rupee funds provided to him by sale of forex to an AD or a money changer in India.
   (b) Against a foreign bank cheque, draft, travellers cheque or foreign currency notes. The forex so received shall be sold to an AD or a money changer within 7 days of its receipt.
   (c) By a postal or money order issued by a post office outside India.

3. A Resident, to make any payment in rupees —
   (a) Towards meeting expenses of a ROI who is on a visit to India on account of boarding, lodging and related services or travel to and from and within India.
   (b) To an ROI, by means of a crossed cheque or a draft for purchase of gold or silver in any form imported by such person in accordance with the Foreign Trade (Development and Regulations) Act, 1992 or under any other law, rules or regulations for the time being in force.
   (c) To bear the medical expenses of a visiting NRI / PIO who is a close relative.

4. A company in India, to make payment in rupees to its whole time director who is an ROI and is on a visit to India for the company's work and is entitled to payment of sitting fees or commission or remuneration, and travel expenses to and from and within India, provided the requirements of any law, rules, regulations, directions for making such payments are duly complied with.

19

~

Forex Availability — Residents

RBI permits more than sufficient forex for specific needs of all Residents, inclusive of those who have permanently returned to India. Therefore, it is advisable not to have any RFC, RFCD and EEFC accounts or leave forex abroad only for availing forex or maintaining its repatriability.

General Conditions

All forex transactions have been classified either as capital or current account transactions. Those which do not alter the assets or liabilities of a person, including contingent liabilities, outside India are current account transactions.

Remittances of forex to Nepal, Bhutan, Mauritius, Pakistan or Bangladesh, Cook Islands, Egypt, Guatemala, Indonesia, Myanmar, Nauru, Nigeria, Philippines and Ukraine are prohibited. There are no restrictions towards remittances to Mauritius and Pakistan for permissible current account transactions.

As per Sec. 5 of FEMA, Residents are free to buy or sell forex for any current account transaction except for specifically prohibited transactions.

Foreign visitors are allowed to convert up to US$ 5,000 in rupees.

It is not mandatory for ADs to endorse the amount of forex sold for travel abroad on the passport of the traveller, unless the traveller himself desires to have the details recorded. For a private visit, it should invariably be endorsed. In the case of a child travelling on a parent's passport, the endorsement is made on the joint passport.

Residents may take or send up to two commemorative coins outside India, other than those covered by the Antique and Art

Treasure Act, 1972. FEMR (Possession and Retention of Forex) allows a Resident to possess foreign coins without any limit.

Traveller's cheques should be signed by the traveller in the presence of an authorised official.

All applications for forex exceeding prescribed limits (as described later) should be referred to — The Regional Office of the Exchange Control Department under whose jurisdiction the applicant is functioning or residing. AP (DIR) Circular 31 dt 18.10.02 states that a Nodal Officer has been appointed at each Regional Office of RBI to dispose of applications on the same day itself and forward by fax or e-mail. The circular lists the name, telephone and fax number and e-mail address of the Nodal Officer at each Regional Office.

There are certain transactions such as cultural tours, advertisements in foreign print media, hiring charges of transponders, membership of P&I Club, etc., where prior approval of the Government of India is required for remittance. This Rule does not apply where the payment is made out of funds held in RFC or EEFC Account of the remitter.

Surrendering Unused Forex

Permissible forex can be drawn 180 days in advance. In case it is not possible to use it within this period it should be surrendered to the AD. Again, on return from a foreign trip, travellers are required to surrender unspent forex held in the form of currency notes and travellers cheques within 180 days of return. Following are the limits for possession or retention of forex —

(a) Possession without limit of foreign coins by any person.

(b) Retention by a Resident of foreign currency notes, bank notes and foreign currency travellers' cheques not exceeding US$ 2,000 or its equivalent in aggregate provided it —

- was acquired while on a visit to any place outside India by way of payment for services not arising from any business in or anything done in India.

- was acquired as honorarium, gift, services rendered or in settlement of any lawful obligation from any person not Resident and who was on a visit to India.
- was acquired by way of honorarium or gift while on a visit to any place outside India.
- represents unspent amount of forex acquired by him from an authorised person for travel abroad.

Current Account Transactions Liberalised

RBI Circular 76 dt 24.2.04 has removed or diluted the requirement of RBI's prior approval relating to current account transactions on remittances by Residents in following cases —

1. Payment for securing health insurance from a company abroad.
2. Earnings of artistes e.g., wrestler, dancer, entertainer, etc.
3. Commission to agents abroad for sale of residential or commercial plots in India, exceeding 5% of the inward remittances. ADs now may freely allow such remittances up to US$ 25,000 or 5% of the inward remittance, per transaction, whichever is higher.
4. Short-term credit to overseas offices of Indian companies.
5. Where export earnings of the advertiser were less than ₹10 lakh during each of the preceding 2 years.
6. Where the agreement for technical collaboration had not been registered with RBI. Henceforth, ADs may allow remittances for royalty and payment of lump sum fee, provided the royalty does not exceed 5% on local sales and 8% on exports and lump sum payment does not exceed US$ 2 million.
7. Use of trademark or franchise in India. However, RBI's prior approval will continue to be required for remittance towards purchase of trademark or franchise.
8. Henceforth, the proposal for hiring of transponders by TV Channels and internet service providers will require prior approval of the Ministry of Information & Broadcasting.

Foreign Assets of a Resident

U/s. 6(4) of FEMA, a Resident may hold, own, transfer or invest in forex, foreign security or immovable property situated outside India if such assets were acquired, held or owned by him when he was an ROI or inherited these from an ROI. Circular AP (DIR) 90 dt 9.1.14 has clarified that such assets cover —

1. Forex accounts opened and maintained by such a person.
2. Income earned through (i) employment or business or vocation outside India taken up or commenced or (ii) from investments made or (iii) from gift or inheritance received.
3. Forex including any income arising therefrom, and conversion or replacement or accrual to the same, held outside India by a Resident acquired by way of inheritance from an ROI.

Such a Resident may freely utilise all his eligible assets abroad as well as income therefrom or sale proceeds thereof received after his return to India for making any payments or any fresh investments abroad, provided the cost of such investments and/or any subsequent payments received therefrom are met exclusively out of funds forming part of eligible assets.

Liberalised Remittance Scheme (LRS)

Resident individuals including minors can remit up to US$ 2,50,000 for any permitted capital or current account transactions or a combination of both. If the remitter is a minor, the LRS declaration form must be countersigned by the minor's natural guardian.

There are no restrictions on the frequency of remittances under LRS. However, the total amount of forex purchased from or remitted through, all sources in India during the FY should be within the cumulative limit of US$ 2,50,000.

Remittance is on a gross basis and not on net of repatriation from abroad. This means that once a remittance has reached the LRS limit, no further remittance is possible during the FY even if some of the proceeds of the investments have been brought back into India during the same year.

Resident (but not permanently Resident) individuals who have remitted their entire earnings and salary and wish to further remit "other income" may approach RBI through their AD bank for consideration.

The individual will have to designate a branch of an AD through which all the remittances under the Scheme will be made. The applicants should have maintained the bank account with the bank for a minimum period of one year prior to the remittance only for capital account transactions (not for current account transactions). He has to furnish Form A-2 regarding the purpose of the remittance along with all other documentation as required by the AD. The remitter needs to possess a PAN card.

However, if the amount does not exceed US$ 25,000 or its equivalent and the payment is made by a cheque or demand draft drawn on the applicant's bank account, a simple letter from the applicant (containing the basic information, viz., names and the addresses of the applicant and the beneficiary, amount to be remitted and the purpose of remittance) will suffice as long as the forex being purchased is for a permissible current account transaction. ADs shall prepare dummy A-2 for statistical inputs for Balance of Payment.

Note that there are no restrictions towards remittances for current account transactions even to Mauritius and Pakistan.

The permissible capital account transactions by an individual under LRS are —

1. Opening forex account with a bank abroad.
2. Purchase of immovable property abroad.
3. In case members of a family pool their remittances to purchase a property, then the said property should be in the name of all the members who make the remittances. It can also be purchased with balances held by the Resident in his RFC bank account.

4. Making investments abroad (for acquisition of shares, ESOPs, ESOPs linked to ADR/GDR qualification shares, investment in units of Mutual Funds, Venture Funds, unrated debt securities, promissory notes, etc.).
5. Setting up Wholly Owned Subsidiaries and JVs abroad.
6. Extending loans in INR to NRI relatives.

For remittances pertaining to permissible current account transactions, if the applicant is a new customer of the bank, ADs should carry out due diligence on the opening, operation and maintenance of the account. Further, the AD should obtain bank statement for the previous year from the applicant to satisfy themselves regarding the source of funds. If such a bank statement is not available, copies of the latest Income Tax Assessment Order or Return filed by the applicant may be obtained. He has to furnish the "application-cum-declaration" for purchase of forex in the specified format along with Form A-2 regarding the purpose of the remittance and declare that the funds belong to him and will not be used for purposes prohibited or regulated under the Scheme.

Fund or non-fund based facilities (= loans) can be entertained by the ADs to their resident individual customers to facilitate remittances only for current (not for capital) account transactions under LRS.

Remittance can be consolidated in respect of close family members subject to the individual members being compliant. However, clubbing is not permitted of other family members for capital account transactions such as opening a bank account, making investment, purchasing property, etc., if they are not the co-owners or co-partners of the transaction. Further, a Resident cannot gift forex to another Resident, for the credit of the latter's forex account held abroad under LRS.

An offshore banking unit in India cannot open forex accounts in India for Residents under the Scheme.

Expenses incurred by individuals for the following purposes are subsumed under LRS w.e.f. 26.5.2015:

(a) Private visits to any country (except Nepal and Bhutan).
(b) Gift or donation.
(c) Going abroad for employment.
(d) Emigration.
(e) Maintenance of close relatives abroad.
(f) Travel for business, or attending a conference or specialised training or for meeting expenses for meeting medical expenses, or check-up abroad, or for accompanying as attendant to a patient going abroad for medical treatment / check-up.
(g) Expenses in connection with medical treatment abroad.
(h) Studies abroad.
(i) Any other current account transaction.

In respect of such activities, note the following:

1. Any Resident individual or entity such as a trust, company, partnership firms, etc., may remit up to US$ 2,50,000 in one FY as gift to a person or as a donation to an organization outside India. A Resident cannot gift to another Resident for the credit of the latter's forex account held abroad under LRS.

2. A Resident is free to send outside India (export) any gift article, which may be free to be exported as per the extant Foreign Trade Policy, of value not exceeding ₹5 lakh. Such gifts may be sent outside India without furnishing the declaration in Form EDF / SOFTEX, as the case may be.

3. Receiving grant / donation from abroad is under the Foreign Contribution Regulation Act, 1976 which is administered and monitored by the Ministry of Home Affairs whose address is — Foreigners Division, Jaisalmer House, 26, Mansingh Road, New Delhi-11001. No specific approval from RBI is required.

4. For medical expenses, or check-up abroad, AD banks may allow amount exceeding the LRS limit provided the request is supported by an estimate from a hospital or doctor in India or abroad. Otherwise, a self-declaration in Form A2 and

"Application cum declaration for purchase of forex" is sufficient. Additionally, an amount up to the LRS limit is available to an attendant accompanying the patient.

5. The Scheme also covers expenses incurred in going abroad for employment, emigration, maintenance of close relatives abroad, studies abroad and any other current account transaction. However, for expenses in connection with emigration, medical treatment or studies abroad, individuals may be permitted to exceed LRS limit, if it is so required by the country of emigration, medical institute offering treatment or the university.
6. A Resident individual may give a loan (or a gift) to a close NRI relative under the LRS by way of crossed cheque or electronic transfer, subject to —
   (a) It is free of interest and the minimum maturity is 1 year.
   (b) It should be credited to the NRO account of the NRI.
   (c) It shall not be remitted outside India. It should be utilised for the borrower's personal requirements or his own business in India.
7. Where an AD in India has granted loan to an NRI, a Resident close relative is permitted to repay the loan taken by NRI.
8. General permission is available to persons other than individuals to remit towards donations up to 1% of their forex earnings during the previous 3 FYs or US$ 5 million, whichever is less, for (a) creation of Chairs in reputed educational institutes, (b) contribution to funds (not being an investment fund) promoted by educational institutes and (c) contribution to a technical institution or body or association in the field of activity of the donor company.

Other Investments Outside India

Resident individuals can use LRS for making investments in —

(a) MFs, Venture Funds, unrated debt securities, promissory notes, immovable property, shares of both listed and unlisted overseas company, debt instruments and any other asset outside India such as objects of art subject to the Foreign Trade Policy.

(b) ESOPs and ESOP-linked ADRs / GDRs offered by a foreign company to a Resident employee or a Director of an Indian office, etc. (Refer Chapter *Employees' Stock Option*). Purchase of foreign securities under ADR/GDR linked stock option schemes by Resident employees of Indian companies in the knowledge based sectors, including working directors provided purchase consideration does not exceed US$ 50,000 or its equivalent in a block of 5 calendar years.

(c) Qualification shares for becoming a director of a company outside India to the extent prescribed as per the law of the host country where the company is located provided it does not exceed the limit prescribed under the LRS.

(d) Shares of a foreign entity in part / full consideration of professional services rendered to the foreign company and also in lieu of Director's remuneration.

Remittance facility under the Scheme is not available for—

(a) Margins or margin calls to overseas exchange counterparty.

(b) Purchase of FCCBs issued by Indian companies in the overseas secondary market.

(c) Trading in forex abroad.

(d) Remittances directly or indirectly to Nepal, Bhutan, Mauritius, Pakistan and to countries identified as non co-operative countries and territories.

(e) Remittances directly or indirectly to those individuals and entities identified as posing significant risk of committing acts of terrorism as advised separately by RBI to the banks.

International Credit & Debit Cards

ADs are permitted to issue International Debit Cards (IDCs) which can be used by a Resident individual for drawing cash or making payment to a merchant establishment overseas during his visit abroad. IDCs can be used only for permissible current account transactions and the usage of IDCs shall be within the LRS limit.

AD banks can also issue Store Value Card, Charge Card, or Smart Card to Residents travelling on private or business visit abroad which can, besides the above facilities, be also used for drawing cash from ATM terminals. the use of such cards is limited to permissible current account transactions and subject to the LRS limit.

Resident individuals maintaining a forex account with an AD in India or a bank abroad, are free to obtain International Credit Cards (ICCs) issued by overseas banks and other reputed agencies. The charges incurred against the card either in India or abroad can be met out of funds held in such accounts or through remittances from India only through a bank where the card holder has a current or savings account. Such remittances should be made directly to the card-issuing agency abroad, and not to a third party. The applicable credit limit will be the limit fixed by the card issuing banks. The LRS limit shall not apply to the use of ICC for making payment by a person towards meeting expenses while such person is on a visit outside India. Use of ICCs/ IDCs can be made for travel abroad in connection with various purposes and for making personal payments like subscription to foreign journals, internet subscription, etc.

Incidentally, if an individual holds two or more ICCs, his limit on usage gets forex increased.

Use of these instruments for payment in forex in Nepal and Bhutan is not permitted.

Foreign Securities & Residents

General permission has been granted to a Resident for purchase or acquisition of securities —

(a) Out of funds held in RFC account.
(b) Bonus or Rights shares on existing holding of forex shares.

(c) Gift from a person Resident Outside India.
(d) Under Cashless ESOP of a company incorporated outside India, provided it does not involve any remittance from India.
(e) Inheritance from a person whether resident in or outside India.
(f) When not permanently Resident, out of his forex resources outside India.
(g) Purchase of shares of a JV / WOS abroad of the Indian promoter company by the employees or directors of Indian promoter company which is engaged in the field of software where the consideration for purchase does not exceed US$ 10,000 or its equivalent per employee in a block of 5 calendar years.

A Resident individual holding qualification or rights shares may sell these provided the sale proceeds are repatriated to India through normal banking channels and documentary evidence thereof is submitted to the AD.

The investor can retain and reinvest the income earned on investments made under the LRS. He is not required to repatriate the funds or income generated out of investments made.

Dividends as well as STCG received from abroad are chargeable to tax in India in the hands of the investor at the normal rates of tax, based on their slab rate. LTCG in the case of foreign companies is charged to tax @ 20% after claiming the benefits of indexation. The investor has the right to claim the benefit of DTAA.

Acquisition or Setting up of a JV or WOS Abroad

A.P. Dir 106 dt 23.5.13 permits w.e.f. 5.8.13 a Resident individual (single or in association with another Resident individual) may make overseas direct investment in the equity shares and/or compulsorily convertible preference shares of a Joint Venture (JV) or Wholly Owned Subsidiary (WOS) outside India within the overall ceiling of LRS. The investment made out of the balances held in EEFC/RFC account shall also be restricted to the limit prescribed under LRS.

The Resident individual, making overseas direct investments shall submit Part I of the Form ODI, duly completed, to the designated authorised dealer, within 30 days of making the remittance. The JV / WOS, to be acquired or set up shall be an operating entity only and no step down subsidiary is allowed. Any financial commitment by the Resident individual to or on behalf of the JV / WOS other than the overseas direct investments is prohibited. Any alteration in shareholding pattern of the JV or WOS may be reported to the designated AD within 30 days including reporting in the Annual Performance Report.

The individual may disinvest (partially or fully) by way of transfer, sale, liquidation or merger of the JV or WOS only after one year from the date of making first remittance for setting up or acquiring the JV / WOS abroad. The disinvestment proceeds shall be repatriated to India not later than 60 days from the date of disinvestment. No write off shall be allowed.

The individual may disinvest (partially or fully) by way of transfer, sale, liquidation, or merger of the JV/WOS only after one year from the date of making first remittance for setting up or acquiring the JV/ WOS abroad. The disinvestment proceeds shall be repatriated to India not later than 60 days from the date of disinvestment and the same may be reported to the designated AD. No write off shall be allowed in case of disinvestments by the resident individuals.

Gifts of Securities

As per AP (DIR) Circular 14 dt 15.9.11, a Resident who proposes to gift to an ROI any security including shares or convertible debentures requires RBI's prior approval. The limit on value of security to be gifted together with any security already gifted by the transferor, has been raised from US$ 25,000 during a calendar year to US$ 50,000 per FY.

Pledge / Sale of Foreign Securities

The shares acquired by Residents in accordance with the provisions of FEMA are allowed to be pledged for obtaining credit facilities in India from an AD Category-I bank or a Public Financial Institution. He may also sell such shares provided the proceeds are repatriated not later than 90 days from the date of sale.

Facilities to Persons Other than Individuals

Donations up to 1 % of their forex earnings during the previous three FYs or US$ 5,000,000 whichever is less, for — (a) creation of Chairs in reputed educational institutes; (b) contribution to funds (not being an investment fund) promoted by educational institutes; and (c) contribution to a technical institution or body or association in the field of activity of the donor Company.

Commission, per transaction, to agents abroad for sale of residential flats or commercial plots in India up to US$ 25,000 or 5% of the inward remittance whichever is less.

Remittances up to US$ 10,000,000 per project for any consultancy services in respect of infrastructure projects and US$ 1,000,000 per project, for other consultancy services procured from outside India.

Remittances up to 5% of investment brought into India or US$ 100,000 whichever is less, by an entity in India by way of reimbursement of pre-incorporation expenses.

Miscellaneous Provisions

In addition to all this, exchange to the extent needed may be released by the ADs for the following purposes:

- Remittance by tour operators or travel agents to overseas agents, principals, hotels, etc.
- Fee for participation in global conferences and specialised training.

- Remittance for participation in international events and competitions (towards training, sponsorship and prize money).
- Film shooting.
- Disbursement of crew wages.
- Remittance towards fees for examinations held in India and abroad and additional score sheets for GRE, TOEFL, etc.
- Skills / credential assessment fees for intending migrants.
- Visa fees.
- Processing fees for registration of documents as required by the Portuguese (or other) Governments.
- Registration, subscription and / or membership fees to International Organisations.
- Other permissible current account transactions without any limits subject to the AD verifying the bona fides.
- Securing health insurance from an insurer abroad.

Small Value Remittances

ADs may release forex not exceeding US$ 25,000 for all miscellaneous non-trade current account transactions on the basis of a simplified application-cum-declaration version of Form-A2 in place of the normal Form-A2. The payment should be made by a cheque drawn on the applicant's bank account or by a DD.

Post Office

GSR 405(E) 3.5.2000, of RBI permits anyone to buy forex from any post office, in the form of postal orders or money orders.

Export and Import of Indian Currency

This is covered in Chapter, *Baggage Rules*.

Tax Clearance Certificate No More Required

Ministry of Finance & Company Affairs declared that from 9.1.03 onwards, any person who is not domiciled in India or who is domiciled in India at the time of his departure but intends to leave India as an emigrant or intends to proceed to another country on a work permit will not be required to obtain a tax clearance certificate. However, in some cases, the authorities will notify the emigration authorities that some specified persons should not be allowed to leave India without obtaining a tax clearance certificate. Excellent! This has nullified the rampant corruption that existed while issuing such clearance.

Expenses of an ROI

A Resident can pay in Indian Rupees towards meeting expenses on account of boarding, lodging and services related thereto of an ROI who is on a visit to India, including tickets for his visits within India or even to any third country. For instance, Residents can book ticket for his travel from London to New York, through domestic or foreign airlines in India. This would be a part of the traveller's overall entitlement under LRS.

Where the medical expenses in respect of NRI close relative are paid by a Resident individual, such a payment being in the nature of a Resident to Resident transaction may be covered under the term "services related thereto"

20

~

Baggage Rules

Each and every person coming to or going out of India, whether a resident or tourist, an Indian or foreigner, must know the Baggage Rules in India to avoid subsequent heartaches.

General Provisions

- No import license or Customs Clearance Permit (CCP) is required for the clearance of goods as bona fide baggage.
- There is no provision in the baggage rules to endorse the value of the baggage in passports. Passenger desiring a proof can request for endorsement at the back of the return ticket.
- The allowances are per individual and cannot be pooled with that of another, even between husband and wife.
- A passenger may request the customs for issue of an import/export certificate for articles of high value such as video cameras, cassette recorders, jewellery, etc., at the time of his arrival or departure to facilitate its re-import or re-export subsequently, without affecting the free allowance available. Normally, such goods are packed and therefore, it is inconvenient to take these out for inspection of the officer. In such cases, the certificates can be issued in advance, valid for 1 year in custom houses, international airports and sea ports.
- Carrying narcotic drugs is strictly prohibited and the punishment can be very serious.
- Import of consumer goods in commercial quantity is not treated as part of bona fide baggage.
- Goods brought through a carrier or courier are not "gifts" or "personal baggage" of the carrier. These will be classified as imported goods requiring a valid import licence. The rates are

governed under the Courier Imports (Clearance) Regulations, 1998 (Circular 56/95-Cus. dt 30.5.95).

- There is a procedure prescribed whereby the passengers leaving India can take the export certificate for the various high value items such as camera, video camera, as well as jewellery from the Customs authorities. Such an export certificate facilitate re-importation of such goods while bringing back the things to India as no duty is charged. The advantage of having the Export Certificate is that the concessions you are entitled to, when you return, are not affected.
- Passenger may request detention of dutiable or prohibited articles for being returned to him while leaving India. The request can be made either for payment of duty or for re-export or subsequent production of documents. The request for detention cannot be entertained after the goods have been confiscated and/or penalty imposed.
- If the passenger does not come for clearance of the goods within the specified period as indicated in the receipt, the authorities can dispose of the goods, deduct customs duty and incidentals and refund the balance.

Classes of Articles

Articles specified in Annexure-I are prohibited. Only one unit of the first 14 items specified in Annexure-II can be imported whereas items in Annexure-III can be imported in any quantity, subject to the overall limit applicable to the passenger. Quantities exceeding the limit are subject to a concessional duty (Refer *Valuation of Goods & Custom Duty*).

Items which attract general allowance for duty-free imports are given in Table-1. Items for personal use are available in Table-2 whereas household items are available in Table-3.

Annexure-I (Applicable to Rule 3, 4 or 6)

1. Fire arms.
2. Cartridges of fire arms exceeding 50.

3. Cigarettes exceeding 100 or cigars exceeding 25 or tobacco exceeding 125 grams.
4. Alcoholic liquor or wines in excess of two litres.
5. Gold or silver, in any form, other than ornaments.
6. Flat Panel (LCD/LED/Plasma) Television.

Annexure-II (Applicable to Rule 6)

1. Colour Television or Monochrome Television.
2. Video Home Theatre System.
3. Dish Washer.
4. Domestic Refrigerators of capacity above 300 litres.
5. Deep Freezer.
6. Video Camera with or without combination of one or more of (a) Television Receiver; (b) Sound recording or reproducing apparatus; (c) Video reproducing apparatus.
7. Cinematographic films of 35 mm and above.
8. Gold or Silver, in any form, other than ornaments.

Annexure-III (Applicable to Rule 6)

1. Video Cassette Recorder or Video Cassette Player or Video Television Receiver or Video Cassette Disk Player.
2. Digital Video Disc Player.
3. Music System.
4. Air Conditioner,
5. Micro Oven.
6. Word Processing Machine.
7. Fax Machine.
8. Portable Photocopying Machine
9. Washing Machine.
10. Electrical or Liquefied Petroleum Gas Cooking Range.
11. Personal Computer (Desktop Computer).
12. Laptop Computer (Notebook Computer).
13. Domestic Refrigerator of capacity up to 300 litres.

Table-1 : General Duty Free Allowance Items

Airconditioner	Exposure meter	Processed food
Bedding	Films	Radio
Bicycle	Fishing rod	Rain coat
Binocular	Flash units	Razor & blades
Blanket	Food processor	Record player
Blender	Frying pan	Refrigerator
Calculator	Games	Room heater
Car coat	Garments	Rotisserie
Car stereo	Glassware	Service trolley
Carpet sweeper	Gloves	Sewing machine
Cassette player	Golf set	Shoes & socks
Cassette recorder	Hair clipper	Slide projector
Cassette tape	Hair dryer	Smoking pipe
Cheese tins	Hand bag	Sports equipment
Chewing gum	Handkerchief	Stationery
Chocolates	Wall pictures	Still camera
Cigarette	Head-gear	Tape recorder
Cigarette lighter	Headphone	Telephone set
Clock	Health equipment	Textiles
Coffee maker	Heating tray	Time piece
Confectionery	Iron	Toaster
Cooking stove	Iron board	Toiletries
Cosmetics	Juice extractor	Toys
Costume jewellery	Kitchen utensils	Tuner
Crockery	Knitting machine	TV Set
Curios	Lacquer-ware	Two-in-one
Cutlery	Meat grinder	Umbrella
Decoration pieces	Medicines	Under garments
Deep freezer	Mixer	Vacuum cleaner
Deck amplifier	Mosquito destroyer	Vase
Dictaphone	Movie camera	Video camera
Digital audio disc	Movie projector	Video player
Digital clock	Music system	Video tape
Dinner set	Musical Instrument	Voltage regulator
Dish washer	Nail cutters	Wall paper
Door bell	Ordinary typewriter	Washing machine
Dry fruits	PC	Water cooler
Electric fan	Perfume	Water heater
Electric iron	Phonograph records	Water/air purifier
Electric toaster	Photographic outfits	Weighing scale
Electric micro oven	Playing cards	Wig
Electronic typewriter	Polish	Wrist watch
Embroidery	Pressure cooker	

Table-2: Personal Effects

Bedding	Handkerchiefs	Pants	Sarees
Blankets	Hair dryer	Petticoats	Salwars
Bedsheets	Hair curler/styler	Perfumes	Shoe polish
Sleeping bag	Hearing aids	Toilet articles	Shoe brush
Boiler suits	Headgear	Cosmetics	Spectacles
Blouses	Chair for Invalid	Suits	Tops
Dresses	Jeans	Shirts	Towels
Dentures	Lungis	Shoes	Underwear
Frocks	Neckties	Socks	Umbrella
Gloves	Nighties	Shaving kit	Walking stick

Table-3 : Household Effects

Blender	Kitchenware	Toaster	TV
Crockery	Linens	Utensils	Music System
Cutlery	Liquidizer	Air Conditioner	Camera
Iron	Oven	PC	Typewriter
Egg beater	Pressure cooker	Refrigerator	Tapes
Glassware	Rotisserie	Deep Freezer	Films
Juicer	Tablewares	VCR/VCP	Vehicles

As per Circular 72/98-Cus. dt 24.9.98 personal effects would also include the following:

(a) Personal jewellery.

(b) One camera with film rolls not exceeding twenty.

(c) One video camera / camcorder with accessories and with video cassettes not exceeding twelve.

(d) One pair of binoculars.

(e) One portable colour television (not exceeding 15 cm in size).

(f) One music system including compact disc player.

(g) One portable typewriter.

(h) One perambulator.

(i) One tent and other camping equipment.

(j) One computer (laptop/note book).

(k) One electronic diary.

(l) One portable wireless receiving set (transistor radio)

(m) Professional equipments, instruments and apparatus of appliances including professional audio/video equipments.

(n) Sports equipments — one fishing outfit, one sporting firearm with 50 cartridges, one non-powdered bicycle, one canoe less than 5·1 metres long, one pair of skids, two tennis rackets, one golf set consisting of 14 pieces with a dozen golf balls.

(o) One cell phone. Satellite phone is not permitted to be imported except against a licence to be issued by the WPC wing of Ministry of Communication and Information Technology.

(p) Cinematographic films, exposed but not developed.

Duty-Free Items

All over the world, no duty is levied on used personal effects, (excluding jewellery), required for satisfying daily necessities. Though there is no limit, the number of items should be reasonable. One wrist watch, irrespective of its value, is personal effects. The Indian Customs Baggage Rules, 2016 have done away with different allowances for persons under or over 10 years of age. Infants can have freedom only for used personal items and not any duty-free allowance.

Residing in India (Rule-3)

A Resident tourist is a person with an Indian passport or a foreigner normally residing in India, who has gone abroad on a short trip. The duty-free allowance for such a tourist returning after a trip abroad is ₹50,000 and ₹15,000 for the foreigner. This is in addition to the items mentioned in Annexure-I.

Nepal, Bhutan or Myanmar (Rule-4)

For passengers coming from Nepal, Bhutan or Myanmar (Burma) other than by land route, and also for those coming from Pakistan by land route, the allowance is ₹15,000.

Professionals (Rule-5)

A person who is engaged in a profession abroad or is transferring his residence to India shall be allowed, in addition to the allowances mentioned in Rule-3 and Rule-4 above, the following additional concessions—

1. 3 to 6 months: ₹60,000.
2. 6 months to 1 year: ₹1,00,000.
3. 1 year to 2 years: ₹2,00,000, provided the passenger should not have used this concession in preceding 3 years.
4. Over 2 years: ₹5,00,000, provided —
   (a) The minimum stay abroad is 2 years immediately preceding the date of arrival in India. Shortfall up to 2 months in stay abroad can be condoned by Deputy or Assistant Commissioner of Customs if early return is on account of (i) terminal leave or vacation (ii) any other special circumstances for reasons to be recorded in writing.
   (b) Total stay in India during the two preceding years should not exceed 6 months. This condition can be wavered by Principal Commissioner or Commissioner of Customs for reasons to be recorded in writing.
   (c) Passenger should not have availed this concession in the preceding 3 years. No condensation of this condition is possible.

This concession is not available to those who were merely on training abroad, unless the passenger is a government official deputed on training abroad.

This concession cannot be availed in conjunction with TR concessions specified by Rule-8. These allowances are in addition to those offered by Annexures I, II and III.

"Professional equipment" consists of portable equipment, instrument, apparatus and appliance as are required in the profession by a carpenter, plumber, welder, mason, and the like and shall not include items of common use such as cameras, cassette recorder, dictaphone, personal computer, typewriter, and other similar articles.

Jewellery (Rule-6)

The limit to import, free of duty, on jewellery is up to weight of 20 gms with a value of ₹50,000 for males and up to weight of 40 gms with ₹2,00,000 for females. This rule is also applicable to a person transferring residence.

Even an infant can enjoy this full concession provided the jewellery is for bona fide use of the infant. The value of jewellery is determined at the prevailing international rates. Import of old jewellery for conversion into new one and subsequent re-export is not permitted.

There is no value limit on the export of gold jewellery through baggage, if it constitutes the bona fide baggage of the passenger (F. 495/19/93-Cus VI, dt 6.10.94). Note that incentives for export of jewellery through legal commercial channels are more attractive.

Commercial export of gold jewellery through the courier mode is permitted subject to observance of prescribed procedures.

Foreign Tourists (Rule-7)

Foreign Tourist is a person not normally Resident who enters India for a stay of not more than 6 months, in the course of any 12 months, for legitimate non-immigrant purposes, such as touring, recreation, sports, health, family reasons, study, pilgrimage or business. Such a tourist, either of Indian origin or otherwise is allowed used personal effects and travel souvenirs if these are for his personal consumption. Balance should be re-exported when he leaves India.

Tourists of Indian origin can avail the general allowances available to passengers who are Indian Resident or a foreigner residing in India as per Rule-3 or Rule-4. Tourists of foreign origin can bring articles up to ₹8,000 and travel souvenirs (other than those mentioned in Annexure-I) for personal use or gifts.

There is no free allowance for tourists of Nepalese or Bhutanese origin coming from their respective countries.

A tourist of (i) Pakistani origin coming from Pakistan other than by land routes and (ii) of any origin coming from Pakistan by land route, can bring articles up to ₹6,000 for making gifts.

The land routes are —

Amritsar	Amritsar Railway Station, Attari Roads, Attari Railway Station & Khalra.
Baroda	Assara Naka, Khavda Naka, Lakhpat, Santalpur Naka & Suigam Naka.
Delhi	Delhi Railway Station.
Ferozepur	Hussainiwala.
Jodhpur	Barmer & Munabao Railway Stations.
Baramullah	Adoosa.
Poonch	Chakan-da-bagh.

Under Public Notice 34-ITC(PN)/78 dt 16.5.78, an NRI or a PIO, major or minor, who is normally Resident abroad is entitled to import articles of personal and household effects up to ₹5,000, subject to certain conditions. Baggage of family members may be pooled or treated separately. This allowance should be allowed irrespective of educational qualification or profession of the tourist. For example, goldsmith can bring with him his plumbing tools.

Transfer of Residence (Rule-8)

A person on *Transfer of Residence (*TR) to India is a person whose minimum stay abroad is of 2 years immediately preceding the date of his arrival on TR. He can bring with him any used personal and household articles, other than those listed at Annexure I or II, but including all the items in Annexure III. The total stay in India on short visits during these 2 preceding years should not exceed 6 months and he should not have availed this concession in the preceding 3 years. The concessions can be availed only once in 3 years. This condition cannot be relaxed.

In case there is a shortfall of up to 2 months in the stay abroad and if his early return is on account of terminal leave or vacation or any other special circumstances, it can be condoned by Assistant or Deputy Commissioner of Customs. Only the Commissioner can extend the period of stay in India of 6 months in deserving cases.

Persons who had availed TR were required to stay in India for minimum one year after their return; not any more.

Indian diplomats, if called back to India in public interest before the stay of 2 years, are also eligible for the concessions provided a certificate to that effect from the ministry of external affairs is produced and the items have been in use and possession of the diplomat for more than 6 months.

Articles allowed free of duty are — used personal and household articles, other than those listed in Annexure I or Annexure II but not Annexure III. This is in addition to the allowances offered by Rule-3 and Rule-4 and Rule-6.

TR is not available to each member of the family if they are having a common establishment and staying together. Not more than one unit of each item can be imported by a family.

The passengers, including foreign nationals, will have to pay duty on brand new items for personal use or gifts. Any article will be presumed to be in use if it has been in possession of the passenger for one year. Physical appearance that an article looks new is no ground for denying TR benefit. Purchase bill is to be taken as sufficient evidence. TR benefit must be allowed unless the revenue has sufficient evidence to prove otherwise — *Jiwa Singh* v. *Union of India and Another 1990 (45) ELT 229 (Del.)*.

Even if the goods are liable to confiscation, exemption of TR cannot be denied — Naresh Lokumal Serai v Commissioner of Customs (Export) Raigad 2006 (203) ELT 0580 Tri-Bom.

TR for Foreigner Specialist

A foreigner with special technical knowledge or experience, finding that he cannot take the benefit of TR for one reason or another, (e.g., his resident permit of visa is for less than one year) may be allowed with prior approval of RBI, to get his goods released on giving a suitable bond. Other conditions of TR would prevail. The bond can be cancelled if and when he gets the visa extended.

The Indo-Pak Baggage Rules

The Baggage Rules, 1998 (as amended in 2006), are applicable also to Indians and Pakistanis arriving from Pakistan ever since the Indo-Pak Baggage Rules have been rescinded. For export of baggage of those proceeding to Pakistan, export trade control concessions contained in Handbook of Import-Export Procedure are applicable. All the provisions regarding the Baggage Rules, 1998 will be applicable to passengers arriving from Pakistan.

TR of Persons from Nepal or Bhutan

There is no passport and visa restrictions between India and Nepal or Bhutan. Therefore, it is difficult to enforce provisions of TR. Nevertheless, persons employed in the Indian Embassy or the Indian Co-operation Mission, can obtain certificates about their bona fide transfer. For other individuals the concessions are given on the basis of certificate given by the Indian Embassy in Nepal.

Unaccompanied Baggage (Rule-9)

Passengers are allowed to send their baggage through cargo as unaccompanied baggage provided it has been in possession abroad of the passenger and has been dispatched 1 month after his arrival in India or such further period as Deputy or Assistant Commissioner of Customs may allow. The baggage may land in India 2 months in advance before the arrival of the passenger or within such period not exceeding 1 year as the Commissioner or Deputy Commissioner may allow, for reasons to be recorded in writing.

These Rules shall apply to such baggage, unless specifically excluded. There is no free allowance for such baggage which is chargeable to Customs duty @ 35% ad valorem + 3% Education Cess .

Avoid sending used personal effects through unaccompanied baggage. The provisions of Rule-8 are extended to unaccompanied baggage, except where they have been specifically excluded. Consequently, in our opinion, the concessions to the extent of shortfall availed on the accompanied baggage can be claimed on unaccompanied baggage.

The unaccompanied baggage should be in the possession abroad of the passenger and shall be dispatched within one month of his arrival in India and land in India up to two months before the arrival of the passenger. The Deputy / Assistant Commissioner of Customs may allow an extension of this period not exceeding one year, for reasons to be recorded, if he is satisfied that the passenger was prevented from arriving in India within the stipulated period due to circumstances beyond his control.

Such baggage can also be received by a friend or relatives of the passenger.

NRIs passing through India in transit may also pay the freight in rupees only if it was obtained by sale of forex by the traveller.

The freight rates are normally half the usual cargo rates with a minimum charge for 10 kgs. Freight on accompanied baggage can be accepted in rupees if the fare of the traveller to India was collected in rupees either in India or abroad.

Public Notice 29/86 states that no demurrage is chargeable for storage of baggage since it is baggage and not cargo. This also applies to cases where the goods were detained at the instance of the customs — *R. K. Pariyar* v. *International Airport Authority of India, 1993 (63) ELT 411 (Del).*

Crew Members (Rule-10)

Any individual coming to India for a short stay who typically makes more frequent visits, and also an airline crew, may bring petty items like chocolates, cosmetics, cheese, and other petty gift items up to ₹1,500 per visit.

He is not allowed to bring costly gadgets like air conditioners, music system, refrigerators, etc., on payment of baggage duty without an import licence, except where such items have been specifically permitted under the Exim Policy in force or under public notice or order issued by the DGFT.

A crew member of a foreign-going vessel is treated on par with Resident passengers for his baggage at the final pay off on termination of his engagement and Rule-3 to Rule-9 would be applicable. In addition, he would also be eligible to the concessions related with import of gold and silver, since a retired employee ceases to be a member of the crew.

A foreign-going vessel includes a vessel —

(a) of a foreign government taking part in a naval exercise;
(b) or aircraft proceeding to a place outside India for any purpose whatsoever; and
(c) engaged in fishing or any other operation outside the territorial waters of India.

Prohibited or Restricted Items

Certain goods are prohibited (banned) or restricted (subject to certain conditions) for import and/or export. These are goods of social, health, environment, wild life and security concerns. While it is not possible to list all the goods, more common of these are :

1. Export of most species of wild life and articles made from wild flora and fauna, such as ivory, musk, reptile skins, furs, shahtoosh, etc.
2. Trafficking of narcotic drugs and psychotropic substances.

3. Export of goods purchased against forex brought in by foreign passengers are allowed except for prohibited goods.
4. Carrying of Indian currency notes in the denomination of ₹500 and ₹2,000 to Nepal is prohibited.
5. Export of Indian Currency is strictly prohibited. However Indian residents when they go abroad are allowed to take with them Indian currency not exceeding ₹25,000.
6. Tourists while leaving India are allowed to take with them foreign currency not exceeding an amount brought in by them at the time of their arrival in India. As no declaration is required to be made for bringing in forex / currency not exceeding equivalent of U.S. $ 10,000, generally tourists can take out of India with them at the time of their departure forex/ currency not exceeding the above amount.
7. Indian residents going abroad are permitted to take with them foreign currency without any limit so long as the same has been purchased from an authorised forex dealer.
8. Pornographic material and pirated goods and good infringing any of the legally enforceable.
9. Intellectual property rights.
10. Antiquities.
11. Live birds and animals including pets.
12. Plants and their produce, e.g. fruits, seeds.
13. Endangered species of plants and animals, whether live or dead.
14. Any goods for commercial purpose: for profit, gain or commercial usage.
15. Radio transmitters not approved for normal usage.

Following items are prohibited from being carried either in checked-in or hand baggage —

- Briefcase with built-in alarms or lithium batteries and/or pyrotechnic materials.

- Compressed gases, toxic, refrigerated liquids, like camping gas devices.
- Corrosive products, acids, mercury, alkali and wet batteries.
- Flammable liquids, coal gas, paints and thinners.
- Asbestos materials.
- Oxidising agents such as chloride of lime and peroxide.
- Flammable solids, matches and material which ignite easily substances capable of spontaneous combustion or which on contact with water emit flammable gases.
- Poisonous and infectious substances.
- Radioactive substances.

Hand bag cannot carry — Gels, Alcohol, Liquids, Creams, Lotions, Sharp articles, etc.

Satellite phone is not permitted to be imported except against a licence issued by the WPC wing of Ministry of Communication and Information Technology

Fire Arms

Import of fire arms is strictly prohibited. Import of cartridges in excess of 50 is also prohibited. However, in the case of persons transferring their residence (as per conditions specified in the rules) to India for a minimum period of one year, one firearm of permissible bore can be allowed to be imported subject to the conditions that: (i) The same was in possession and use abroad by the passenger for a minimum period of one year and that such firearm can be disposed of after ten years of its import. However, this facility can be availed only once. (ii) The passenger has a valid arms licence from the local (Indian) authorities. (iii) The customs duties as applicable shall be paid.

Thanks to the terrorists, it is very difficult to get any permission.

Renowned shooters and rifle clubs can import arms and ammunition, of permissible bore for their own use and even for gift purpose, on the recommendation of the Department of Youth

Affairs and Sports. An application has to be made using Form given in Appendix-8 of the Handout of Procedures to DGFT.

Export of Antique items is prohibited. Artifacts / items over 100 years old are considered antiques.

One Laptop Computer Imported as Baggage Exempt

Notification 11/2004 dt 8.1.04 has exempted from the duty one laptop computer (notebook) when imported into India by a passenger of the age of 18 years or above (other than a member of the crew).

Import of Baggage of Deceased Person

Used, bona fide personal and household effects belonging to a deceased person are allowed to be imported free of duty subject to the condition that a Certificate from the concerned Indian Embassy or High Commission is produced regarding the ownership of the goods by the deceased person — MoF Notification 103 (F. 56/7/Cus VI) dt 19.7.69. In such a case, the value should be ignored, especially when the person is the widow of the deceased person — *Padma K. Fokul Fandhi* v *Collector of Customs, Mumbai* 1995 (78) ELT 265 (Tribunal).

Replacement of Defective Items

Notification 49/96 Cus dt 23.7.96 exempts articles and component parts thereof when imported for replacement of defective items.

Pets, Wild Animals

Export of most species of wild life, exotic birds, wild orchids and articles made from flora and fauna such as ivory, musk, reptile skins, furs, tiger skins, shahtoosh, etc., is prohibited.

Import of pets up to two numbers per passenger are allowed as baggage only to persons transferring their residence to India after two years of continuous stay abroad in terms of Baggage Rules, 1998 subject to production of required health certificate from country of origin and examination of the said pets by the animal quarantine officer without an import licence issued by DGFT.

Gifts

A Resident is free to send outside India (export) any gift article, which may be free to be exported as per the extant Foreign Trade Policy, subject to the exporter submitting a declaration that the gifted goods are not more than ₹5,00,000. Such gifts may be sent outside India without furnishing the declaration in Form EDF/ SOFTEX, as the case may be.

Any person may buy from any post office any forex in the form of postal orders or money orders. Import of goods which are otherwise freely importable is also permitted without requiring a CCP. In other cases the permit is issued on an application by the Licensing Authority on merits of each case.

A gift to an entity in India can be made subject to —

(a) It is made for donee's personal use.

(b) It is made by post or otherwise.

(c) It does not contain vegetable seeds exceeding one pound in weight, bees, tea, books, literature which is prohibited, canalised items, alcoholic beverages, and consumer electronic items (except hearing aids, life saving equipments, apparatus and appliances and parts thereof).

(d) Consumer goods made to charitable, religious or educational institutions and others specified by central government.

(e) CIF value of the gift parcel does not exceed ₹5,000, vide Notification 87/99 Cus dt 6.7.99. Postal charges or the air freight shall not be taken into account for determining the value limit.

(f) Under para 11.4 of Import Export Policy 1997-2002, goods of value not exceeding ₹15,000 in a licensing year may be exported as a gift. Items in the negative list of exports require a licence except in the case of edible items.

Postal Imports

Remittances against bills received for imports by post parcel may be made by ADs, provided such goods are normally despatched by post parcel. The parcel receipts must be produced as evidence of despatch through the post and an undertaking must be furnished in Postal Appraisal Form or Customs Assessment Certificate as evidence of import within 3 months from the date of remittance, even if the parcel has already been received in India. Where goods are not of a kind normally imported by post parcel or where the AD is not satisfied about the bona fides of the applicant, the case should be referred to the RBI for prior approval with full particulars together with relative parcel receipt and Postal Appraisal Form or Customs Assessment Certificate.

ADs may make remittances towards import of books by post parcel by booksellers or publishers against bills received for collection, irrespective of the amount involved, against endorsement on the import licence wherever applicable in the normal course. They may also make remittances even if import licences covering the imports have been issued subsequent to the date of import subject to endorsement on such licences.

Import & Export of Currency

Travellers going out of India are allowed to purchase forex currency notes and coins up to US$ 3,000 per visit. Balance amount can be carried in the form of store value cards, travellers cheque or banker's draft. This facility is per individual, including children, major or minor.

However, travellers proceeding to Iraq and Libya can draw up to US$ 5,000 or its equivalent per visit and those proceeding to the Islamic Republic of Iran, Russian Federation and other Republics of Commonwealth of Independent States can draw entire forex (up to US$ 250,000) in the form of notes or coins. For travellers proceeding for Haj / Umrah pilgrimage, full amount of entitlement (US$ 250,000) in cash or up to the cash limit as specified by the Haj Committee of India, may be released by the ADs and FFMCs.

Normally, tourists, while leaving India, are allowed to take with them forex not exceeding an amount brought in by them at the time of their arrival in India. As no declaration is required to be made for bringing in currency notes up to equivalent of US$ 5,000, generally they can take with them at the time of their departure currency notes not exceeding this limit.

A resident of India, who has gone out of India on a temporary visit may bring into India at the time of his return from any place outside India (other than Nepal and Bhutan), Indian currency notes up to ₹25,000.

Any person resident outside India, not being a citizen of Pakistan and Bangladesh and also not a traveller coming from and going to Pakistan and Bangladesh, and visiting India may bring Indian currency notes up to ₹25,000 while entering only through an airport. Any person Resident who had gone to Pakistan and / or Bangladesh on a temporary visit, may bring into India at the time of his return, Indian currency notes up to ₹10,000 per person.

A person coming into India from abroad can bring with him forex without any limit. However, if the aggregate value in the form of currency notes, bank notes or travellers cheques brought in exceeds US$ 10,000 and/or the value of foreign currency alone exceeds US$ 5,000 or its equivalent, it should be declared to the Customs Authorities at the Airport in the Currency Declaration Form (CDF), on arrival in India. ADs and their exchange bureaux are required to issue Encashment Certificates (EC) in Form-ECF in all cases of purchase of forex from the public, irrespective of whether the Currency Declaration Form (CDF) has been submitted or not by the tenderer of the forex and whether the tenderer requests for the certificate or not. In the absence of encashment certificate, unspent local currency held by non-resident visitors will not be allowed to be converted into forex.

Since Indian notes and coins (other than ₹500 or ₹2,000 notes) are acceptable currency in Nepal and Bhutan, travellers can carry Indian currency without any limit but in denomination not above ₹100. There is no necessity of carrying forex.

Permissible forex can be drawn 180 days in advance by an individual, Resident. Forex for travel abroad can be purchased from an authorized person against rupee payment in cash below ₹50,000. However, if the sale of foreign exchange is for the amount equivalent to ₹50,000 and above, the entire payment should be made by way of a crossed cheque, banker's cheque, pay order, demand draft, debit card, credit card or prepaid card only.

Note that there is no forex exchange counter after immigration.

Weight & Size of Baggage

This is based on weight or number of bags, depending upon the airline. Each passenger is normally allowed to carry as free baggage allowance 40 kgs in first class, 30 kgs in executive class and 20 kgs in economy class. However, a lady's hand bag, reasonable reading material, purse, overcoat, wrap, blanket, umbrella, walking stick, a small camera, binoculars, infant's carrying basket, infant's *en-route* food for consumption, any prosthetic device for passenger's use such as crutches, collapsible wheel chair, etc., are allowed free.

Each passenger is allowed to checked-in bags, each one not exceeding linear dimension (length + breadth + height) of 158 cms and weighing not more than 32 kgs. Passengers in any class with infants (paying 10% of adult fare, not entitled to a separate seat) are allowed one extra piece of checked-in bag up to 10 kgs with total linear dimension not exceeding 115 cms, plus other items as they are allowed under the weight system.

First class and Executive class passengers are allowed to carry two hand bags in the cabin, the total weight of which should not exceed 12 kgs. The economy class passenger can carry only one bag of not more than 8 kgs. The individual dimensions of each piece should not exceed 55 cms × 40 cms × 20 cms. One stroller per child within the allowance is permitted.

A passenger can book additional seat at normal fare to carry hand baggages, the total weight of which is under 75 kgs per seat.

If the bag exceeds the prescribed limits in weight or dimensions, the excess baggage rate is charged which is normally @1% of the normal first class one way fare per kilogram. This slightly varies depending upon the airline and the destination.

Travellers on flights originating from Jammu, Srinagar and Leh are not allowed to carry any hand baggage.

Loss, Delay or Damage of Baggage

The airlines reimburse the loss arising out of delay or damage of lost baggage but the rates differ depending upon the air line. Air India pays US$ 20 per kilo for checked baggage and US$ 400 per passenger for unchecked baggage, unless a higher value is declared in advance. No liability is undertaken for goods which are fragile or perishable. For travel wholly between one US point to another, the US law requires the airlines to pay at least US$ 1,250 per passenger.

If a passenger wishes to cover the risk comprehensively, he may go in for insurance of unbreakable articles at a nominal premium of approximately 1% of the insured value declared. Insurance companies make payment on depreciated value of the goods. The passenger is also entitled for compensation if his goods are damaged provided they were properly packed. The payment towards settling the claim may take between 3 weeks and 3 months.

Until the baggage is traced, the airlines meets the essential expenses of the passenger. The amount depends on the profile of the passenger including the class in which he was travelling and the distance from his residence.

In case the baggage has been lost or mishandled by the Airlines, a simplified procedure is in place for clearance of such baggage which allows the passenger to have delivery of his baggage at his door step by the Airlines. There is no need to handover the passport or the keys of the bag to the airlines. The passenger has to first file a property irregularity report (PIR) along with a declaration indicating contents in the missing baggage. The passenger is required to obtain a certificate to that effect from the airlines and get it countersigned by Customs indicating specifically the unutilized portion of the free allowance. This would enable the passenger to avail the unutilized portion of the duty free allowance when his baggage is delivered by the airlines. The examination of the mishandled baggage would be carried out in the presence of the passenger.

Detained Baggage

A passenger may request the Customs to detain his baggage either for re-export at the time of his departure from India or for clearance subsequently on payment of duty. The detained baggage would be examined and full details will be inventorised. Such baggages are kept in the custody of the Customs. If he does not come within the time limit specified in the detention receipt, the Customs can dispose the goods.

When a contraband article is seized, a panchanama should be made at spot. Sometimes, it may not be possible to do so because of lack of facilities. Panchanama has to be witnessed by persons who are locally available for giving evidence later, if required. Merely because some employees were called as they happened to be available, it is no ground to view their evidence with suspicion — Sec. 108, para 13 of the Custom Act, 1962.

Take Care

Some touts and unauthorised persons operate, particularly in the unaccompanied baggage centre of Air Cargo Complexes. It may be quite possible that some of the assessing officers are hand in gloves with them. How else can you explain the presence of these shady characters in the complex? If you keep your list ready, you have nothing to worry. However, the procedures are quite complicated and it is better to employ a recognised clearing agent.

Whenever a dispute arises in respect of bona fide nature of the baggage sought to be cleared under TR, the matter can be brought to the notice of the additional deputy collector of customs for appropriate decision.

Valuation of Goods & Custom Duty

In view of the difficulty encountered in fixing the value of used items, the government has fixed tariff value of a number of items usually imported by the passengers as baggage. In other cases, the value is fixed on the basis of purchase bills, depreciation (mostly in the case of cars) and other available data. Normally, the value as declared by the passenger is accepted unless proved otherwise. The burden of proof lies on the Department. The rate of exchange as in force on the date on which a bill of entry is presented will be taken for ascertaining allowances and duty.

If there is any unutilised portion of duty-free allowance, a set-off of that portion is allowed before charging the duty. No such set-off is allowed on unaccompanied baggage.

Duty Rates

The goods over and above the free allowances shall be chargeable to customs duty @ 35% + an education cess of 3%, i.e. to say the effective rate is 36.05%.

The rate of duty applicable on these products over and above the above mentioned free allowance is as under:

(i) Cigarettes BCD @100%+ educational cess @ 3%.
(ii) Whisky BCD @150% + ACD @ 4% + no education cess.
(iii) Beer BCD @100% + ACD NIL + 3% education cess.

The rates of duty are liable to frequent changes and therefore you will do well by checking the latest rates applicable.

Misdeclaration or non-declaration attracts penal actions. Goods up to ₹500 in excess of the declared quantity may be allowed clearance on payment of duty. Excess beyond this limit up to ₹2,000 may be allowed on payment of duty and fine. Goods beyond this limit up to ₹5,000 may attract penalty besides confiscation whereas goods in excess of ₹5,000 may attract, besides other actions, prosecution.

Special Concession

As per Notification 13/2004-Cus dt 8.1.04 w.e.f. 9.1.04, total exemption on items listed in Annexure-II and concessional duty @15% ad valorem for those in Annexure-III is charged to —

(a) any person returning to India after having stayed abroad for at least 365 days during the 2 years immediately preceding the date of arrival in India. Refer Rule 5 for whom duty-free allowance is ₹75,000. The person should declare in writing that the goods have been in his possession abroad or the goods are purchased from a duty-free shop located in the arrival hall.

(b) any person on a bona fide Transfer of Residence (TR) to India as part of his bona fide baggage. Refer Rule-8 for whom duty-free allowance is ₹5,00,000. The person should give an additional declaration affirming that no other member of the family has availed of or would avail of this benefit.

Notification 48/2007-Cus dt 12.11.07 permits Government of India officials proceeding abroad on official postings to carry along with their personal baggage, food items strictly for their personal consumption.

Clearance Channels — Green & Red

The green channel is for those not having any dutiable or restricted goods whereas the red is for others. If the goods pass the conditions applicable to the green channel, only 10% of the packages will be opened for examination by the customs. Full examination will be resorted to only in cases of doubts arising out of such percentage examination. Passengers are normally cleared on an oral declaration. It is prudent to have a list of the articles giving their description and value along with all purchase receipts for articles brought as baggage.

Mishandled Baggage

In case the baggage has been lost or mishandled by the Airlines, a simplified procedure is in place for clearance of such baggage which allows the passenger to have delivery of his baggage at his door step by the Airlines. There is no need to handover the passport or the keys of the baggage to the airlines. The passenger has to first file a property irregularity report (PIR) with the airlines for the missing baggage. At the same time, he has to file a declaration indicating contents in the missing baggage. The passenger is required to obtain a certificate to that effect from the airlines and get it countersigned by Customs indicating specifically the unutilized portion of the free allowance. This would enable the passenger to avail the unutilized portion of the duty free allowance when his baggage is delivered by the airlines. Finally, the passenger is required to submit all these documents with the concerned airlines for clearance and delivery of goods on his behalf. The examination of the mishandled baggage would be carried out in the presence of the passenger.

Mandatory Declarations

It is obligatory for disembarking passengers to declare details of plants, seeds, other planting materials, meat and meat products, dairy products, live or ornamental fish, poultry and poultry products. It is also obligatory to declare goods in excess of the free allowance, prohibited or restricted goods, including narcotic drugs, wildlife and its products, arms, explosives, and also commercial goods at the Red Channel Counter. Attempt to import these goods through non-declaration can lead to penal consequences, including arrest.

Registration for Foreign Nationals

Anyone entering India on a student, employment, research, medical, medical attendant or missionary visa, which is valid for over 180 days, is required to register with the Foreigners Registration Officer under whose jurisdiction he proposes to stay, within 14 days of arrival in India.

Foreigners visiting India on any other category of visa that is valid for over 180 days are not required to register themselves if their actual stay does not exceed 180 days on each visit. If such a foreigner happens to find that his stay would go beyond 180 days, he should get himself registered before he crosses the limit.

Foreign nationals who are exempt from registration are —

(a) those having visa for 180 days or less;
(b) children under 16 years of age, irrespective of the type of visa;
(c) those holding OCI card.

Irrespective of the type of Visa, Pakistani nationals are required to register within 24 hours and Afganistan nationals within 14 days of their arrival in India.

If at any time, a foreigner proposes to be absent from the registered address for a continuous period of 8 weeks or more, or is changing the address or is finally departing from India, he shall, before leaving inform in person, or through an authorised representative, or by registered post to his jurisdictional Registration Officer.

For updated information and in case of any difficulty or complaint, you can contact the Customs Officer (PRO).

Motor Vehicles

Cars are excluded from definition of baggage. Import of passenger cars, Jeeps, multi-utility vehicles and motor cycles, etc., both new and second hand, can be imported against an import licence and on payment of customs duty. However, the following persons do not require licence —

(a) Individuals coming to India for permanent settlement after 2 years of continuous stay abroad provided the car has been in his possession for a minimum of 1 year abroad. Short visits to

India are to be ignored as provided for in the baggage rules. Consequently, such individuals cannot import brand new cars.

(b) Legal heirs or successors of a deceased relative residing abroad.

(c) A physically handicapped person if the vehicle is specially designed for him. Only one vehicle is allowed and it shall not be sold within 2 years.

A second hand or used vehicle means a vehicle that has been sold, leased or loaned prior to its importation into India. It shall not be older than 3 years from the date of manufacture and shall have a minimum road-worthiness for 5 years.

In all the cases, the new as well as the old vehicles shall have:

(a) A speedometer indicating the speed in kilometres per hour.

(b) Right hand steering and controls. Manufacturers can import left hand drive vehicles only for testing and research.

(c) Photometry of the head lamps to suit keep-left traffic.

Motor cars, motor cycles and scooters, new or old, are chargeable to customs duty on the basis of their list price prevailing in the country of their manufacture on the date on which the bill of entry is presented. Trade discount and depreciation are to be adjusted. Depreciation for used cars is taken from the date of registration to the date of shipment or the date of departure of the owner from abroad, whichever is earlier. Freight, insurance and landing charges are to be added to the price to arrive at the final assessable value.

Import of new vehicles is permitted only through Customs ports at Nhava Sheva, Kolkata, Chennai, Delhi Air Cargo and at ICD Tughlakabad.

Depreciation Rates

Per quarter in	%
1st year	4.0
2nd year	3.0
3rd year	2.5
4th year & onwards*	2.0

*Subject to overall limit of 70%

This structure of depreciation is applicable to all the used items imported as baggage. The depreciation for each year is to be computed on the Written Down Value method. However, where the straight line method is used to save time it is accepted even if it benefits the passenger.

FA12 has increased the basic customs duty from 60% to 75% on completely built units of large cars, MUVs, SUVs permitted for import without type approval of value exceeding US $ 40,000 and engine capacity exceeding 3,000 cc for petrol and 2,500 cc for diesel.

Car Registration Licensing and Insurance

You must register and license your vehicle unless you are visiting India for less than 3 months. This is required even if you have been exempted from import duty. You will have to submit a Customs Declaration Form and an undertaking for the re-export of the vehicle. You must take your vehicle for registration to the Regional Transport Office as soon as possible and obtain a licence. An international driving license is valid in India.

You will be required to show to the RTO that you are adequately insured covering all the risks, including third party liabilities before you register your vehicle.

21

PAN is PAIN

As per Sec. 139A (5a & b), from 1.1.05 it is mandatory to quote PAN on challans for any payments due to the Department. Moreover, Sec. 139A(5c) read with Rule 114B makes it compulsory to quote PAN in all documents pertaining to some financial transactions, mainly purchase and sale of shares and MF schemes. Because of the distance, NRIs find it very difficult to obtain a PAN mainly due to lack of understanding of the exact requirements. This is an attempt to clarify the position in detail.

Though NRIs are not mandatorily required to possess a PAN, it is advisable to possess a PAN.

How to Obtain PAN

UTI Investor Services Ltd. (UTIITSL) and National Securities Depository Ltd. (NSDL) are authorised to issue PAN cards. The fee for preparation and delivery of a tamper proof card is ₹107 plus courier charges, if any, to be paid at IT PAN Service Centre or the TIN Facilitation Centre. Details of service charges and delivery time are available on their respective websites.

Addresses

UTIITSL —
The Vice President
IT PAN Processing Centre
UTI Investor Services Ltd.
Plot No. 3, Sector - 11
CBD, Belapur
Navi Mumbai-400 614
Tel 022-27561690
Fax 022-27561706

NSDL —
The Vice President
Income Tax PAN Services Unit, NSDL
4th Floor, Trade World, A Wing
Kamala Mills Compound
S. B. Marg, Lower Parel
Mumbai-400 013
Tel 022-2499 4650
Fax 022-2495 0664

Coupon number or Acknowledgement number, as the case may be, should be mentioned in all communications.

Application Form-49A can be downloaded from the websites

of Department	:	www.incometaxindia.gov.in, or
UTIISL	:	www.utiisl.co.in or
NSDL	:	tin.nsdl.com

or photocopied (on A4 size 70 GSM paper) or obtained from any other source. The Form is also available at IT PAN Service centers and TIN Facilitation centers.

If an application is submitted through Internet and payment made through a "nominated" credit card, the PAN is allotted on priority (TATKAL) and communicated through e-mail.

It is illegal to obtain or possess more than one PAN.

Filling the Application Form

- Form must be filled and signed using black ink only.
- Individual applicants will have to affix 2 recent coloured photographs (Stamp Size: 3.5 cms × 2.5 cms). Three signatures are required — 1. At the left side of the photograph across the photograph. 2. Box provided below the photograph, and 3. On page two in the box at end of the form.
- Full Name is required in the order of Surname, First name and middle name. However, provision is available in the form for you to select the style in which your name is to appear in PAN card. For instance, if your name is Sunil Raghav Shah, you can ask for S. R. Shah to be printed on the card. Only father's name is required to be filled in the Form, even by female applicants, irrespective of their marital status.
- Assessing Officer (AO) code pertaining to International Taxation Directorate is available on the website of service providers. In the case of doubts the first international taxation AO of Delhi is a default.
- NRIs not having any Indian residential address may provide a foreign address. Such applicants should indicate the address at which the PAN card should be sent and also invariably mention their email-id.

- Codes 99 and 999999 should be entered for State and PIN fields respectively by those who do not have any Indian address. However, actual foreign ZIP/PIN code should be mentioned in any of the 5 address fields (preferably last) along with the name of the country.

Proofs of Identity & Address

S.O. 2394(E) dt 17.10.11 has stipulated that copy of any one of the following documents is sufficient for the purpose —

(a) Passport or visa.
(b) PIO/OCI card.
(c) NRE account statement.
(d) Other national or citizenship identification number.
(e) Bank account statement (not more than 2 months old) in country of residence.
(f) Certificate of residence in India or Residential permit issued by the State Police Authority.
(g) Registration certificate of the Foreigner's Registration Office showing Indian address.
(h) Appointment letter or contract from Indian company or certificate (in original) of Indian service providers,
(i) Taxpayer Identification Number duly attested by "Apostille" (in respect of countries which are signatories to the Hague Apostille Convention of 1961) or by Indian embassy or High Commission or Consulate in the country where the applicant is located and finally,
(j) Every applicant has to submit self-attested copies of proof of identity, address and date of birth documents along with original documents for verification.

In case the applicant is a minor, any of above documents of any of the parents or guardian shall serve as proof of Address. In case PAN application is made on behalf of a HUF, any of above documents of the Karta will serve as proof of Address.

Non-individuals having no office in India should submit a copy of registration certificate of their country duly attested by Indian Embassy in the country where applicant is located.

Aadhaar Card

The FA17 has introduced a new Sec. 139AA requiring every person eligible to obtain Aadhaar number shall, on or after 1.7.17, quote it in the return of income furnished by him. Circular 6-1/2016-UIDAI (DBT) dt 15.11.17 draws attention to Sec. 2(v) of the Aadhaar Act which defines "resident" as an individual who has resided in India for a period of periods amounting in all to 182 days or more in the 12 months immediately preceding the date of application for enrolment. This definition is entirely different from that as defined either by ITA or FEMA. However, in a circular issued by UIDAI, it is clarified that NRIs/PIOs/OCIs are exempt from obtaining Aadhar. Yes, they can, if they choose to do so obtain it when they are in India.

Depository Participant

It is also necessary to have a PAN while opening an account with a DP for share transactions in demat format.

NRIs/PIOs who are not able to obtain PAN for one reason or the other but are holding securities in physical form and desire to sell the same, may be permitted to open a "limited purpose account" without PAN subject to —

- These accounts will be "suspended for credit" which means, only credits arising out of corporate benefits and demat of physical certificates will be permitted.
- These accounts cannot be used for getting credit from IPOs, any off-market or secondary market transactions, etc.
- These accounts can remain operational only for a limited period of 6 months to regularise the account. The DPs shall freeze non-regularised accounts thereafter.
- The account holders can sell the securities lying in these accounts only through a registered broker on the stock exchange.
- Where there is difference in the maiden name and current name of the investor (predominantly in the case of married

women), DPs can collect the PAN card proof as submitted by the account holder. However, this would be subject to the DPs verifying the veracity of the claim of such investors by collecting sufficient documentary evidence in support of the identity of the investor.

KYC Norms for Mutual Funds

It is compulsory for all the MFs w.e.f. 3.3.08 to comply with KYC norms for all the applications including New Fund Offer applications of ₹50,000 or more. This requirement is applicable even to joint holders. This is grossly unjustified, inconvenient and unfriendly measure involving a national waste and benefits none. AMFI exists to protect the investors in MFs and we are surprised to find that this particular diktat has been issued by AMFI itself.

Application forms are separate for individuals and non-individuals. These can be downloaded from the website of AMFI/MFs or obtained from any distributor.

If you have multiple folios within one Fund, you can instruct the MF to update the KYC against all the folios. A copy of the receipt allotted while submitting the KYC Form is required to be attached along with all new investment applications.

Power of Attorney (PoA)

Though the purchases can be made through direct remittances, it is obvious that an NRI requires to have a person in India to whom he has donated his PoA to dabble in shares on his behalf. Can he arrange for a PoA from abroad? Of course yes. Let us take the case of UK. All that he has to do is to —

(a) Print the PoA on a stamp paper of the required denomination as per UK Law and contact the Indian Embassy in UK.

(b) The person executing the PoA will sign in the presence of a notary who countersigns every page of the PoA.

(c) Arrange to send the PoA to the stamp office in India for getting it stamped for a denomination of ₹100.

(d) The person accepting the PoA will sign in the presence of the notary who attests his signature.

The authorities may feel that this is very easy. We do not.

To Sum

On reading my previous article one of my NRI readers, Mr. M. T. Antony observed, "Our stupid ministers and ridiculous bureaucracy outlandish, meaningless, counter-productive, self destructing bureaucracy continues unabated. Sorry to inject my personal philosophy. India is (next to China, USA and Japan) I am told, a super power. Why and for what reason India needs my hard earned money? If India needs it and if I am stupidly 'patriotic' can't they make it practical, easy for me to invest?"

We share his deep indignation and we are sure, almost all the NRIs are also reeling under same or similar reactions towards investment in India.

Dr. Manmohan Singh, during his address to Pravasi Bharatiya Divas symposium in 2006 had stated that it is the Indian diaspora which has rendered health to the Indian economy and has brought the capital account convertibility within its reach.

Unfortunately, the regulators appear to be repelling them.

22

~

Insurance and NRIs

Policies Issued by Insurers Outside India

A Resident may take or continue to hold a life or general insurance policy, including health insurance issued by an insurer outside India provided aggregate remittance including amount of premium does not exceed limit under the Liberalised Remittance Scheme for health insurance and RBI specific or general permission for life insurance.

No person shall take or renew any policy covering any property in India with an insurer whose principal place of business is outside India without IRDA permission.

Where the premium on a general or life insurance policy has been paid by making remittance from India, the policy holder shall repatriate to India through normal banking channels, the maturity proceeds or amount of any claim within 7 days from the receipt thereof.

Medical insurance policies in forex can be issued to Indian citizens who have gone abroad for employment and studies. Even when the premium can be paid in Indian rupees, some foreign insurers insist on payment in forex. Such payments are covered under the maintenance quota released by ADs.

Policies Issued by Indian Insurers

Resident of India may take general/health insurance policy permitted by IRDA from Indian insurer on payment of premium in INR, where claims arising under the policies outside India are to be settled in foreign currency.

Resident outside India may take general/health insurance policy as permitted by IRDAI from Indian Insurers. Claims arising under the policies are to be settled in INR if payment of premium is in INR and in any currency if payment of premium is in foreign currency. However, Insurance cover on risks inside India (including All Risks Insurance) on assets in India owned by Indian branches/offices of foreign companies, banks, etc., may be issued only in INR.

Insurers may issue general as well as life policies denominated in forex through their offices in India or abroad to NRIs provided the premiums are collected in forex or out of NRE accounts of the insured or his family members. For policies denominated in rupees, premium through NRO accounts can be accepted.

Policies may be issued in forex to Residents of Indian nationality or origin who have returned to India after being NRIs, provided the premiums are paid out of forex remittances or from their RFC accounts.

Foreign currency Policies issued by overseas offices of Indian insurers may be transferred to Indian register, together with the related actuarial reserves, when the policy holder returns to India. However, if the policy is in force for at least 3 years prior to policy holder's return to India and the policy holder wishes to retain and continue the forex policy, ADs can accept premium payments through foreign remittances or the RFC account of the policy holder. If the premiums are continued to be paid in forex, the maturity proceeds or the amount of claim can be credited to his account abroad or the RFC account in India.

Resident beneficiaries of forex life insurance policies are being permitted to retain the proceeds in their RFC/RFCD Accounts.

Proceeds of policies denominated in forex or the rupee policies for which premia are paid in forex or out of NRE accounts can be credited to NRE Account of the NRI.

The restrictions in regard to export of policies stand withdrawn.

Conversion of life policies of Resident in rupees into forex or transfer of records of such policies to a country outside India requires RBI prior approval.

Settlement of Claims — Maturity, Surrender Value, etc.

The basic rule for settlement of claims on rupee life insurance policies in favour of claimants resident outside India is that payments in forex will be permitted only in proportion in which the amount of premiums paid in forex in relation to the total premiums payable. Where such a person is an NRI, the amounts can be credited to his NRE account, if it is so desired. Resident beneficiaries may credit proceeds to their RFC/RFCD accounts, if they so desire.

Claims in respect of rupee life insurance policies issued to NRIs for which premia have been collected in non-repatriable rupees may be paid only by credit to NRO account if the claimant is NRI and ordinary account if he is a Resident.

If a beneficiary residing outside India desires remittance abroad, he should apply to RBI for its approval in Form-A2 together with Form-LIM(1), through his bank for the approval.

Where the policies are assigned to an overseas bank, the credit in rupees of any claim to the overseas assignee's account with an AD, requires RBI permission.

In case of cashless international health insurance products remittances may be allowed to the hospital which has provided the treatment/Third Party Administrator with which the insurer or the hospital has entered into a contractual arrangement in accordance with applicable IRDAI regulations or to the insured person resident outside India.

Notes:

Where rupee policies are issued on life of a non-resident Indian national under the Married Women's Property Act, the beneficiaries will be the wife and/or children of the policy holder. He may appoint a bank in India or a relative as special trustee to receive the claims and distribute the same to the beneficiaries.

RBI's prior approval is required for assignment of rupee life insurance policies held in Indian register by a Resident in favour of an NRI or by an NRI in favour of another NRI in a different country, except where the assignment is without consideration in favour of the policy holder's non-resident wife or dependent relatives. Applications to RBI should contain full details regarding beneficiaries and exact manner in which their shares will be disposed of by the special trustee.

Foreign Nationals not Permanently Resident

Policies denominated in forex or rupees may be issued to foreign nationals not permanently Resident provided the premiums are paid out of forex or from their income earned in India or repatriable superannuation and pension funds in India. Claims, maturity proceeds or surrender value in respect of rupee policies may be paid in rupees or allowed to be remitted abroad, if the claimant so desires.

In the case of foreign nationals employed in India, the insurer may accept a certificate from an AD to the effect that the foreign national was availing of recurring remittance facility.

Miscellaneous

- Premiums due on rupee policies issued to Indian nationals Resident in Myanmar may be accepted in rupees in India from friends, relatives of the policy holders subject to the condition that all payments under the policies will be made to the policyholders only in rupees after their arrival in India for permanent settlement. Cases of Chinese and Pakistani policyholders should be referred to RBI.
- Indians, Nepalese and Bhutanese resident in Nepal and Bhutan as well as offices and branches of Indian, Nepalese and Bhutanese firms, companies or other organizations in these two countries are treated as Resident for purpose of transactions in INR. Payments in foreign currency towards claims under general/health insurance policies will require prior approval of Reserve Bank, except where premium thereon was also collected in foreign currency.
- Life insurance policies are regarded as securities.

- Units located in Special Economic Zones (SEZs) to take any general policy issued by an insurer outside India provided the premiums are paid by the units in forex. Similar permission is granted for some marine and aviation insurance.
- AP (DIR) Circular 76 dt 4.2.04 states that approval from Ministry of Finance (Insurance Division) for securing insurance on health from a company abroad is no more required and ADs may freely allow such remittances.
- Insurers may pay commission in forex to their agents who are permanently resident outside India regardless of the fact that part of the business booked by them may be on the lives of Residents and related premiums are paid in rupees.

23

~

Gold Does Not Glitter

The most important reason for India being a poor country is its richness in gold. It is estimated that Indian households hold over 20,000 tonnes (= US$ 1,100 billion!) of the yellow metal. This is an unproductive asset. Everyone realises that even if a part of it is converted into productive capital, it will be a great help in poverty eradication. As per World Gold Council, Indian demand has averaged 838 tonnes over the last 10 years. Around 90-95 tonnes of gold was smuggled into the country in 2018, down from 115-120 tonnes a year earlier.

Gold Import Scheme

To curb this menace, the government had promulgated Gold Import Scheme, granting general permission to those NRIs and PIOs who have stayed abroad for at least 6 months to bring as a part of their baggage gold up to 10 kilos and silver up to 100 kilos in any form, including ornaments or articles, provided the import duties are paid in forex, either abroad or here in India. Short visits up to 30 days shall be ignored unless the passenger has availed of the exemption under this scheme during this period. The prescribed quantity cannot be brought in installments within the prescribed period of 6 months.

Originally, the scheme was designed to discourage those indulging in hawala and smuggling. There was a yawning gap between the landed cost of gold or silver and its market price in India.

To begin with, the import duty was ₹250/10 gms on gold and ₹500/kg on silver. It was an instant success. This duty was raised almost each and every year under one pretext or another. The recent FA19(2) has raised it by a whopping ad volerum 12.5% (= 13.0% with 4% cess) which translates into duty of ₹4,600/10 gm. Imports over these limits, duty would be charged @ 35% (=36.4% with cess).

To avoid any disputes arising from under invoicing, the government fixes import tariff value which is the base price at which the customs duty is determined through notifications issued from time to time (normally on fortnight basis).

Has the Scheme Remained Attractive? See following Table.

NRI IMPORT SCHEME : PRECIOUS METALS **Computed on : 01.08.2019**		
Overseas Price		
Gold	$ 1,450.15	Per Ounce
Silver	$ 16.3400	Per Ounce
Import Duty - ₹		
Gold - 12.5% ad valorem	₹4,201	per 10gms
Silver - 12.5% ad valorem	₹4,733	per Kilo
1 Ounce =	31.1034768	gms
1 $ =	₹69.31	rupees
	Gold — 10 gms ₹	**Silver — 1kg** ₹
Price - Indian	35,750	44,100
Overseas	32,315	36,412
Margin	3,435	7,688
Duty	4,201	4,733
Profit	(766)	2,955

It is obvious that no one would like to import any gold or silver through their baggage. The hike in the customs duty on precious metals will certainly boost smuggling.

Most importantly, the government has reduced the quantity of gold allowed to be brought by such eligible passengers returning from abroad from 10 kgs to 1 kg and of silver from 100 kg to 10 kg. w.e.f. 18.4.12.

This is not the end of story. It should be noted that when you purchase gold, you are charged Goods and Service Tax (GST) at 3% on the value of gold plus making charges, if any.

There are some more kinks. When you sell the precious metals in India and earn a profit, it would be considered as either a short-term gain or a long-term gain if you sell it after 3 years of its purchase by you or as business income since your intention while buying it was to sell. In any case, you may be entitled to claim expenses incurred "wholly and exclusively" for the purpose of earning the profit or the capital gains. We claim that the cost of the airline ticket is definitely an expense incurred for this transaction. Whether or not it is incurred wholly and exclusively for buying and selling gold can be a matter of dispute between you and your ITO.

All this has rendered the precious metal import scheme unattractive and we are back at square one where smugglers thrive.

The passenger is allowed to bring the precious metals himself or import it within 15 days of his arrival. To avoid the hazards of carrying the gold personally, he can use customs bonded warehouses of SBI or Metal and Mineral Trading Corporation at Mumbai, Delhi, Thiruvananthapuram and special delivery centres. If he has paid the duty abroad and is found ineligible to import it after his arrival in India, refund would be given to him. He has to file a declaration on a prescribed form before the customs officer at the time of his arrival stating his intention of using the warehouses and pay the duty before clearance.

New Solutions of the Government

FA15 has attacked the problem through a 3-pronged attack by —

1. **Gold Monetisation Scheme**: This new scheme will replace both the present Gold Deposit and Gold Metal Loan Schemes and handled by some banks and gold dealers. It will enable the depositors to earn interest in their metal accounts and the jewellers to obtain loans in their metal account. We hoped that the interest rate would be much higher than the one offered by SBI at 0.755-1% over tenures ranging from 3 to 5 years for the old schemes.
2. **Sovereign Gold Bond**: This will be an alternative to purchasing gold directly. The Bonds will carry a fixed rate of interest, and also be redeemable in cash at the face value of the gold, at the time of redemption.
3. **Indian Gold Coin**: It will carry the Ashok Chakra on its face. Such an Indian Gold Coin would help reduce the de-

mand for coins minted outside India and also help to recycle the gold available in the country.

Yes, these steps are likely to offer an official and easy alternative to invest white money into gold. However, it has to be realised that the battle is against black money, havala and smuggling. The 10% import duty surely renders smuggling a better option, in spite of the various risks involved.

We strongly feel that the one and only way of curbing this menace is to give fillip to recycling of precious metal by providing a window where ornaments can be sold without getting fleeced. At present the buyer faces discount over 20% (!), and strangely, the authorities are oblivious of this menace.

Then again, will someone up there, look at the real estates which are purchased and kept locked up, for one reason or another? Can the government not take custody of all such flats and rent them out with a guarantee to the owner of reclaiming the premises for his own use, if and when he needs it? There is no reason on earth for the government to subsidise the financing cost of the white portion of the real estate cost since it serves as a convenient vehicle to invest his black money.

Smugglers have found ways to outsmart customs officials. All that they do is to declare bentex jewellery as gold, while going abroad. This jewellery is then dumped in the visiting country, and real gold jewellery is brought while returning to India. Some enter India from neighbouring countries like Nepal and Bangladesh.

Smuggling of gold, an illegal activity, is coupled with hawala transaction, another illegal activity. Forex for purchase of gold is picked up from NRIs who desire to send funds regularly to their relatives in India for their subsistence. Indian Rupees are paid to the relative in India at a premium over the forex exchange rate prevalent for normal banking channels. Needless to state that these routs give rise to a parallel black money market.

It is obvious that the increase in the import duty of precious metals is a retrograde step.

Tax Collected at Source

The current Sec. 206(C) (1D) requires TDS @1% to be applied by the seller of bullion if the total sale value exceeds ₹2 lakh for bullion and ₹5 lakh for jewellery. Moreover, there is 1% excise duty on articles of jewellery (excluding silver).

Export of Gold Jewellery

There is no value limit on the export of gold jewellery by a passenger through baggage if it constitutes the bona fide baggage of the passenger. He may request the customs for issue of an export certificate while departing to facilitate its reimport on his return.

Final Nail in the Coffin

From the spurt of imports at various airports in past across the country the government felt that some unscrupulous elements were smuggling gold by hiring eligible passengers to import gold on their behalf.

Seeking to check this route of smuggling, the government, tightened baggage rules, requiring inbound Indian passengers to provide details such as source of funds for importing the metal as well as their air tickets. According to a Revenue Department circular, the baggage receipt issued by the Customs will now include the engraved serial number on gold bars and the item-wise list of ornaments. "Wherever possible, the field officer, may ascertain the antecedents of such passengers, source for funding for gold as well as duty being paid in the foreign currency, person responsible for booking of tickets, and the like," it said, adding that the decision is aimed at preventing misuse of the gold import facility.

To Sum

We are surely back at square number one. Smuggling coupled with hawala has become once more extremely rewarding.

24

~

Overseas Citizenship of India (OCI)

Good news for all PIOs. FA15 has merged the PIO cards into OCI cards. The Government had introduced on 31.03.1999 PIO Cards for PIOs settled throughout the world. Now OCI cards have come into existence and have little better features.

OCI facility is available to any overseas Indian (other than a person who was a citizen of Pakistan or Bangladesh any time) as long as his home country allows dual citizenship under their local laws. On the other hand, the OCI card is not available to a person who was or is a citizen of Afghanistan, Bangladesh, Bhutan, China, Nepal, Pakistan or Sri Lanka at any time.

Such a foreign national should have been —

(a) Eligible to become citizen of India on 26.01.1950. Any person who or either of whose parents or any of whose grandparents was born in India as defined in the Government of India Act, 1935 (as originally enacted), and who was ordinarily residing in any country outside India was eligible to become citizen of India on 26.01.1950, or

(b) Was a citizen of India on or after 26.1.50, or

(c) Belonged to a territory that became part of India after 15.08.1947. Such territories are — (i) Sikkim from 26.04.1975, (ii) Pondicherry from 16.08.1962, (iii) Dadra & Nagar Haveli from 11.08.1961, and iv) Goa, Daman and Diu from 20.12.1961.

(d) His children and grand children, even if minors are also eligible.

A person who is already holding more than one nationality can also be an OCI as long as the local laws of at least one of the countries allow dual citizenship in some form or other.

An OCI card holder does not possess dual citizenship or nationality. He shall not be entitled to the following rights:

(a) Equality of opportunity in matters of public employment.
(b) Be a (i) President, (ii) Vice-President, (iii) Judge of the Supreme Court or High Court or (iv) a member of the House of the People, the Council of States, Legislative Assembly, Legislative Council.
(c) Be registered as a voter.
(d) For appointment to public services and posts in connection with the affairs of the Union or of any State.

As per Sec. 5(1g) of the Citizenship Act, 1955, a person who is registered as OCI for 5 years and is Residing in India for 1 year out of the above 5 years, is eligible to apply for Indian Citizenship to the Ministry of Home Affairs, Central Government. The same rule applies to minor children (even foreign-born) and spouses of foreign origin, married to Indians.

The benefits of OCI are —

- Multi-purpose, multiple entry, life-long visa for visiting India.
- OCI does not require registration with local police authority.
- An NRI or a PIO is prohibited from acquiring agricultural or plantation properties. The press note dt 2.12.05 by Ministry of Home Affairs states that one of the benefits of OCI is — Parity with NRIs in respect of all facilities to the latter in economic, financial and educational fields except in matters relating to the acquisition of agricultural/plantation properties. This implies that an NRI or a PIO does not have the right to purchase an agricultural land but an OCI card holder has the right. We feel that this is an aberration. How can a person with foreign nationality (PIO) have better rights than an Indian citizen (NRI)?
- Facilities as available to children of NRIs for obtaining admission to educational institutions in India, including medical colleges, engineering colleges, institutes of technology, institutes of management etc., under the general category.

Procedure

Every registered OCI will be issued a registration certificate which is printed like an Indian passport in different colours and an OCI visa sticker will be pasted in the person's foreign passport. Both these will have all necessary security features, including photograph.

An eligible person may apply to the Indian Mission or Post of the country of his nationality or of any other country if he is ordinarily residing there, along with the necessary proofs of his eligibility.

Application Form-XIX can be used directly on-line or downloaded from www.mha.nic.in and submitted through post. It can be jointly used by a family consisting of spouses and up to two minor children. Part-A of the Form can be filed on-line. A bar code and a reference number will be generated automatically as an acknowledgement. Part-B can be downloaded and printed on computer or written by hand in Block letters. Printed Part-A and Part-B of the application form have to be submitted in duplicate with all necessary enclosures. The concerned office will issue an acknowledgement number which can be used for enquiries in future.

If the applicant is not in the country of citizenship, the application can be submitted to the Indian Mission or Post of the country where he is ordinarily residing. If the applicant is in India, it can be submitted to the FRRO Delhi, Mumbai, Kolkata or Amritsar or to CHIO, Chennai or to the Under Secretary, OCI Cell, Citizenship Section, Foreigners Division, Ministry of Home Affairs (MHA), Jaisalmer House, 26, Mansingh Road, New Delhi-110011. Central processing of applications will occur in New Delhi. Ministry sends OCI cards to embassy / consulate.

An application where there is no reporting of criminal case against the applicant will be granted OCI within 30 days whereas in other cases it may take 120 days. An OCI certificate acquired on the basis of concealed information or misrepresentation, will be cancelled and such persons will be blacklisted for entry into India.

A registration certificate in the form of a booklet will be issued and a multiple entry, multipurpose OCI "U" visa sticker will be pasted on the foreign passport of the applicant. For this purpose, the applicant has to send the original passport after receipt of the acceptance letter or verification of the application on-line.

In the case of loss of or damage to the certificate, an application has to be made to the same Indian Mission or Post which issued the certificate. A new OCI "U" visa sticker will be issued. However, the applicant can continue to carry the old passport wherein OCI "U" visa sticker was pasted along with new passport for visiting India without seeking a new visa, as the visa is valid for lifelong. Ditto for renewal of the foreign passport.

In the unlikely case of a person desiring to renounce OCI, he can use Form-XXII and send it to the Indian Mission or Post where OCI registration was granted.

Cost of OCI Card

An OCI card cost is US$ 275 for US citizens and US$ 295 for others. If the application is rejected, the amount will be returned after deducting US$ 25 for US citizens and US$ 45 of others as processing fees. Issue of duplicate OCI card costs US$ 25.

Letter of Mr. Ashwin Kalbag

The following letter of Mr. Ashwin Kalbag published in *Economic Times* of 18.3.10 is a testimony of the fact that the OCI Card, leave alone the PIO Card, is useless. We have taken the liberty to drop and edit certain portions for conserving space —

"I ran into trouble in February 2010, at the Mumbai International airport. I had arrived with a newly issued US passport and an OCI card. As it turned out, I needed the class "U" visa issued along with the OCI card, which was stamped in my expired US passport that I had not brought with me. I was made to pay US$

40 for a 5-day temporary entry visa known as Temporary Landing Facility (TLF).

"The Bureau of Immigration (BOI) under the Ministry of Home Affairs (MHA) has a link 'Instructions (Foreigners)' on its website, http://www.immigrationindia.nic.in, clearly stating, 'On production of bona fide proof and on satisfaction of the FRRO/FRO cum District Superintendent of Police, a TLF may be granted for up to 15 days. Yet, I was granted only a 5-day TLF. The same link categorically states "foreigners carrying a valid PIO or OCI card along with their valid national passport are authorised to enter India without obtaining India visa separately.

"As an OCI card holder, I have a life-long visa to enter and exit India. I am purportedly free not to register with the FRRO even for stays lasting longer than 180 days. Yet, in a single swoop, in effect, my OCI card was rendered useless.

"It is impossible to obtain an OCI card without also being given a corresponding class 'U' visa. In that case producing the OCI card should be perfectly equivalent to producing the visa itself. OCI card grants a life-long visa. Unfortunately, when a passport expires, the OCI or PIO card needs to have the new passport linked to it, creating an entire bureaucracy around this process.

"It would perhaps be a better idea to model the OCI card after the US green card, as an Indian green card. The US green card is a standalone document that supersedes the permanent visa given at the time of its issuance. It may be produced at US immigrations without its concomitant visa.

"I went to several banks during my subsequent visit to Mumbai asking whether I could open an on-line trading account with which to trade Indian securities. Most banks had no knowledge of how to deal with OCI card holders!

"As recently as December 2009, the MHA implemented new regulations that affect visa holders' periods of authorised stay and registration in India, targeted at travellers with tourist visas, who have been in India for more than 90 days before travel abroad, or for more than 180 days within the past year. The regulation mandates a 2-month gap between successive visits to India.

“A lot of NRIs have long-term (5 or 10 years) tourist visas. They now have to apply for a re-entry permit from the appropriate CGI office in the US. The information on governmental websites is not specific enough to determine whether this affects PIO or OCI card holders. The US State Department’s webpage http://travel.state.gov/travel/cis_pa_tw/cis/cis_1139.html states — Citizens are advised to carefully review the latest regulations, which are included under the section titled ‘Instructions (Foreigners)’, and to be aware that implementation at ports of entry may be inconsistent.

“It took me 4 trips to the FRRO to get a visa extension covering my stay. If I were an NRI interested in doing business in India, this experience would give me a pause.”

To Sum

We thank Mr. Ashwin Kalbag for warning the Indian diaspora about the various dangers associated with the use of OCI Card. It is really sad that the US State Department warns its citizens that “implementation at ports of entry may be inconsistent”. This implies that the authorities at the ports are either not trained properly or are allowed to take different actions under the same situations depending upon whether they like the face of the card holder or not. And worst — the higher authorities do not appear to be interested in taking any corrective action for reasons best known to them.

25

Double Taxation Avoidance Agreement (DTAA)

In today's era of globalisation, movement of personnel across countries is commonplace. An individual may work in India for some part of the year and the rest of the year in another country. In such cases, a question arises as to the taxability of the income of the individual, received overseas as well as in India. One country may want to tax the income on account of the residential status whereas the other country may want to tax, at least that part of the income on source basis.

DTAA between two countries supersedes their respective domestic tax laws. In other words, the assessee is entitled to higher benefit as is available under the DTAA and the domestic tax laws.

DTAA normally determines which country reserves the right to tax a particular stream of income. Sometimes, it may so happen that the DTAA may not give exclusive privilege to any one country to tax the income. For example, the resident country may have a right to tax some certain income whereas the source country also has a right to tax the same income. In such cases, double taxation is normally avoided by means of the resident country giving credit for the taxes paid in the source country.

There are two ways of granting DTAA reliefs —

(a) Exemption: A particular income is taxed in only one of the two countries and is exempt in the other.

(b) Tax Credit: An income is taxed in both the countries as per their respective tax laws read with the DTAA.

Example

Take the instance of the DTAA between India and the USA. An employee has worked till October 15th in India and the rest of the year in USA. Let us explore the way DTAA protects the employee from paying tax twice.

Article 16 of the DTAA deals with Dependent Personal Services, which is a jargon for salary income. The following is the relevant clause of the Article —

> "Subject to the provisions of article 17 (Director's Fees), 18 (Income Earned by Entertainers and Athletes), 19 (Remuneration and Pensions in Respect of Government Service), 20 (Private Pensions, Annuities, Alimony and Child Support), 21 (Payments Received by Students and Apprentices) and 22 (Payments Received by Professors, Teachers and Research Scholars), salaries, wages, and other similar remuneration derived by a resident of a Contracting State in respect of an employment shall be taxable only in that State unless the employment is exercised in the other Contracting State. If the employment is so exercised, such remuneration as is derived therefrom may be taxed in other State."

Consequently, the primary right of taxation is with India and the secondary right is with the USA. But since the income is being taxed twice, Article 25 of the agreement, states —

> "Where a resident of India derives income which, in accordance with the provisions of this Convention, may be taxed in the United States, India shall allow as a deduction from the tax on the income of that resident an amount equal to the income-tax paid in the United States, whether directly or by deduction. Such deduction shall not, however, exceed that part of the income-tax (as computed before the deduction is given) which is attributable to the income which may be taxed in the United States."

This means that on the tax to be paid in India, the assessee is entitled to a deduction of the tax paid in the USA on the income earned there.

The Residentship Rule

We have already discussed the fact that tax depends upon Residential status. What happens when a person is a Resident in both the countries as per their respective domestic laws? For example, a country may determine a person to be a Resident if he stays in that country for more than 150 days. In such a case, it may be possible that he spends 182 days in India, and the rest in that country, thereby making him a Resident of both.

As per Article-4(1) of the UN Model Convention, dealing with Residentship rules which prescribes tie-breaking tests for persons who may qualify as Residents of both countries. Accordingly —

"1. For the purposes of this Convention, the term 'resident of a Contracting State' means any person who, under the laws of that State, is liable to tax therein by reason of his domicile, residence, citizenship, place of management, place of incorporation, or any other criterion of a similar nature . . .

"2. Where by reason of the provisions of paragraph 1, an individual is a resident of both Contracting States, then his status shall be determined as follows:

(a) he shall be deemed to be a resident of the State in which he has a permanent home available to him; if he has a permanent home available to him in both States, he shall be deemed to be a resident of the State with which his personal and economic relations are closer (centre of vital interests);

(b) if the State in which he has his centre of vital interests cannot be determined, or if he does not have a permanent home available to him in either State, he shall be deemed to be a resident of the State in which he has a habitual abode;

(c) if he has a habitual abode in both States or in none, he shall be deemed to be a resident of the State of which he is a national; and

(d) if he is a national of both States or of neither of them, the competent authorities of the Contracting States shall settle the question by Mutual Agreement Procedure (MAP) . . ."

DTAA confers the right of taxation either to the Resident or to the Source country (or distributes it between the two).

Procedure

Those availing of treaty benefits have to file returns of their income in India, even if those aren't liable to be taxed here. Prior to FY 10-11, those who didn't pay taxes in India, owing to the provisions under the double taxation avoidance agreement between India and the country of origin concerned, didn't have to file returns in India.

The taxpayer has to bifurcate his incomes to which provisions of a tax treaty apply. For instance, if he earns income from interest on bank deposits in India as well as abroad, he would have to state the interest earned on foreign income separately. He has to quote the Tax Identification Number (TIN) in case tax has been paid in a foreign country. If the TIN is not allotted by that country, he has to furnish his passport number. It is mandatory for a taxpayer with total annual income of more than ₹25 lakh to declare his domestic assets, including land, buildings, bank deposits, shares, insurance policies, loans, jewellery, bullion, drawings, paintings, yachts, boats, etc. As part of foreign asset reporting norms, an assessee also has to state his foreign bank account number and the details of the trusts in which he is a trustee.

The individual needs to submit a signed declaration, in a prescribed format to the ITO in India. He also needs to submit proof of his residence in the country abroad. This can either be a Tax Residency Certificate issued by the government of the country of residence or a copy of IT returns filed in that country. Further, such NRI investor would also be required to furnish Form 10F along with TRC, if such TRC does not contain information prescribed by the CBDT vide its Notification No. 57/2013 dt 1.8.13. In countries like UAE where there is no income tax, a self declaration is sufficient.

The advantage to the investor is that when he files his returns in his country of residence, he can claim the benefit of the TDS and the advance tax already paid in India and only needs to pay the extra tax (if any) in that country. For example, if in that country the tax rate is 40% and he has paid TDS @15%, he only needs to pay the balance 25% tax in that country and not the entire 40%.

This is the general vein followed by all DTAAs. Some fine tuning may be required depending upon the exact provisions of DTAA between India and the host country. Such agreements are available on — www.incometaxindia.gov.in. Since such a fine tuning is a very complex exercise, you will do well by employing a consultant specialising in the field in your normal place of residence in India.

DTAA with Tax Havens

As per AAR, only liability to pay tax, both in India and the foreign country entitles a taxpayer to claim relief under the rules laid down in the DTAA. If a taxpayer pays tax or is liable to pay tax under the laws in force in one country alone, he cannot claim any relief from a non-existent burden of double taxation under the DTAA. The DTAA is for the benefit of taxpayers who are liable to pay tax twice on the same income. Therefore, no question of granting relief to the applicant from double taxation can arise.

In, *88ITR169 (SC)*, it was held that "doubly taxed income should be understood as income actually charged to tax". Since no tax is paid on income exempt u/s 10(38), there can be no presumption of tax having been paid u/s 112. Only the income on which tax has been paid abroad and which is again taxed in another country, is entitled to DTAA relief.

Taking into consideration these rulings, on incomes such as dividends, interest and capital gains, the rates specified in Finance Act in India have to be used.

Payments to NRIs in UAE

In respect of payments to be made to NRIs at the UAE, tax at source must be deducted at the following rates —

(a) Dividends: 5% of the gross amount of the dividends if the beneficial owner is a company which owns at least 10% of the shares of the company and 15% in all the other cases.

(b) Interest: 5% of the gross amount of the interest if such interest is paid on a loan granted by a bank carrying on a bona fide banking business or by a similar financial institution and 12½% of the gross amount of the interest in all other cases.

(c) Royalties: 10% of the gross amount.

Circular 734 dt 24.1.96 proclaims that the above rates which are enshrined in the DTAA between India and UAE are to be strictly adhered to so as to avoid unnecessary harassment of tax-payers.

DTAA with USA

In the case of taxation of income earned in the US, credit will be available in respect of taxes paid in the US. Such credit is available only in respect of federal taxes. No credit is available in respect of state tax and payment in respect of social security, insurance, etc.:

- If a person is on a short term deputation of an Indian employer to the US and who has all other personal and economic connection attached to India, then he is regarded as a Resident even as per the treaty. India retains the right to global taxation in such a situation, as per treaty provisions.
- The scope of the DTAA covers only certain incomes and certain kinds of taxes. If there is a particular income or a tax in the domestic law which is not envisaged in the DTAA, then the DTAA would not apply. The Indian Fringe Benefit Tax is a case in point.
- It may be noted that US tax laws allow exemption on capital gains from sale of "Main House".

- The first thing to determine is the source and the residence country. This makes things simpler. In the case of Indians in the USA the source country is the USA which defines the source of the income. The residence country is of course India.
- There are several ex-NRIs who get some pension from abroad after returning to India permanently. As per Article 20(2) of the DTAA between India and the US, Social Security Benefits and Public Pensions paid by the US, even to an ROR are taxable only in the US and not in India. Other pensions would be taxable in the country of residence — that is India.
- Contributions of the foreign companies towards social security are mostly of two types. Generally, the contributions would accrue to the credit of the employees and would be payable only on superannuation. However, some countries have compulsory social security contributions which go as a premium for insuring the employment. The insurance company would make a lump sum payment or an annuity to the employee as and when there is any curtailment of earning capacity. Barring such special circumstances, such contributions do not entail any benefit to the employees.

Mumbai bench of the ITAT in the case of *Gallotti Raoul* v *ACIT* 61ITD453 dealt with the taxability of compulsory contributions to be made to French Social Security Fund according to which every French national is under an obligation to affiliate with social security organisation and contribute a prefixed percentage of salary irrespective of the place of employment. It held that compulsory contributions to the extent to which the assessee has no domain over it, cannot be said to be an income in the hands of the employee. This is an instance of diversion of income by overriding title.

Such agreements between India and other countries, are available on — www.incometaxindia.gov.in.

The Countries with Whom India has DTAA are —
India has entered into such agreements with more than 90 countries and has been engulfing many new countries. The up-to-date list is available on www.incometaxindia.gov.in.

Case Law
The judicial pronouncements made by ITAT Pune Bench "B" in the case of *ACT* v *EPCOS AG Germany,* IT Appeal 398 (Pune) of 2007 is important and have a far-reaching effect.

The German company had two subsidiaries in India, namely, EIPL and EFPL. It provided support services to them in field of product marketing, sales and information technology from its centralised infrastructure in Germany. In the relevant previous year, assessee had disclosed receipts of the fees as well as interest on ECB loans. Assessee had accepted a tax liability on said receipts @10% on the basis of Article 12 of Indo-German tax treaty.

AO held that each and every activity of Indian subsidiaries was done under active supervision of assessee in India, and hence, assessee had a PE in India in form of its subsidiaries. He further held that even if the receipts in question were in nature of royalties those receipts were taxable on gross basis @20% u/s 44D, read with Sec. 115A.

The main pronouncements were —

- A tax treaty is primarily a detailed instrument assigning taxing rights between two or more competing tax jurisdictions over a tax subject and unless a tax jurisdiction has a right to tax an income, it is irrelevant whether or not, under domestic tax legislation of that tax jurisdiction, income-in-question is taxable
- In the case of cross-border tax situation between treaty partner States, logically first thing for a source tax jurisdiction is to establish right to tax under applicable tax treaty, and only if such a source tax jurisdiction indeed has right to tax, next

thing is to be examined is taxability under domestic laws of that State.

- The first step towards examining taxability of business profits in source country is to ascertain whether or not foreign enterprise has a Permanent Establishment (PE). And if it does have one, the quantum of business profits attributable to such a PE.
- A PE means a fixed place of business through which business of foreign enterprise should be carried on. Merely because an Indian company conducts its business in India with help and guidance it receives from a foreign company that gives help and guidance, it does not follow that the foreign company will be deemed to have a PE. In case an assessee receives "royalties" and "fees for technical services" but these receipts do not have an effective nexus with PE, and are not, therefore, attributable to PE, exclusion clause under Article 5(5), as also taxability under Article 7(1) and (2), is not triggered. Since no part of work of assessee was carried out in India in as much as there was no billing raised by assessee in connection with any services rendered in India and moreover Indian subsidiaries merely acted upon advice so given in e-mails and letters which were sent from outside India, action of subsidiaries could not alter sites of activities of assessee, and it could be said that assessee did not have a PE in India in form of Indian subsidiaries.

In view of above, it could be said that receipts in question were not attributable to PE in India and, therefore, there was no question of applicability of Sec. 44D, read with Sec. 115A.

Double Taxation Relief

If income is not taxable and there does not exist any tax liability of assessee as per regular provisions of Act, DTAA cannot be invoked to create any such tax liability — Xelo Pty. Ltd. v. Deputy Director of Income-tax (International Taxation) — [2009] 32 SOT 338 (MUM.) [IT APPEAL NOS. 4107, 4108, 4380 AND 4381 (MUM.) OF 2002]

Form-8938 & FBAR

To contain tax evasion and avoidance by US citizens and residents, particularly Green Card holders, in respect of foreign assets, Form-8938 is introduced by US tax authorities, from the tax year 2011.

This Form needs to be filed if the value of your foreign financial assets exceeds —

- For a single assessee: $50,000 at end of year or more than $75,000 during the year.
- For Married joint assessee: $100,000 at end of year or more than $150,000 during the year.

There are higher limits if you do not live in the United States.

Foreign Financial Assets include —

- Financial account maintained by a foreign financial institution.
- Stocks or securities issued by someone other than a US person.
- Financial instrument or contract where the issuer or counter party is someone other than a US person.

These encompass almost all the accounts that you may hold back in your home country such as Banks, Brokerage and securities, Commodity futures & options, MFs, DPs, Insurance policy with cash surrender value, Annuities with cash value, and most importantly, Pension Funds. Note that a state pension like the US social security is not included in the value.

Filing Form-8938 does not stop the requirement to file Form-TD F 90-22.1, otherwise known as the FBAR (Foreign Bank and Financial Accounts Reporting). This form still needs to be filed with the US Treasury by June 30 each year if you have certain financial accounts exceeding US$ 10,000 in value.

If you meet the following conditions, you must file an FBAR —

- You are a US citizen or a Resident or an entity, including but not limited to corporations, partnerships, or limited liability companies, created or organised in the US under the laws of the United States and trusts or estates formed under the laws of the United States.
- You have a financial interest or signature authority over the account by way of holding a legal title to the account. This means that you, either by yourself or jointly with others, control the disposition of assets held in the foreign accounts. This will apply even if the foreign account is owned by an agent or nominee on your behalf. In case of corporate, partnerships or trusts, they must own more than 50% of voting rights, capital or beneficial interest respectively.
- The total of all your non-US bank and financial accounts exceeds US$ 10,000 even for a single day during the relevant calendar year. This is rather harsh. For instance, suppose you desire to buy a property in India. Surely, your Indian account will hold funds only for a few days before the money is paid to the seller of the property. But since the balance in the account would have exceeded US$ 10,000 for those few days, you must file FBAR.
- The basic penalty for failing to file the Form is $10,000 going up to a maximum of $50,000 for continuing failure to file. Also if you fail to report income from the foreign financial assets the IRS will have up to 6 years to assess the tax rather than the normal 3 years.

Take care!

Indian banks cannot issue Form-1099 to their customers in the USA. However, on your request a certificate indicating the details of your deposit and interest earned during a calendar year (January-December) or a FY (April-March) can be provided.

Where DTAA does not Exist (Sec. 91)
Sec. 91(1) provides for relief in respect of income tax on the income which is taxed in India as well as in the country with which there is no DTAA. Accordingly an Indian Resident is entitled to a deduction from the Indian income tax of a sum calculated on such doubly taxed income, at the Indian rate of tax or the rate of tax of said country, whichever is lower. In cases of the 92 countries with which India has a DTAA, a relief on doubly taxed income is available as per the respective DTAAs. The Act does not provide the manner for granting credit of taxes paid in any country outside India. Therefore, FA15 has amended Sec. 295(2) to provide that CBDT makes rules to provide the procedure for granting the necessary reliefs.

FATCA and CRS

Each and every government across the length and breadth of the globe desires to catch hold of money flowing out of their country specifically for avoiding taxes. With this aim, India has signed an Inter-Governmental Agreement with the USA under their Foreign Account Tax Compliance Act (FATCA) effective from 1.9.15.

Many "reportable" persons in both the countries have started receiving inquiries related with their assets and income causing some anxiety. This is an attempt to give such persons the most desired related information.

We shall deal with only the administration of the disclosures that India has undertaken with persons related with USA who have investments in India. The USA has also to take corresponding action with persons related with India.

FATCA Details
A reportable person means an individual who is (i) a citizen or resident of USA (ii) US entity such as a partnership or corporation organised in the USA, US trusts etc., and (iii) a person that

is resident of any country outside India under the tax laws of such country other than the prescribed entities.

A reportable Account is the one which has been held by a Reportable Person.

The date from which the procedure for New Accounts would be applicable is —

1st July, 2014 in case of U.S. Reportable Accounts

1st January, 2016 in case of Other Reportable Accounts

For individuals, the threshold on Pre-Existing US Reportable Accounts (before the above dates) is US$ 50,000 whereas there is no threshold for other reportable accounts. For all the entities, US or others, the threshold is US$ 250,000.

High value accounts are those which are over US$ 1 million.

New Accounts are those which are opened after the dates mentioned above.

Because of the delay in signing, there are intermediate New Accounts (opened between 1.7.14 and 31.8.15) and actual New Accounts opened from 1.9.15 onwards.

The Reporting Financial Institutions must review electronically searchable data maintained on indicia covering —

- Identification of the account holder as a resident of any country outside India for tax purposes or unambiguous indication of a place of birth in USA.
- Current mailing or residence address (including a post office box) in any country outside India, or
- At least one telephone number in a country outside India and no number in India, or
- Standing instructions (other than with respect to a depository account) to transfer funds to an account maintained in a country outside India, or

- Currently effective power of attorney or signatory authority granted to a person with an address in a country outside India, or
- A "hold mail" instruction or care-of address in a country outside India if the reporting financial institution does not have any other address on file for the account holder.
- If none of the indicia are discovered in the electronic search, no further action is required, but if there is a match, then a confirmation needs to be obtained from the Investors around whether s/he is a US Reportable / Other Reportable Account.

For high value pre-existing individual accounts, apart from the above procedures, a paper search for 5 years and a confirmation is also necessary from customer. There are also different reporting deadlines, though the procedures are the same.

In the case of accounts opened from 1.7.14 to 31.8.15 (date when FATCA was signed), the self-certification required for New Accounts should be obtained by 31.8.16 and if it is not obtained, the accounts need to be closed.

An Entity becomes a Reportable Person if it is —

- a non-participating financial institution by the USA, or
- a financial institution from a country / territory which has not entered into an IGA with USA,
- a financial institution from a country/territory which has entered into an IGA with USA (a partner jurisdiction FI) but has not registered with US IRS or obtained GIIN, and
- a passive Non-Financial Entity and whether its controlling persons are residents of countries / territories outside India. Broadly, this is a non-financial services company that derives income from dividends, interest, royalty, capital gains, etc.

What Needs to be Reported

The following information needs to be maintained and reported to the US tax authorities:

- The name, address, taxpayer identification number (assigned to the account holder by the country of his residence for tax purposes) and date and place of birth (in the case of an individual) of each reportable person.
- In the case of any entity which is an account holder and which is identified as having one or more controlling persons that is a reportable person —
  (i) The name and address of the entity, taxpayer identification number assigned to the entity by the country of its residence.
  (ii) The name, address, date and place of birth of each such controlling person and taxpayer identification number.
- The account number and balance.
- In the case of any account other than custodial or depository accounts, including accounts held by investment entities and cash value insurance contract and annuity, the total gross amount paid or credited to the account holder with respect to the account during the relevant calendar year with respect to which the reporting financial institution is the obligor or debtor, including the aggregate amount of any redemption payments made to the account holder during the relevant calendar year.

CRS

India has also signed on 3.6.15, with over 100 G-20 countries for exchanging similar information popularly known as the Common Reporting Standards (CRS) on Automatic Exchange of Information

For Pre-existing Accounts under CRS, the cut-off date for Pre-existing accounts is 31.12.15. Due diligence procedures for high accounts existing on that date under CRS would need to be completed by 30.6.16 and low value accounts by 30.6.17. Non-confirmation will lead to Account reporting and closure by 31st May of the next year.

Comments

A more immediate consequence of FATCA is that all people who are tax resident of the US/Canada and are FATCA compliant can invest in any MF Schemes. However, at present, some of the MFs allow investments from all foreign citizens only when they are physically present in India, to ensure that they are really FATCA (or CRS) compliant. Other MFs depend upon their declarations. In any case, those who had invested their funds without declaring these to the tax authorities in the country of their nationality, are running away with their money parked in India to those havens where FATCA or CRS is not applicable and there are many such countries.

26

~

India has become a Tax Haven

Yes, India has become a tax haven.

You can arrange your affairs in such a fashion that irrespective of the size of your funds, you can earn much higher returns than those available anywhere else across the globe with high degree of safely and little tax.

If you are ready to take market related risks, go for Equity-based MF Schemes which are endowed with excellent tax concessions. For those who are risk averse, go for Debt-based FMPs of MFs with a term of over 3 years to earn the benefit of low tax on long-term capital gains.

NRE deposits carry exchange risk. Under the new government, the economy is surely slated to improve fast and along with it, the rupee will go from strength to strength.

In any case, those who do not want to take the exchange risk, FCNR is a good bet.

To Sum

For sure, India has become a tax haven for an informed NRI.

There are different courses for different horses.

Bibliography

~

1. *Taxmann's Foreign Exchange Management Manual*, An Authorised Publication of RBI.
2. FEMA Foreign Exchange Management Manual & Ready Reckoner, D. T. Khilnani, Snow White Publications Pvt. Ltd.
3. *Direct Taxes Law & Practice*, Dr. V. K. Singhania, Taxmann Publications Pvt Ltd.